Ernst Walter Andrae
Rainer Michael Boehmer

BILDER EINES AUSGRÄBERS

Die Orientbilder von
Walter Andrae 1898–1919

SKETCHES BY AN EXCAVATOR

2., erweiterte Auflage
2nd enlarged edition

GEBR. MANN VERLAG · BERLIN

Englische Übersetzung: Jane Moon, Cambridge

Die Deutsche Bibliothek – CIP-Einheitsaufnahme

Bilder eines Ausgräbers : die Orientbilder von Walter Andrae 1898–1919 =
Sketches by an excavator / [Deutsches Archäologisches Institut, Abteilung Baghdad].
Ernst Walter Andrae ; Rainer Michael Boehmer. [Engl. Übers.: Jane Moon].
– 2., erw. Aufl. – Berlin : Gebr. Mann, 1992
ISBN 3-7861-1651-2
NE: Andrae, Walter; Andrae, Ernst Walter; Deutsches Archäologisches
Institut ›Berlin‹ / Abteilung ›Baġdād‹; PT

© 1992 Gebr. Mann Verlag · Berlin
Deutsche Erstveröffentlichung der 1. Aufl.: Baghdader Mitteilungen 20, 1989
Alle Rechte vorbehalten. Photomechanische Wiedergabe
nur mit ausdrücklicher Genehmigung durch den Verlag
Farbreproduktionen: O.R.T. Kirchner + Graser · Berlin
Satz und Reproduktionen: Hellmich KG · Berlin
Druck: H. Heenemann · Berlin
Verarbeitung: Dieter Mikolai · Berlin
Umschlaggestaltung: Wieland Schütz · Berlin
Printed in Germany · ISBN 3-7861-1651-2

INHALT

CONTENTS

ERNST WALTER ANDRAE
RAINER MICHAEL BOEHMER

DIE ORIENTBILDER VON WALTER ANDRAE

EINLEITUNG

Als ich im Frühjahr 1988 Ernst W. Andrae, den ältesten Sohn Walter Andraes, kennenlernte – er besuchte unser Institut in Berlin – wurde mir bewußt, daß ein großer Teil der Bilder Andraes sich noch im Besitz der großen Familie Andrae befindet. Diese Werke bilden einen Teil des breiten, vielseitigen Schaffens Walter Andraes, der der Orientalistik bislang nur andeutungsweise in wenigen ausgewählten Bildern vorlag. Ehe diese noch unbekannten Zeugnisse eines Tages auf einen noch größeren Personenkreis verteilt sind, sollen sie hier in einer repräsentativen, ungefähr zwei Drittel der Gesamtzahl umfassenden Auswahl der Öffentlichkeit vorgelegt werden*.

Herrn E. W. Andrae ist es zu verdanken, daß er die in der Familie befindlichen Bilder zusammenbrachte und nicht nur seine Einwilligung zur Veröffentlichung gab, sondern auch aktiv an dieser mitarbeitete. Dank gebührt auch den Verantwortlichen der Handschriftenabteilung der Staatsbibliothek, SPK, Berlin, Dr. Brandis und Frau Dr. Stolzenberg, und dem Leiter der Plansammlung der Technischen Universität Berlin, Herrn Dipl.-Ing. D. Radicke, die Druckerlaubnis für die hier vorgelegten Bilder Andraes aus ihren Beständen gaben. Weitere Danksagung geht an Frau Barbara Grunewald für die mühevolle Erstellung der meisten Ektrachrome, die als Grundlage für die Farbreproduktionen verwendet wurden, und Herrn B. Fischer, Offset-Repro-Technik (Berlin) sowie die Herren D. Eckert und Dr. F. Redecker vom Gebr. Mann Verlag (Berlin) für

---

*Abkürzungsverzeichnis

Bell, AtA	Gertrude Lowthian Bell, Amurath to Amurath (1911)
LE	Walter Andrae, Lebenserinnerungen eines Ausgräbers (1988) (2. Auflage)
Le 1. Aufl.	Walter Andrae, Lebenserinnerungen eines Ausgräbers (1961) (1. Auflage)
MDOG	Mitteilungen der Deutschen Orientgesellschaft
RK	Walter Andrae, Babylon. Die versunkene Weltstadt und ihr Ausgräber Robert Koldewey (1952)
Sarre-Herzfeld	Friedrich Sarre-Ernst Herzfeld, Archäologische Reise im Euphrat- und Tigris-Gebiet I (1911). II (1920). III (1911).
SPK	Stiftung Preußischer Kulturbesitz
WVDOG	Wissenschaftliche Veröffentlichungen der Deutschen Orientgesellschaft

den sorgfältig ausgeführten Druck. Ganz besonders danke ich Frau Dr. Beate Salje für ihre geduldige redaktionelle Hilfe bei der Drucklegung.

Walter Andrae begegnete mir erstmalig als hochgewachsener, ungebeugter Endsiebziger während meiner ersten Studienjahre. Bei abendlichen Vorträgen im Saal der stark kriegsgeschädigten Zentrale des Deutschen Archäologischen Instituts in der Maienstraße zu Berlin (Ende der 50er Jahre wurde das Gebäude dann völlig abgerissen) wie auch in Hörsälen der Fakultät für Architektur der Technischen Universität Berlin nahm er als Zuhörer teil. Obwohl stark sehbehindert – 1948 hatte sich der damals 73jährige beim Hacken von Brennholz ein Auge verletzt, die Sehkraft des anderen Auges hatte dann infolge Überanstrengung nachgelassen – folgte er auch Lichtbildreferaten und wußte in der anschließenden Diskussion stets Wesentliches beizutragen und die richtige Wertung zu geben, gleich, ob es dabei um archäologische Fakten, allgemeine oder besondere Dinge des Lebens ging wie beispielsweise einen Bericht von H. J. Lenzen über noch im Winter 1955/56 erfolgte kriegerische Auseinandersetzungen zwischen den arabischen Stämmen bei Larsa-Senkere und denen bei Uruk-Warka.

Stark sehbehindert: was das für Andrae als Künstler, als Maler, als Mann des wachen Auges bedeutet haben muß, kann man nur erahnen. Aber seine starke Persönlichkeit, die ein Leben lang auf dem Weg nach innen war, hat auch diesen Schicksalsschlag ertragen und getragen, wissend, daß Leid reif macht. Ließ sein äußeres Sehorgan nach, so verstärkte sich doch der Blick seines inneren Auges.

In der Vielzahl seiner erhaltenen Skizzen und Bilder nehmen neben denen aus seiner Heimat, aus Böhmen, Österreich, Italien, Portugal die des Orients aus den Jahren 1898–1919 den größten Raum ein. Die hier vorgelegten bilden eine recht umfassende Auswahl der letzteren. Sie sind zeitgeschichtlich bedeutsam. Vieles, was er noch gesehen hat, existiert heute nicht mehr. Städte haben sich völlig verändert, geradezu winzig waren beispielsweise vor 90 Jahren noch Beirut und Iskenderun (Nr. 9. 10. 19. 20).

Die Bilder sind überwiegend in zeitlicher Abfolge angeordnet. So bildet diese Arbeit eine gute Ergänzung zu Andraes eigenen Lebenserinnerungen (LE) und der Biographie seines Lehrers Robert Koldewey, die Andrae selbst herausgegeben hat (W. Andrae, Babylon. Die versunkene Weltstadt und ihr Ausgräber Robert Koldewey, Berlin 1952). Auf beide Bücher wird im folgenden immer wieder, teilweise in wörtlichen Zitaten, hingewiesen. Durch die chronologische Anordnung der Bilder wird auch die Entwicklung des Künstlers Andrae sichtbar.

Daß Andrae echter Künstler und nicht nur ein gut zeichnender oder aquarellierender (LE 77) Archäologe war (obwohl er sich selbst bescheiden nur als Dilettant empfand), wird der Betrachter schnell erkennen. Dabei handelt es sich bei manchen Skizzen um schnell hingeworfene (z. B. Nr. 39), um Beilagen von Briefen nach Hause (Nr. 40), je nach der ihm zur Verfügung stehenden Zeit. Er verstand meisterhaft, mit dem Bleistift, der Kreide, der Feder und dem Pinsel umzugehen. Landschaft und Himmel wie Tier und Mensch, bis zum Portrait, alles findet sich in seinen Arbeiten, für alles gibt es im folgenden Belege. Erstaunlich auch die Stärke seiner inneren Vorstellungskraft, die ihn zu den klaren und deutlichen und gleichzeitig dabei im Detail sich nicht festlegenden

Federzeichnungen befähigte, in denen er aus den unansehnlichen, in seinen Grabungen in Assur festgestellten (Lehm-)Ziegelmauerresten die alte Stadt zum neuen Leben erweckte und dem Beschauer ganze Ansichten derselben oder einzelne Bauwerke vor Augen führte (vgl. Nr. 126–131, auch Abb. 20).

Andrae, der als Arbeitsloser nach dem 1. Weltkrieg kurze Zeit erwog, sich völlig der Kunst zu widmen, hat dann später kaum noch gemalt. In seinen archäologischen Fach-publikationen finden sich allerdings zahlreiche hervorragende Rekonstruktionszeich-nungen der eben beschriebenen Art, die erweisen, wie stark die innere Schau dieses Mannes war, dem wir nicht nur die Durchführung der Grabung in Assur (unter sparta-nischen Bedingungen), die Einrichtung der Vorderasiatischen Abteilung der Berliner Museen und eine ganze Generation von ausgezeichneten Bauforschern verdanken. Unter diesen ist zuerst sein Schüler und Nachfolger auf dem Lehrstuhl für Bauge-schichte an der Technischen Universität Berlin, Ernst Heinrich, zu erwähnen. Dessen Nachruf auf Andrae ist eine der besten Würdigungen dieses großen Vertreters der sog. Koldewey-Schule; sie ist deshalb hier am Ende noch einmal abgedruckt.

R. M. B.

WALTER ANDRAE
18. 2. 1875–28. 7. 1956

Leben und Werk

»Er grub Assur aus. Er richtete die Vorderasiatische Abteilung der Staatlichen Museen ein.«

Dies ist die kürzeste Zusammenfassung seiner vita, geschrieben von ihm im Jahre seines Todes 1956, im Testament.

Kindheit und Jugend 1875–1893

Andrae war es bestimmt, seinen Lebensweg im letzten Viertel des 19. Jahrhunderts zu beginnen. Geboren wurde er am 18. 2. 1875 als Sohn eines Eisenbahn-Ingenieurs in Anger bei Leipzig. Der Vater – er leitete einige Jahre lang den Bau einer Umgehungs-bahn – war in Leipziger Bürgerkreisen bekannt und beliebt als virtuoser Klavierspieler, als Sänger und Laienschauspieler. Seine Laufbahn beendete er als Eisenbahndirektor der Sächsischen Staatsbahnen. Diesem bürgerlichen Elternhaus entstammend begann

Walter Andrae nach einer humanistischen Vorbildung in den Gymnasien von Chemnitz und Grimma und nach der einjährigen Militärdienstzeit das Studium der Architektur an der Technischen Hochschule in Dresden. Sein Zeichentalent hatte sich in frühester Jugend zwar geregt, wurde aber während der Schulzeit so gut wie nicht gefördert.

Studienzeit 1893–1898

Auf die weitere Entwicklung der zeichnerischen Begabung hatten die Begegnungen mit Künstlern während seines Studiums an der Technischen Hochschule in Dresden erheblichen Einfluß. Andrae nennt die Jugendstil-Zeichner und Radierer Otto Greiner und Max Klinder,[1] die er bewundert und nachahmt. Seine Schwester Elisabeth, die Malerin,[2] die später für die ständige Ausstellung im Vorderasiatischen Museum die Großbilder von Assur, Uruk und Boğazköy-Ḫattuša malte, studierte an der Kunstakademie in Dresden, was Verbindungen schuf zu deren Schülern und Lehrern.

Von seinen Lehrern nennt er Cornelius Gurlitt (Baukunstgeschichte),[3] Karl Weißbach,[4] Ernst Giese[5] und Paul Wallot.[6] Gurlitt regt seinen Schüler an zum Skizzieren der Barockbauten in Dresden und Wien. Das gehört freilich schon zur ernsthaften Seite des Architekturstudiums. Paul Wallot, der in Berlin mit dem Bau des Reichstagsgebäudes betraut worden war, zeigt dem Studenten, wie mit großen Baumassen umzugehen sei – zunächst einmal auf Papier und Reißbrett. Andrae bewunderte Wallot. In dessen Sinne entstand die Arbeit für die Staatsprüfung als Regierungsbauführer (Dipl.-Ing.), die er nach acht Semestern mit »sehr gut« bestand. Wenige Wochen war er in einem Staatsbauamt tätig, als ihm sein Studienfreund und späterer Schwager Paul Ehmig die Zeitungsannonce schickte: Zeichner für Expedition nach Vorderasien gesucht. Andrae hatte damals gerade einen Geräteschuppen für ein Forstamt zu entwerfen, nachdem er doch wenige Wochen zuvor bei der Staatsprüfung gelobt worden war für den Entwurf eines Landtagsgebäudes, das durchaus größer sein mußte als das Berliner Reichstagsgebäude seines Lehrers Wallot. Andrae bewarb sich sofort um die Teilnahme an der Babylon-Expedition Koldeweys. Unter 16 Bewerbern wurde er ausgewählt.

---

1 Otto Greiner, Maler, Lithograph, Stecher, 16. 12. 1869–24. 9. 1916, vgl. Allgemeines Lexikon der Bildenden Künstler von der Antike bis zur Gegenwart. Begründet von Ulrich Thieme und Felix Becker (im folgenden abgekürzt: Thieme-Becker). Band 14 (1921) 588 f. – Max Klinger, Graphiker, Maler, Bildhauer, 18. 2. 1857–5. 7. 1920, vgl. ebenda 20 (1927) 513 ff.

2 Elisabeth Andrae, Landschaftsmalerin und -lithographin, 3. 8. 1876 – Mai 1945, Thieme-Becker 1 (1907) 442; H. Vollmer, Künstlerlexikon des 20. Jahrhunderts (1953) 47; L. Jakob-Rost – E. Klengel – R.-B. Wattke – J. Marzahn, Das Vorderasiatische Museum (1987) 61 Abb. 56 (= E. Andrae ebenda vor ihrem Bild des sog. Königstores in Boğazköy-Ḫattuša).

3 *Cornelius* Gustav Gurlitt, 1. 1. 1850–25. 3. 1938, Kunsthistoriker, Prof. Dr., vgl. Otto Schubert, Neue deutsche Biographie 7 (1966) 327 ff.

4 *Karl* Robert Weißbach, 8. 4. 1841–8. 7. 1905, Architekt, Prof., vgl. Thieme-Becker 35 (1942) 22.

5 Ernst Giese, 16. 4. 1832–12. 10. 1903, Architekt, Prof., vgl. Thieme-Becker 14 (1921) 5.

6 Paul Wallot, 26. 6. 1841–10. 8. 1912, Architekt, Prof. Dr., Geh. Baurat und Geh. Hofrat, vgl. Thieme-Becker 35 (1942) 103 f.

Abb. 1 Walter Andrae, Selbstportrait 1902 in Babylon

Der Vater, um die Karriere des Sohnes besorgt, riet dringend ab, den »sicheren« Staatsdienst aufzugeben. Auch noch später, 1903 und 1908, als Andrae seine Urlaubszeiten in Europa verbrachte, versuchte der Vater, ihn von der Ausgräbertätigkeit im Morgenlande zur beamteten Architekturtätigkeit in Deutschland zurückzubringen.

Am 12. Dezember 1898 fuhr Koldewey mit Andrae auf der »Cleopatra« vom Österreichischen Lloyd in Triest ab und erreichte nach einem Zwischenaufenthalt in Alexandria (Nr. 4) am 20. Dezember Port Said (Nr. 5). Dort stieg man auf den »uralten syrischen Küstenklepper ›Nettuno‹, ebenfalls vom Lloyd« um, der sie, zusammen mit

Bruno Moritz von der khedivialen Bibliothek in Kairo über Jaffa (Nr. 6–8), Haifa nach Beirut brachte (Nr. 9. 10).

Babylon 1899–1903

Für eine Assistententätigkeit an der Seite des erfahrenen Bauforschers Robert Koldewey war Andrae (Abb. 1) so gut wie nicht ausgebildet. Das bemerkte Koldewey schon bei der von Kaiser Wilhelm II. gewünschten Untersuchung der Ruine Baalbek (Nr. 11–17. 21), als es um die Bauaufnahme ging. Er schrieb darüber Anfang Januar 1899 in einem Brief an seinen Freund Otto Puchstein: »Wären wir doch beisammen wie dort in den Tempeln von Sizilien. Ich habe hier einen harmlosen Jüngling bei mir, der kann nicht einmal ein Stemmloch von einem Wolfloch unterscheiden – aber er malt und zeichnet entzückend.«[7]

Von Baalbek zurück nach Beirut, von dort mit dem Schiff nach Alexandrette (Nr. 19. 20), dem heutigen Iskenderun, wo man am 22. Januar 1899 eintraf, ging es nach Aleppo (Nr. 18. 22), das am 25. Januar 1899 erreicht wurde (MDOG 1, 1898/1899, 10).

Martha Koch, die Gattin des deutschen Kaufmanns Carl Koch (vgl. Kat. zu Nr. 22 und 160), gab jede erdenkliche Hilfe, so wie sie es auch später 1915 und 1916 noch tat, als sie »dem vollkommen hilflos gewordenen Generalstabe zum Weiterkommen nach Baghdad« half: »Frau Koch zuliebe taten die Aleppiner Leute alles, dem Kommandoton der hohen Herren wollten sie sich gar nicht fügen« (LE 229). Sie hat sich in jener Zeit auch mutig für die Armenier eingesetzt, bis hin zum deutschen Oberkommandierenden v. Falkenhayn. Doch das ist Vorgriff auf spätere Zeiten. Von dieser hervorragenden Frau besitzen wir aus Andraes Hand leider nur die Rückansicht (Nr. 22). Zunächst brach man am 8. Februar in Aleppo zu einem 26tägigen Karawanenmarsch nach Baghdad auf (Nr. 23–41, Abb. 2–4), das am 5. März erreicht wurde. Die Lehrzeit Andraes begann.

Koldewey führte längs des Euphrats so, daß er zwei bis dahin noch nicht erforschte Ruinenstätten berührte: Halebije, das alte Zenobia (Nr. 29, Abb. 3), und Islahije – Kan Kalessi, das alte Dura Europos (Nr. 31).[8] Zur provisorischen Bauaufnahme umschritten Koldewey und Andrae die Ruinen routierend. Für den Assistenten war dies die erste Aufnahmepraxis in Mesopotamien. Die damals wüstenähnliche Öde weiter Strecken des Euphrattales hat Andrae, wie zuvor die Landschaften der Mittelmeerküste und Baalbeks, nahezu täglich zeichnend und aquarellierend festgehalten (Nr. 23–36). In Babylon wurde er dann von Koldewey in dessen erprobte, für die archäologische Arbeit notwendige Art der zeichnerischen Darstellung eines Grabungsfeldes eingeführt: »Noch etwas anderes hatte ich bei Koldewey gelernt. Die Oberfläche unserer so prosaischen Ruinenhügel s o darzustellen, daß sie plastisch vor dem Auge des Betrach-

---

7 LE 34 nach C. Schuchhardt, Ernste und heitere Briefe aus einem Archäologenleben (1925).
8 Vgl. Katalog Nr. 31.

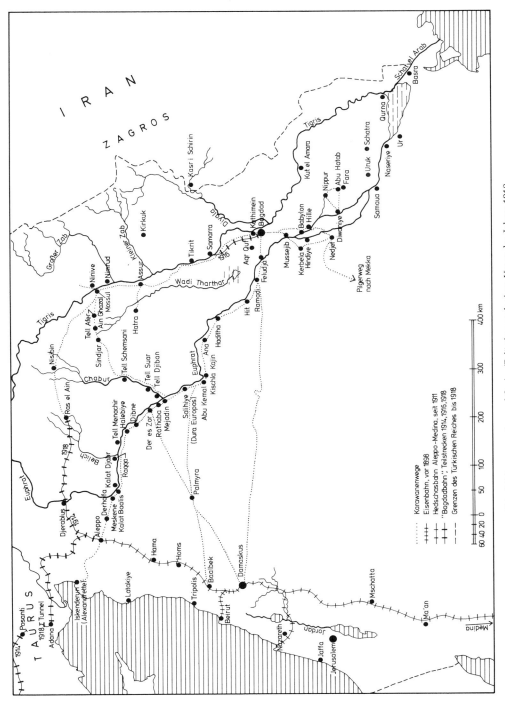

Abb. 2 Mesopotamien und Syrien/Palästina nach einer Karte des Jahres 1918

Abb. 3 Halebije, 15. 2. 1899

ters zu liegen schienen, nämlich immer so, als seien sie von der Sonne aus Südosten beleuchtet. Von Fernerstehenden ist diese Finesse oft genug für überflüssig oder gar skurril erklärt worden. Uns erschien sie notwendig, denn diese Oberfläche der Erde galt uns als der letzte, eben der heutige Ruinenzustand von Babylon.

Das Wesentliche bei diesen Gelände- und Bauwerkaufnahmen nach Koldeweyscher Art ist n i c h t das Schattieren, sondern das Zeichnen *vor der Natur,* also nicht am Tisch zu Hause, wo man nur die trigonometrischen Festpunkte aufträgt. A l l e s andere wird draußen vor dem Objekt zu Papier gebracht. Das ist die einzige Methode, alle Fehlerquellen zu vermeiden, die entstehen müssen, wenn man Skizzen von draußen mitbringt und zu Hause ›einträgt‹. Wir haßten geodätische Isohypsenpläne und schattenlose, wenn auch noch so ›steingerechte‹ Ruinendarstellungen!

Da wir alles in unser trigonometrisch bestimmtes Gradnetz eingepaßt hatten, konnten dann die Ausgrabungen in dieses Oberflächenbild an der richtigen Stelle eingetragen werden. Da erschienen dann Gebäudeteile. Auch diese erhielten in der Darstellung die Südost-Beleuchtung und warfen Schatten von der Länge der Gebäudereste-Höhe.

Wer sich in diese fest angenommene Methode hineingesehen hat, braucht nicht erst lange zu rechnen, sondern überschaut die Situation mit e i n e m Blick. Bei allen deutschen Ausgrabungen im Irak ist diese Methode beibehalten worden.«[9]

---

9 LE 78 f.

Abb. 4 Lager östlich Kischla Kajin

Am 22. 3. 1899 war die Expedition in Babylon eingetroffen (Nr. 42–90, Abb. 5). Hier hatte Andrae bei Koldewey das Ausgraben zu lernen an einem Objekt, das so leicht von keinem anderen an Größe und Tiefe, räumlich und geistig gesehen, übertroffen werden kann. Sehr bald wurde dem damals 24jährigen Architekten bewußt, daß dieser Anfang zugleich eine Schicksalswende war, nämlich von der schaffenden Baukunst zur Bauforschung. Sie sollte das ganze Leben bestimmen. Im höchsten Alter blickt er zurück auf die beiden ersten Jahre in Babylon: Er sieht sich als Adept, der in die Geheimnisse der Altertumsforschung eingeweiht werden sollte. Die Schule Koldeweys nahm ihren Anfang und damit die wissenschaftliche Ausgrabungstechnik in Mesopotamien.

Schon zu Beginn der Arbeit in Babylon hatte Koldewey seinem Mitarbeiter eine Arbeit zugewiesen, deren Ergebnis diesen lebenslang bewegte, ja ihm zur Lebensaufgabe wurde.

Auf dem Kasr-Hügel (Nr. 85–87) hatte Koldewey die Grabung angesetzt, weil dort eine Menge farbig-emaillierter Ziegelbrocken zu finden waren, mit klaren, leuchtenden Farben, Reste unbekannter, zerstörter Kunstwerke.[10] Viele dieser Brocken konnten relativ rasch aufgrund ihrer Relieform »identifiziert« werden: Sie entsprachen den Formen der Drachen und Stiere, die als nicht-emaillierte Ziegelreliefs an den Mauern der freigelegten Fundamente des Ischtar-Tores ans Tageslicht kamen. Aber es blieb ein Rest an farbigen Ziegelbrocken mit und ohne Relief-Formen aus dem Bereiche der Prozessionsstraße und eines Palasthofes. Sie paßten nicht zu den Stier- und Drachenbildern. Ihre Bestimmung herauszufinden war Andraes Aufgabe. Nach einjähriger, geduldiger Arbeit des Zusammensetzens hatten die Versuche Erfolg (vgl. Hintergrund von Nr. 2 und Nr. 80). Die Löwen der Prozessionsstraße mit den Rosettenornamenten, die Löwen der Thronsaalfassade mit den Ranken-, Blüten- und Palmenornamenten waren gefunden. 27 Jahre später konnte Andrae etwa 300 000 dieser farbigen Ziegelbrocken nach Verhandlungen mit dem Irak von Babylon nach Berlin bringen lassen.[11]

Koldewey hat sich bald auf seinen Assistenten voll verlassen. Sonst hätte er nicht von 1901 an ihm, dem 20 Jahre Jüngeren, zeitweise die Grabungsleitung in Babylon, Borsippa-Birs Nimrud (Nr. 91, Abb. 5) und Fara (vgl. Abb. 6) anvertraut.

Diese »Nebengrabungen« begannen mit Birs Nimrud. Koldewey und Andrae wechselten sich dort und in Babylon in der Leitung ab.[12] Schon ein Jahr später (1902) war Andrae in Fara ganz auf sich gestellt und mußte beweisen, was er an Menschenführung von Koldewey gelernt hatte.[13] In Fara war man fern von den Anfängen moderner Zivilisation, die es in den Städten Mesopotamiens in Form von Polizei und Verwaltungsbe-

---

10 Vgl. Katalog Nr. 80.
11 Vgl. unten S. 34 ff.
12 Vgl. RK 149 ff., LE 91 ff., 96 ff. und Katalog Nr. 91 sowie R. Koldewey, Die Tempel von Babylon und Borsippa, WVDOG 15 (1911).
13 RK 195. Andrae hat später die Befunde und Funde der Grabung in Fara Ernst Heinrich zur Bearbeitung überlassen, vgl. E. Heinrich, Fara (1931).

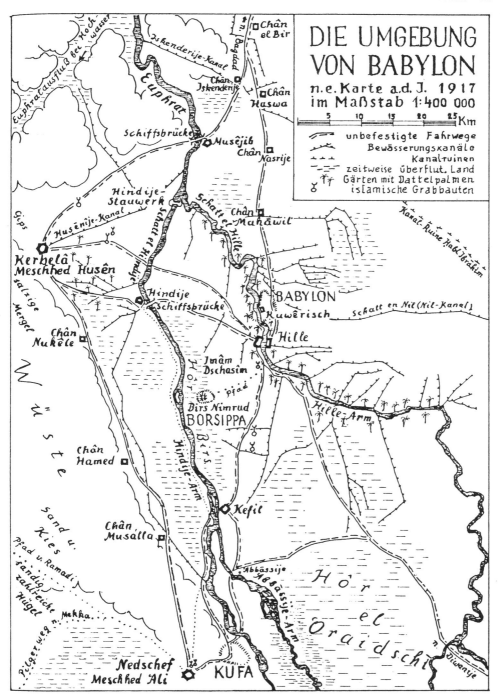

Abb. 5 Umgebung von Babylon nach einer Karte des Jahres 1917

hörden, von Post und Telegraf schon gab. Man lebte mit einer Landbevölkerung, die von diesen Errungenschaften völlig unberührt war. In der abgelegenen Farahana gab es Konflikte, die hervorgingen aus der Begehrlichkeit von Sippen- und Stammesführern, welche an den Einkünften der Grabungsarbeiter, die sie zu stellen hatten, beteiligt waren.[14] Der Europäer mußte unter allen Umständen mit den Schechs im guten auskommen. In den Biographien Koldeweys und Andraes sind die Konflikte in Fara und Assur geschildert – auch ihre Beilegung. Auf heutige Leser mögen die beschriebenen Ereignisse erheiternd wirken, was aber an der humorvollen Art liegt, in der beide Autoren überstandene Strapazen zu beschreiben pflegten. Sie befanden sich in Fara, Assur und Babylon unter Menschen, bei denen selbst ein fahrlässig verursachter Schieß-Unfall mit Todesfolge zu Blutrache, eine Beleidigung durch Worte oder Gesten zu heißblütigen, unberechenbaren Ausbrüchen hätte führen können. Wie schon in Fara hat Andrae sich bei Zwistigkeiten, die sich unter Einheimischen mit und ohne Blutvergießen abspielten und das Wohl der Grabungsmitarbeiter betrafen, durch ruhige Überlegung und angemessene Reaktion Autorität verschafft. Es war eine Autorität, die nicht auf Macht beruhte. Spätere nicht unblutige Zwischenfälle in Assur bewiesen das, denn sie geschahen sozusagen unter den Augen bewaffneter Polizisten, die als Vertreter der türkischen Staatsmacht die Archäologen hätten schützen sollen.

Weder Koldewey noch Andrae haben beschrieben, was sie befähigt hatte, mit arabischen Bauern und Beduinen über Jahrzehnte so friedlich auszukommen. Die lange, kaum unterbrochene Anwesenheit im Lande hat sie mit Sprache, Sitten und Gebräuchen vertraut gemacht. Hätte das genügt? Beide haben die Gepflogenheiten der Menschen, die religiösen Gebote eingeschlossen, mit Taktgefühl beachtet. Vertrauen und Anhänglichkeit waren die Antwort.

Die deutschen Warka-Expeditionen vor und nach dem zweiten Weltkrieg schätzten den Beistand, den ihnen Ismain ibn Dschasim gab (Abb. 9 ganz rechts).[15] Als junger Mann hatte er 1904 Andrae von Babylon nach Assur begleitet, als Diener. Nach dem

---

14 R. Koldewey, MDOG 15, 1902, 8 ff. (zu den Lebensverhältnissen bes. 18 ff.); MDOG 16, 1902/1903, 9 ff.; W. Andrae, ebenda 16 ff. 24 ff.; MDOG 17, 1903, 4 ff. (zu den Lebensverhältnissen bes. 18 ff.); A. Nöldecke, ebenda 35 ff.; RK 153 ff.; LE 112 ff. 123 ff.

15 Vgl. H. J. Lenzen, UVB 22 (1966) 8 f. – Im Besitz der Abt. Baghdad des Deutschen Archäologischen Instituts befindet sich eine Bronzebüste von Ismain ibn Dschasim, die 1955 von Peter Steyer geschaffen wurde. Vgl. LE 154 f., 264 ff. – 154 f.:
»Mit dem Gesinde im Expeditonshofe gut auszukommen, war ohne diplomatische Kunststücke leicht. Das gelang jedoch nur deshalb so gut, weil die Mehrzahl dieser Araber von Natur aus gutwillig, ja z. T. vorbildlich waren. Obenan mein guter Ismain, der in wunderbarer Treue noch heute als Großgrundbesitzer und Kaufmann an mir hängt, obwohl wir uns 20 Jahre nicht mehr haben sehen können. Als Symbol unseres Verhältnisses zueinander kann folgende kleine Geschichte gelten: Eines Tages steht er an meiner Zimmertür wie üblich, mit auf dem Bauch übereinandergelegten Händen: ›Oh Herr, Dir ist heute ein Sohn geboren worden, wie soll er heißen?‹ Ich gab ihm den Namen Ali, und so heißt er fortan und zeugte seinem Vater Ismain 16 Enkel, von denen heute noch 10 leben und ihrem Großvater innige Freude machen, insbesondere der Jüngste. Und auch alle diese Enkel wissen genau Bescheid über unsere deutschen Ausgrabungen und unsere Persönlichkeiten. Damals schon in Assur war Ismain unentbehrlich als Schlichter von Araberstreitigkeiten, die

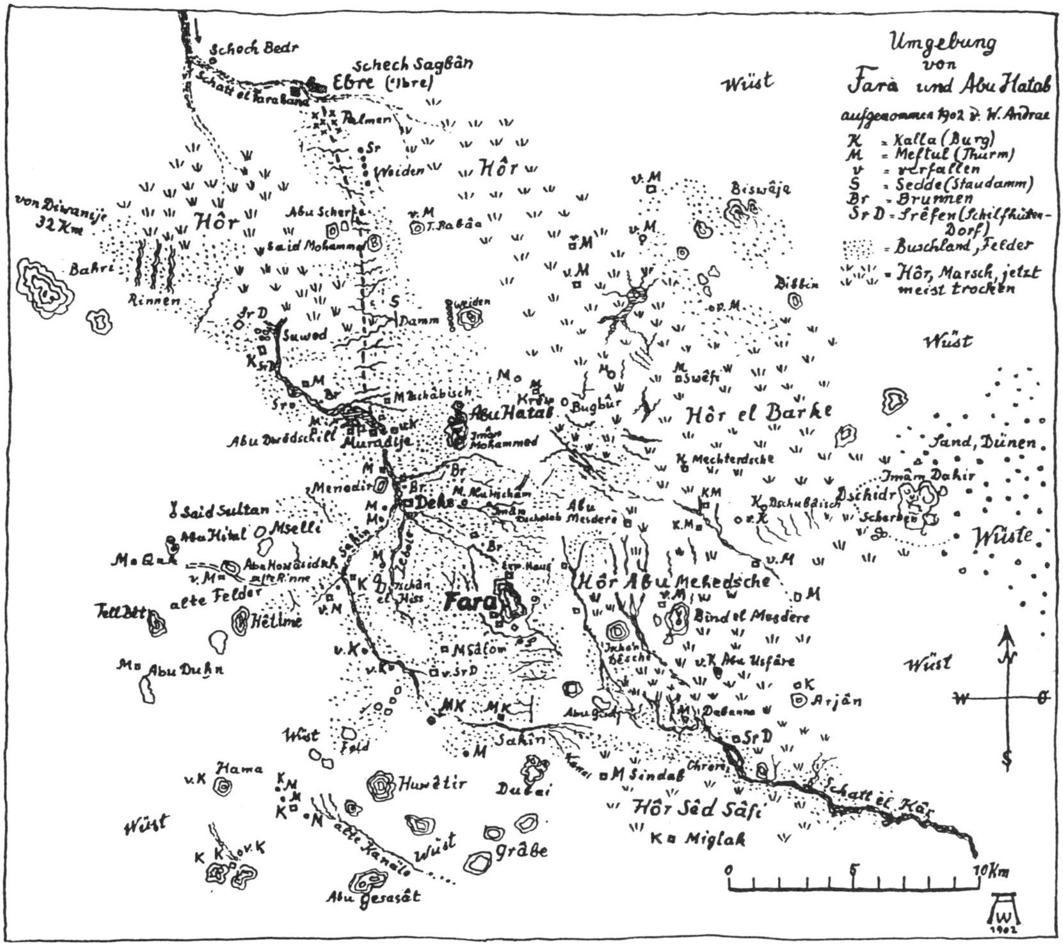

Abb. 6 Umgebung von Fara und Abu Hatab, 1902 aufgenommen von W. Andrae

manchmal bis in unseren Hof brandeten. Wir wußten durch ihn sehr genau, auf welche Leute von dem Völkchen da draußen Verlaß war, auf welche nicht. Es gab da sehr erhebliche Unterschiede.

Nachzutragen ist noch zu Ali ibn Ismain: Als Ali eine Wiege brauchte, hatte mein echter, in Dresden erworbener, ungegerbter Rindlederkoffer durch Feuchtigkeit japanische Dachformen angenommen. Unmöglich, ihn zu schließen, da er auf der Reise in den Regen gekommen war. Ismains Auge fiel auf ihn. Auf seinen Antrag wurde der Koffer im Scharnier zerteilt, und Ali schaukelte in der einen Hälfte, bis er laufen konnte. Auch die andere Hälfte fand Verwendung, aber nicht bei Ismains. Noch heute brennt eine Unterlassungssünde in meinem Erinnern: daß ich damals ganz vergaß, nach dem Befinden der Mutter Alis zu fragen. Das kann jedoch für arabisches Fühlen gerade das Richtige gewesen sein: Geltung haben nur der Mann und der Sohn!«

Ismain war in seinem letzten Lebensjahrzehnt der Uruk-Expedition verbunden, vgl. Lenzen a. O. Sein Sohn Ali übernahm dann seine Stelle als Wirtschaftsführer der Grabung. Am 16. 12. 1981 wurde er mit dem Bundesverdienstkreuz am Bande ausgezeichnet, bei dieser Ehrung wurde auch der Verdienste seines Vaters Ismain gedacht. Ali ibn Ismain starb am 20. 2. 1985 in seinem Haus in Hille.

Ende der Grabung 1914 kehrte er in seinen Heimatort Hille zurück. 1915 kam Andrae als Offizier wieder nach Mesopotamien. Ismain war sofort wieder da und begleitete Andrae bis 1918 wie ein Schatten durch alle gefahrvollen Kriegsereignisse am Tigris, auch am Diyala, in Syrien und in Palästina. Er war nicht nur Diener, sondern auch Berater und hat Andrae vor manchem Unheil bewahrt – aus freien Stücken, denn als Araber brauchte er in der türkischen Armee nicht zu dienen. Es ergab sich eine lebenslang währende Freundschaft.

In Babylon gehörten – außer der Bearbeitung der farbigen Ziegelbrocken – zur Arbeit Andraes u. a. ein großer Teil der Stadtplanaufnahme und die Arbeit am Marduk-Tempel.[16]

Daneben blieb er seiner »Freizeitbetätigung«, seinen Aquarellen und Zeichnungen, treu. Auch in diesen sticht die Gabe exakter Schilderung hervor, daß durch sie die Bilder zu Zeitdokumenten werden. Bereits jetzt in Babylon beginnt das Nachdenken über die Farbe und auch ein Experimentieren mit der Farbe. Andrae schildert uns in den Lebenserinnerungen diesen Weg des Zeichners zum zeichnenden Maler und, wie spätere Bilder ausweisen, zum Maler. Er selbst hat seine Orientbilder bescheiden nur als »Arbeiten« eines Dilettanten bezeichnet.[17]

Diese Betrachtung seiner »Lehrjahre« als Ausgräber geht aus von einer im Alter gestellten Frage: Wie hielten wir es in Babylon mit der Religion? »Obwohl rings um uns Religion ausgeübt wurde, dachte ich nicht mehr an die von mir selbst in der Jugend ausgeübte. Sie war wie verschwunden. Was war an ihre Stelle getreten? Wirklich nur ein Vacuum?[18]« »Riet mir nur deshalb Koldewey, den Schopenhauer kommen zu lassen und zu lesen, damit das Loch ausgefüllt werde? Ich tat es, nicht deshalb, weil ich gespürt hätte, daß etwas auszufüllen war, sondern weil er es besser wissen mußte. Ich konnte ihn in aller Ruhe studieren, den Schopenhauer und seine Welt als Wille und Vorstellung, diese echte Junggesellenphilosophie!

Besonders religiös stimmte mich diese Lektüre freilich so wenig wie die Seitenblicke auf Immanuel Kants ›Träume eines Geistersehers‹ und seine verschiedenen Kritiken, deren allzulange Sätze mich immer wieder abstießen.«[19] »Schon im zweiten Jahre in Babylon ging mir statt dessen ein anderes, mehr irdisches und weniger philosophisches Licht auf: Die Taten und Leiden des Lichtes, wie Goethe die Farben nennt, und die Formen, welche die Natur vor unsere Augen stellte zum Bewundern. Mir scheint fast, als wäre mir diese Erleuchtung als voller Ersatz beschert worden.

Es lag sogar etwas feierlich Begeisterndes über diesem farbigen Einfangen der Natur auf meinen Blättern. An den arbeitsfreien Sonntagen nach der arbeitsreichen Sechstagewoche ging ich am liebsten in die ruinenfreie Landschaft, in die Palmenhaine, an die Flußufer, auf die grünen oder abgeernteten Felder und gewann allmählich auch den

---

16 Vgl. R. Koldewey, Die Tempel von Babylon und Borsippa, WVDOG 15 (1911) 37 ff.
17 Vgl. unten p. 15 (nach LE 77).
18 LE 75 ff.
19 Bisher unveröffentlichte, in LE weggelassene Passage.

Anschluß an die seltsame Schönheit der formlos scheinenden Ruinenhügel, denen der kundiger gewordene Blick doch schon manches Verborgene absehen konnte. Immer mutiger ging ich den spröden Palmen zuleibe, an die ich mich ein ganzes langes Jahr nicht herangewagt hatte. Mancherlei Hemmungen verhinderten das Wagnis. Anfangs die landesübliche vierwochenlange, sehr schwächende Dysenterie, die ebenfalls ortsübliche Bagdadbeule, die man damals noch nicht heilen konnte, sondern ein Jahr lang überstehen mußte und endlich die Arbeit an den sehr farbigen babylonischen Löwen, die mich ein volles Jahr Tag und Nacht in Atem hielt. Jetzt im zweiten Jahr trat ein anderer Rhythmus ein: Sechs Tage Hügelaufnahmen messend und zeichnend und minutiöse Ziegelzeichnerei ausgegrabener Mauerreste, dazu der tägliche Grabungs- dienst zur Beobachtung der Grabungsfortschritte und -resultate. Der Sonntag als Ruhetag mit jener erholsamen Farbenschwelgerei wurde eine wirksame Erholung. Wirksamer als Bücherlesen. Es erhielt frisch und gesund. Ich kann es allen empfehlen, die so seltsam wie ich veranlagt sind. Ich erinnerte mich meiner Studien bei Erwin Oehme[20] in Dresden. Nur tauchten hier ganz andere Probleme der Farbgebung auf als in der Heimat. Vor allem beunruhigte mich lange das überhelle Licht, das sich auch durch die Kontraste nicht bändigen lassen wollte. Es war doch kein Kunststück, Mor- gen- und Abenddämmerungen ohne direktes Sonnenlicht zu malen, so schön die Far- ben auch sein mochten. Nein! Wir erleben doch auch den viel, viel länger sengenden Tag mit dem prallen Sonnenlicht! Wie macht man das? Die meisten Orientmaler schei- tern bei diesem Versuch. Mir gelang es, wie ich glaube, nur ganz selten. Akademisch geschulte Maler würden anders gemalt haben. Meine Malereien sind liebhaberisch ent- standen und haben hie und da Dilettantenwert. Freuden und Leiden des Künstlers stek- ken aber doch in ihnen. Das kann ich ehrlich behaupten...«[21]

»Lieber Leser, Du irrst, wenn Du annimmst, daß mir die Malerei mehr wert gewesen wäre als Forschung und Zeichnung. Ich vergleiche sie vielmehr mit dem ›Unkraut‹ am Rande unserer heimischen Kornfelder, das zugleich den Rand der Straßen und Wege begleitet, auf dem die vollen Erntewagen fahren sollen. Dieses ›Unkraut‹ enthält bekanntlich fast alle die guten Heilpflanzen, mit denen wir uns gesund machen können. Ich könnte meine Malerei auch mit ›Nebenprodukt‹ bezeichnen, obwohl es mir weniger sympathisch ist. Denn es erinnert zu sehr an die chemische Industrie, deren ›Nebenpro- dukte‹ ja ebenfalls mehr schädliche als nützliche ›Medikamente‹ sein können, die leider meist in einer ›Kette‹ mit den wüstesten Spreng- und Giftstoffen entstehen. Ich habe gelernt, sie zu bemißtrauen. Wenn Du, lieber Leser, anderer Meinung bist, magst Du diesen Vergleich dem mit den Heilpflanzen vorziehen. Ich tue es nicht.

Einem gesunden Instinkt folgend habe ich beim Aquarellieren weder in Form noch in Farbe gestrebt, vollkommene ›Naturtreue‹ nach Art der Farbfotografie zu erzielen. Der Stimmungsgehalt der Motive und der symphonische Zusammenklang der Farben

20 Erwin Ernst E. Oehme, Landschafts- und Genremaler (Schüler u. a. von Ludwig Richter), 18. 9. 1831–10. 10. 1907, vgl. Thieme-Becker 25 (1931) 566.
21 LE 76 f.

blieb mir nach einer natürlichen Anlage meiner Sinneswahrnehmung das Wesentlichere. Da ich kein Meister wurde, blieb ich in den Anfängen dieses Strebens stecken. Wären die Bilder im Goetheschen Sinne vom Meister weit über die Natur herausgehoben worden, wenn auch nach Naturgesetzen gestaltet, so hätten sie den Beschauer wegen ihrer »Übernatürlichkeit« ergreifen können. So aber, wie sie durch meine Hand wurden, erfreut das eine oder andere den einen oder anderen Betrachter und sie werden alsdann ad acta gelegt. Mich selbst führen sie behende in die alten Zeiten ihrer Entstehung zurück. Anderen können sie diese Gunst nicht erweisen, es sei denn, der Betrachter hätte jenes Land selbst gesehen. Diese Betrachtung gehört zum notwendigen Streben nach Selbsterkenntnis und ist, wie ich glaube, hier nicht zu entbehren.«[22]

Diese im Alter gemachte Aussage zeigt auf, wie Andrae sein zeichnerisches und malerisches Schaffen selbst charakterisiert hat. Wer das Land kennt, in dem Andrae zeichnete und malte, weiß um jene Schwierigkeit, die er erwähnte. Diese Schwierigkeit stellt sich dem Künstler entgegen; sie ist auch aus den Bildern zu erschließen: Die Überfülle an Licht. Die grelle Helligkeit des Tages zusammenwirkend mit dem fast ständig – nur nach Regenfällen nicht – in der Luft befindlichen Staub, macht das Land fast farblos. E i n e Farbe dominiert, eben die Erdfarbe des weißlich-braunen Staubes, die Farbe der Wüste, die das Grün an den Flußufern wie auch die menschlichen Siedlungen überzieht. Sie verbirgt die Farben, die aber bei bestimmten atmosphärischen Gegebenheiten erscheinen. Sobald nämlich das Licht gebrochen wird, morgens, abends, bei aufziehendem oder abziehendem Gewitter, durch Wolkenschatten, Regen und selbst bei nächtlichen Lichterscheinungen entsteht Farbigkeit, die das Auge des Malers entzückt.

Andrae versuchte, diese meist flüchtigen Farbstimmungen festzuhalten, was wiederum nicht leicht war. Nie hält der Zustand der Farbigkeit in der Atmosphäre oder auf dem Erdboden lange an. Nahe dem nördlichen Wendekreis ist die Zeit der Dämmerung nur kurz. Die Fertigstellung eines Aquarells dauerte länger. Die Farbigkeit des mit dem Gewitter abziehenden Gewölks schwand rasch dahin. Selbst die Feuchtigkeit des Regens, die stets die Farben der Pflanzen und des Erdbodens kräftig hervortreten ließ, verflüchtigte sich in der wiederkehrenden Sonnenhitze schnell – und mit ihr die Farbigkeit.

Eine weitere Schwierigkeit erwähnte Andrae im Briefe an seine Eltern vom 11. 6. 1899:
»Manchmal aquarelliere ich ein wenig, aber nur abends, wenn der heiße, trockene Wind nachgelassen hat. Die Farben trocknen mit unheimlicher Geschwindigkeit, so daß man sehr rasch malen muß. Tuschzeichnungen sind ganz unmöglich, weil die Tusche an der feinen Feder sofort trocknet, sobald sie den Napf verläßt und im Napf selbst sich nur ganz kurze Zeit feucht hält.«
Daneben ist ihm der seit der Schulzeit in Grimma[23] grünende Zweig des karikierenden

---

22 Aus unveröffentlichter Urfassung der LE.
23 Vgl. LE Abb. 3.

Zeichnens nicht verkümmert. Es genügt ein Blick in das noch unveröffentlichte Gästebuch der Babylon-Expedition, in dem Andrae jedem Eintrag von 1900 bis 1902 eine
witzige zeichnerische Umrahmung gab. Auch später im Museumsdienste zu Berlin ver-
anlaßten ihn gewisse Vorkommnisse zu sarkastischer oder satirischer Darstellung, so
z. B. der Dauerstreit der Gelehrten über Aufstellungsart und -ort des Pergamon-Alta-
res. Es sei aber doch bemerkt, daß für einseitige, den Betrachter zum Lachen reizende,
karikierende Darstellungen nicht allzuviele Belege vorhanden sind. Häufiger äußerte
sich eine lebenslang vorhandene Neigung, die komische Seite menschlicher Handlungen – auch der eigenen – zu sehen (vgl. Abb. 9) und sie humorvoll in wenigen Strichen
mit oder ohne begleitende Verse festzuhalten. Grete Güterbock-Auer bemerkt dazu in
Hinblick auf ihre Kinder:

»Er konnte, während er erzählte, die Bilder zu seinen Geschichten in flüchtigen aber
lebensvollen Umrissen vor ihrem Auge erstehen lassen, köstlich humorvoll in Aus-
druck und Bewegung. Er beschenkte sie außerdem mit einigen besonders für sie gefer-
tigten Bilderbüchern, unübertrefflich kindlich, unübertrefflich phantasiereich, und
herrlich in Farbe und Zeichnung. Nicht selten benutzte er die poetischen Einfälle meines älteren Jungen selbst, um Text und Bild danach zu gestalten. Aber auch Volksmär-
chen illustrierte er in reizvollster Weise, hat auch ab und zu eine Publikation versucht,
ohne den Erfolg, den er verdient hätte.«[24]

Im fünften Jahr seiner Archäologentätigkeit übergab ihm Koldewey die Grabung in
Assur.

In Babylon (1899–1903) hat Andrae vorwiegend aquarelliert. In Assur (1904–1914)
gebrauchte er diese Technik selten, es überwiegen die Zeichnungen mit farbigen Kreiden auf getönten Papieren. Der jeweilige Ton des farbigen Zeichengrundes erleichterte
ihm die Darstellung einer Naturstimmung.

Assur 1904–1914

Im Jahre 1903 trat Andrae seinen Urlaub an. Er hatte in Deutschland Militärdienst zu
leisten (Abb. 7). Auf der Reise dorthin wählte er den Weg über Indien (Nr. 108–111).
Auf einer meist bequemen, 6 Wochen langen Eisenbahnreise, manchmal auch auf Och-
senkarren, als Gast im Hotel, im offiziellen Rasthaus für Europäer, als Gast eines Maha-
radjas, fuhr er zu den Zielen, die er sich als Architekt gewählt hatte: Zu Zeugen islami-
scher Baukunst der Mogulkaiser bei Delhi, Agra und Bidjapur, zu hinduistischen Tempeln in Tandschor, Trichinopoli und Madura, zu buddhistischen auf Ceylon, zu den
ältesten sichtbaren Heiligtümern, der Stupa von Sandschi, zum Eisenpfeiler des Ašoka,
zu den Höhlentempeln von Karli und Ellora.

24 J. Renger, in: Deutsches Archäologisches Institut, Berlin und die Antike, Aufsätze, herausggb. von W.
Arenhövel – C. Schreiber (1979) 187.

In seinen »Lebenserinnerungen« fragt sich Andrae nach der Bedeutung dieses Indien-Erlebnisses für sein Leben.[25] Von der alten Geistigkeit hat er nichts erfahren. Zu näherem Kontakt mit den indischen Menschen kam es nicht. Er befindet: Diese Begegnung mit Indien war viel zu früh, er habe sie erlebt wie ein Nachtwandler. Als lebensformendes Element war allerdings das Erlebnis Indien ein so wesentliches, daß er es nicht aus dem Bestande seiner Lebensgüter gestrichen haben wolle.

Im April 1904 ritt Andrae von Damaskus über Palmyra durch die Wüste, über den Euphrat zum Sindjar-Gebirge nach Mossul, von dort gelangte er auf einem Kelek (Floß) nach Kalat Schergat, dem alten Assur (Nr. 113–134, Abb. 8). Koldewey, der 1903 dort zu graben begonnen hatte, war schon wieder in Babylon.

Mit der Leitung der Ausgrabung von Assur erhielt Andrae (Nr. 1) eine Aufgabe, für die er sich damals zu jung fühlte, die er aber, getragen vom Vertrauen Koldeweys und dem seiner Mitarbeiter (Abb. 10), mit vollem Erfolg bewältigt hat. Sie erfüllte ihn ganz, auch lange nach dem Ende der Grabung (1914). Er hat die Aufgabe wieder und wieder unter neuen Aspekten betrachtet, indem er die Funde nicht nur »auszuwerten«, sondern die Ergebnisse davon für die heutige Zeit fruchtbar zu machen suchte. Dabei waren Lasten zu tragen und Schwierigkeiten zu überwinden, gegen die alle Leiden, unter denen heutige Feldarchäologen seufzen, nur ein Kinderspiel sind. Damals war keine größere Stadt, kein Arzt, kein Lebensmittelgeschäft in leicht erreichbarer Nähe. Der Weg nach Mossul dauerte zwei Tage, der nach Bagdad fünf bis sieben Tage. Man lebte wie die Bauern von Schergat, mit Brot von ihrem Korn, mit Fleisch von ihren Schafen, mit Fischen aus dem Tigris, sofern nicht Trockenheit oder Heuschreckenschwärme alles Heranwachsende (vgl. z. B. Nr. 134) vernichteten. In Notzeiten mußte Andrae Karawanen aussenden, um Brotgetreide für die Leute von Schergat herbeizuschaffen.

Für die Grabung in Assur gab es kaum ein Vorbild. Das in Babylon Gelernte ließ sich in der ganz anders strukturierten Ruine von Assur nur in beschränktem Maße anwenden. In Assur stieß man auf ältere Schichten als in Babylon, wo das Grundwasser das Erreichen des gewachsenen Bodens verhinderte. Neue Lösungen mußten für das Vordringen in tiefere Lagen gefunden werden. Als erster hat Andrae in Mesopotamien eine sorgfältige Schichtengrabung durchgeführt. Sie erlaubte es ihm später, komplizierte Ergebnisse, wie die Abfolge der archaischen und der jüngeren Ischtartempel in vorbildlicher Weise mitzuteilen.[26] Im Blick darauf bemerkt der französische Archäologe André Parrot mit Recht, Andrae habe seinen Lehrer Koldewey übertroffen.[27] Dem hätte

---

25 LE 130 ff.
26 W. Andrae, Die archaischen Ischtar-Tempel in Assur, WVDOG 39 (1922); ders., Die jüngeren Ischtar-Tempel in Assur, WVDOG 58 (1935).
27 A. Parrot, Archéologie mésopotamienne. Les Étapes (1946) 214:
»Cependant on ne saurait trop souligner avec quelle maîtrise, W. Andrae dirigea son expédition. A une époque où l'on cherchait une technique, il était impossible de mieux faire et dans tous les domaines, fouille et interprétation, le fouilleur d'Assur fut un étonnant précurseur. Ce n'est pas dénigrer Koldewey, que de dire que l'élève fut supérieur au maître.«

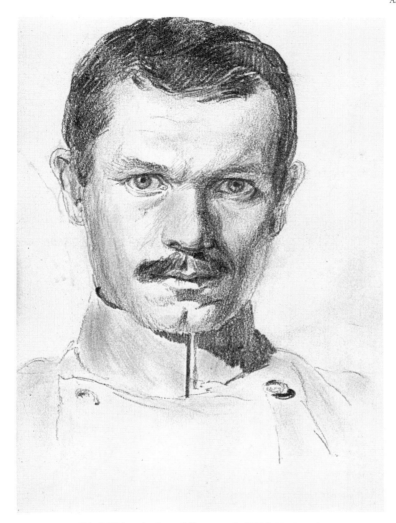

Abb. 7 Walter Andrae, Selbstportrait 1903/04 in Dresden

Andrae nicht zugestimmt. Er sah es als bedeutungsvoll und für die Archäologie in Mesopotamien als glückliche Schicksalsfügung an, daß in Assur die Grabungsmethode entwickelt werden konnte, die es ermöglichte, noch ältere Ruinenstädte wie Uruk zu erforschen.[28]

Was hat elfjährige Arbeit gebracht? Ein Zeit- und Geschichtsbild der Stadt, der Befestigungen, der Paläste, Wohnviertel, Gräber, Klein- und Großfunde, aber auch des Kli-

---

28 Die Leitung übernahm dann dort zunächst der Vertreter W. Andraes in Assur, Julius Jordan.

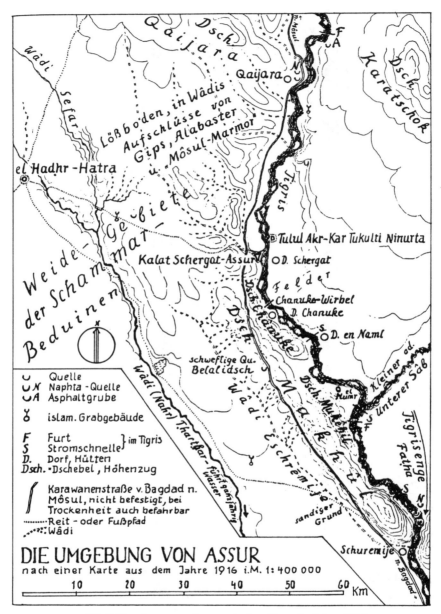

Abb. 8 Umgebung von Assur nach einer Karte des Jahres 1916

mas und anderer physikalischer Verhältnisse hat Andrae zusammenfassend niedergelegt in seinem Buche »Das wiedererstandene Assur«.[29] In den Wissenschaftlichen Veröffentlichungen der Deutschen Orient-Gesellschaft (WVDOG) über Assur sind die Funde und Befunde im Detail beschrieben und ausgewertet.[30] Die Ergebnisse der Nebengrabung Kar Tukulti Ninurta wurden in den Mitteilungen der DOG[31] und die in mehreren, jeweils sehr kurzen Besuchen durchgeführte Untersuchung von Hatra in zwei umfangreichen Bänden der WVDOG[32] von Andrae und seinen Mitarbeitern veröffentlicht.

Zweimal hat Andrae in den 10 Jahren Assur verlassen, 1908 und 1912. 1908 promovierte er an der Technischen Hochschule Dresden zum Dr.-Ing.[33] Daneben war er eingeladen zur Erstaufführung der Historischen Pantomime »Sardanapal« im Königlichen Opernhaus in Berlin. Wilhelm II. hatte Andrae 1907 auffordern lassen, für dieses – von der Kritik verrissene – Theaterstück Bühnenbilder zu entwerfen.[34] Für die Inszenie-

---

29 W. Andrae, Das wiedererstandene Assur, 9. Sendschrift d. DOG (1938); 2. Aufl. (durchgesehen und erweitert von B. Hrouda) (1977). .

30 W. Andrae, Der Anu-Adad-Tempel in Assur WVDOG 10 (1909); ders., Die Festungswerke von Assur, Text und Tafeln WVDOG 23 (1913); ders., Die Stelenreihen in Assur WVDOG 24 (1913); ders., Hethitische Inschriften auf Bleistreifen aus Assur WVDOG 46 (1924); ders., Kultrelief aus dem Brunnen des Assurtempels zu Assur WVDOG 53 (1931); W. Andrae und H. J. Lenzen, Die Partherstadt Assur WVDOG 57 (1933); W. Andrae, Vorwort und Einleitung zu Conrad Preusser, Die Wohnhäuser in Assur WVDOG 64 (1954); ders., Vorwort, Einleitung und der Abschnitt über Gruft 45 in: Arndt Haller: Die Gräber und Grüfte von Assur WVDOG 65 (1954); ders., Vorwort-Überblick: Die Raumformen assyrischer Paläste in: Conrad Preusser: Die Paläste in Assur WVDOG 66 (1955); Arndt Haller, Die Heiligtümer des Gottes Assur und der Sin-Šamaš-Tempel in Assur mit Beiträgen von Walter Andrae WVDOG 67 (1955).

31 W. Andrae – W. Bachmann, MDOG 53, 1914, 41 ff. – Vgl. jetzt auch T. Eickhoff, Kār Tukulti Ninurta, Abhandlungen der Deutschen Orient-Gesellschaft 21 (1985); R. Dittmann – T. Eickhoff – R. Schmitt – R. Stengele – S. Thürwächter, MDOG 120, 1988, 97 ff.

32 W. Andrae, Hatra I. Allgemeine Beschreibung der Ruinen, WVDOG 9 (1908); ders., Hatra II. Einzelbeschreibung der Ruinen, WVDOG 21 (1912).

33 Vgl. MDOG 40, 1909, 1.

34 Vgl. Katalog Nr. 132, 133; LE 180 ff. und J. Renger a. O. (vgl. Anm. 24) 168 f.:

»Sowohl Meissner als auch Zimmern heben in ihren Nachrufen besonders die Mitarbeit Delitzschs an der Aufführung der historischen Pantomime ›Sardanapal‹ hervor. Es scheint, als habe diese Aufführung bei den assyriologischen Zeitgenossen Erinnerungen eigentümlicher Art hinterlassen. Der Stoff des ›Sardanapal‹ ist seit 1698 wiederholt als Oper gestaltet worden (F. Stieger, Opernlexikon III (1975) 1084. Die Pantomime ›Sardanapal‹ geht auf ein Ballett in vier Aufzügen von Peter Ludwig Hertel zurück, der seit 1858 Hofkomponist, seit 1860 Direktor der Königlichen Ballettmusik in Berlin war. Die Uraufführung des Balletts fand am 24. April 1865 in der Königlichen Oper in Berlin statt; es hatte in der Folge das Gefallen von Wilhelm I. gefunden (freundliche Auskunft von Prof. Güterbock, Chicago).

Die Neuaufführung und Umgestaltung zur historischen Pantomime wäre nicht ohne das persönliche Engagement Kaiser Wilhelms II. zustande gekommen, der für sein Interesse an historisch authentisch gestalteten Operninszenierungen bekannt war. Er berichtete darüber: ›Da ich erkannte, daß die Assyriologie, die so viele bedeutende Männer, auch Geistliche beider Konfessionen, beschäftigte, von der Allgemeinheit in ihrer Bedeutung noch nicht verstanden und gewürdigt wurde, ließ ich durch meinen Freund und glänzenden Theaterintendanten, den Grafen Hülsen-Haeseler, das Stück ›Assurbanipal‹ in Szene setzen, das nach langer Vorbereitung unter Aufsicht der Deutschen Orient-Gesellschaft aufgeführt wurde.‹ (Kaiser Wilhelm II., Ereignisse und Gestalten aus den Jahren 1878–1918 [1922] 169.)

Delitzsch gestaltete das Hertelsche Ballett, dessen Choreographie von Paolo Taglioni stammte, zu einer historischen Pantomime um. Die Ballettszenen wurden angereichert durch Rezitationen allegorischer Figu-

rung des Stückes, das vom Ende der assyrischen Dynastie in Ninive handelt, hatte der Kaiser eine historisch genaue assyrische Ausstattung gewünscht. Dafür war nun als zuständig angesehen der Ausgräber von Assur. Seine in Assur angefertigten Aquarelle

ren, wie z. B. der ›Wissenschaft‹ oder der ›assyrischen Vergangenheit‹. Walter Andrae im fernen Assur mußte Bühnenbilder und Kostüme zeichnen. An den Proben und der Inszenierung war Wilhelm II. persönlich beteiligt. Die Aufführung in der Königlichen Oper Unter den Linden fand am 1. September 1908 statt: (F. Stieger a. O. 1084); sie muß – nach Berichten von Anwesenden – sterbenslangweilig gewesen sein. Auf Wunsch des Kaisers mußte die Aufführung mehrere Male wiederholt werden. Jedesmal ergab sich ein leeres Haus (G. Güterbock-Auer, unveröffentlichte Lebenserinnerungen, 187)! Es heißt, daß sich unter den Gästen der Festaufführung der Kaiser von Siam befand. Wenigstens der Schlußteil, als Ninive in Flammen stand, muß einen realistischen Eindruck hinterlassen haben, denn der aus dem Theaterschlaf erwachte Kaiser von Siam wunderte sich laut, daß niemand nach der Feuerwehr rief (freundliche Auskunft von Prof. Güterbock, Chicago).

Delitzsch erhielt noch am Abend der Aufführung vom Kaiser den Roten Adlerorden III. Klasse verliehen (Berliner Lokal-Anzeiger, 2. 9. 1908, 2.). Die extra zur Aufführung eingeladenen Assyriologen Dieulafoy aus Paris, V. Schmidt aus Kopenhagen, M. Jastrow aus Philadelphia, der Rev. Patterson aus London und Hommel aus München äußerten sich am folgenden Tag in Worten überschwenglichen Lobes in den Spalten des ›Berliner Lokal-Anzeigers‹. Eine Begebenheit besonderer Art verbindet sich mit dem Namen Dieulafoy. Grethe Güterbock-Auer, selbst bei der Festaufführung anwesend, weiß zu berichten: ›Um der Feierlichkeit nicht ganz zu erliegen, gab es für Eingeweihte an diesem Abende übrigens noch einen besonderen Spaß. Der französische Archäologe Dieulafoy war mit seiner Frau und Mitarbeiterin erschienen, einem schmächtigen Persönchen, das die Gewohnheit hatte, in Männerkleidung zu gehen, wie das bei Ausgrabungen ja von Nutzen sein mag. Diese Dame hatte schon den ganzen Tag das Hofmarschallamt beschäftigt, denn um keinen Preis der Welt durfte der prüden Kaiserin diese Figur vor Augen kommen. Es wurde ihr also ein Hofbeamter zugeteilt, der sie mit viel Geschick immer dahin zu geleiten verstand, wo die Kaiserin sicher nicht erschien. Und nun betrat dies Unglücksgeschöpf das festliche Haus der Hofoper … im Smoking! Man complimentierte Frau Dieulafoy schnell entschlossen in die Loge, die dicht neben der kaiserlichen lag, und in die man von der Hofloge aus nur blicken konnte, wenn man sich ganz vorbeugte. Eine bängere Aufführung haben die Herren des Hofmarschallamtes und der Intendantur nie erlebt, aber zum Glück dachte der Kaiser nicht daran, sich seine auswärtigen Gäste während der Pause vorstellen zu lassen – er sprach fast nur mit den Herren der Orient-Gesellschaft – und noch weniger, einen Blick in die Nachbarloge zu tun.‹ (G. Güterbock-Auer, 188.)

In der Presse erschien eine Reihe äußerst kritischer Berichte. Das ›Berliner Tageblatt‹ befindet: ›Es ist selbstverständlich, daß die Pantomime gestern mit Beifall aufgenommen wurde. Denn der Kaiser saß in der Loge, ihm gefiel die Aufführung, an der er ja selbst lebhaft mitgearbeitet hatte, und niemand widersprach. Wer aber nicht nur auf das Händeklatschen hörte, …, der konnte deutlich vernehmen, daß das Publikum sich von ganzem Herzen langweilte … Was durch die Mitarbeiterschaft Friedrich Delitzschs erreicht werden sollte, eine Hebung … ins Wissenschaftliche ist vollkommen mißlungen, mußte mißlingen.‹ (Berliner Tageblatt, 2. 9. 1908 2 f.).

An anderer Stelle heißt es: ›Der Verfasser‹ – Friedrich Delitzsch – ›des neuen ›Sardanapal‹ hat sich … zu der Behauptung verstiegen, die Kunst könne sich ›glücklich schätzen, in den Dienst der Wissenschaft zu treten‹. Man kann gewiß Wesen und Zweck der Kunst nicht ärger verkennen, als es mit diesen Worten geschieht.‹

Die ›Vossische Zeitung‹ urteilt: ›Das Unterhaltende … sind die Reste des früheren Balletts.‹ (Vossische Zeitung, 2. 9. 1908, Morgenausgabe, 3.). In einem Leitartikel resümiert das ›Berliner Tageblatt‹: ›Das assyrische Ballett ›Sardanapal‹ ist – nach allem, was man darüber hört und liest – so langweilig, daß jeder, der geduldig bis zum Ende ausharrt, den Kronenorden III. Klasse verdient.‹ (Ballettpolitik, in: Berliner Tageblatt, 7. 9. 1908, 1). Es scheint, daß sich Delitzsch hier auf ein Gebiet begeben hat, das ihm – außer einem Orden – kaum Ruhm, eher Spott und sogar den Vorwurf des ›Byzantinismus‹ eingebracht hat. Aber es wäre falsch, wenn dieses Ereignis, das ja in gewissem Maße auch seine persönliche Haltung und Stellung zum Kaiser widerspiegelt, den Blick von seinen wissenschaftlichen Leistungen in den Berliner Jahren ablenkte. Es erscheint daher angebracht, noch einmal ausdrücklich auf Einzelheiten einzugehen.«

Frau Dr. M. Srocke teilt uns freundlicherweise mit: »Die Staatsbibliothek, SPK, besitzt die Noten. Es handelt sich um ein großes historisches Ballett in vier Akten und sieben Bildern, komponiert von Peter Ludwig Hertel (Ballettmeister: Paul Taglioni) mit den Bühnenbildern von W. Andrae (Uraufführung Berlin 1. 9. 1908). Der Komponist hat einige Ballettmusiken geschrieben.«

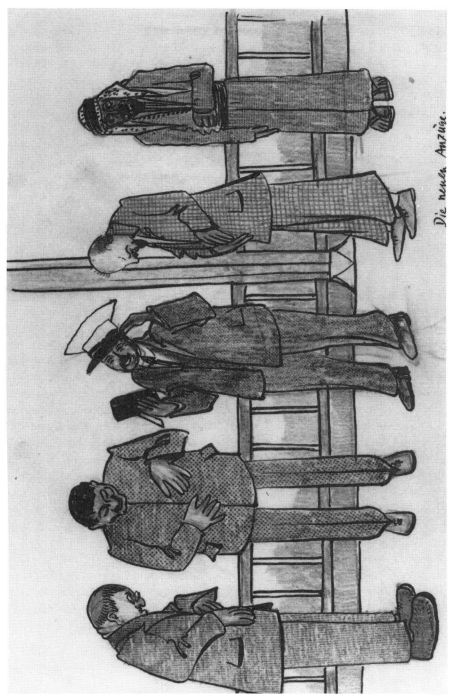

Die neuen Anzüge.

Abb. 9 Die Ausgräber von Assur in neuen Anzügen: Paul Maresch, Walter Andrae, Julius Jordan, Conrad Preußer, Ismain ibn Dschasim, etwa 1908

zu drei Szenen hatten Bühnenmaler in allen Einzelheiten auf das Format der Opernbühne gebracht. Andrae hätte in seiner Biographie diese Episode wegen der Bühnenbilder allein kaum erwähnt. Aber er hatte ja erlebt, mit welcher Anteilnahme Wilhelm II. Koldeweys Tätigkeit in Babylon und von 1904 an auch seine eigene in Assur verfolgt hatte. Der Kaiser hatte sich leidenschaftlich in geschichtliche und dynastische Probleme vertieft. Es war, als ob eine Schicksalsstimme ihn mahnend in die Zukunft weisen wollte. Aber – so schreibt Andrae[35] »was da zu ihm sprach, schien ohne innere Wirkung auf seine Haltung zu bleiben. Das Theaterstück stellt eine gefährliche Koalition der Feinde Assyriens und den Untergang von Reich und Dynastie dar und ausgerechnet derjenige, der solches für sein eigenes Reich und seine Dynastie heraufbeschwor, war zum Regisseur des vorausahnenden Schauspiels bestimmt! Dieser tragische Hintergrund des Spiels wurde damals gewiß von allen Beteiligten übersehen.«

1912 besuchte Andrae in Berlin die Abteilung der Staatlichen Museen, in der die in Babylon zusammengesetzten Tier-Reliefbilder angekommen waren. Beigefügt war eine gehörige Anzahl von emaillierten Ziegelbrocken, die nun in Berlin nach dem Vorbild aus Babylon von Museumsrestauratoren zusammengesetzt werden sollten.[36]

Man präsentierte dem »Mann aus der Wüste« stolz das neueste Werk, einen Löwen ohne Fehl und Tadel. Die Ziegelbrocken waren nämlich mit der Säge bearbeitet worden, so daß sie nahezu fugenlos aneinandergefügt werden konnten. Fehlende Emailleflächen waren durch Ölfarbe ergänzt. Das Tier sah aus wie geleckt. Von der Museumsleitung wurde dieser Löwe für viel schöner gehalten als der in Babylon zusammengesetzte, der die Bruchfugen ehrlich zeigte. Andrae hatte in Babylon eine andere Auffassung von der Behandlung und der Restaurierung antiker Kunstwerke gewonnen und hat sich in diesem Sinne temperamentvoll geäußert. Das verursachte große Aufregung bei den alten Restauratoren und beim Generaldirektor Richard Schoene.[37] Er muß sich beim Kaiser über den jungen Mann aus Babylon beschwert haben. Der Kaiser befahl Schoene und Andrae zu sich, samt den beiden Löwen, sowohl dem gesägten als auch dem in Babylon zusammengesetzten. Andrae sagte nochmals seine Meinung. Auch Wilhelm II. fand den babylonischen Löwen besser. Andrae begab sich auf den Weg nach Assur. Im Museum setzte man so wie vorher »schöne« Löwen zusammen, aber so langsam, daß Andrae noch 24 Jahre später genügend Material vorfand, um die Arbeit, nun als Museumsdirektor, nach seinem wissenschaftlichen Verständnis ausführen zu lassen.

1914 war in Assur alles, was notwendig erschien, aufs sorgfältigste untersucht worden, notiert, inventarisiert und gezeichnet. Die Grabung wurde geschlossen. 700 große Fundkisten mit Inventarlisten mußten 1000 km weit nach Basra transportiert werden. Dafür kam nur der Wasserweg in Frage. Der Tigris ist aber ein unberechenbarer Fluß, besonders oberhalb des Hamrin-Gebirges. Andrae kannte die Tücken, er hatte 1908 ein

---

35 LE 182.
36 Vgl. Nr. 2 und 80; Katalogtext zu Nr. 80 und LE 196 ff.
37 5. 2. 1840–5. 3. 1922.

Dampfmotorboot von Bagdad bis Assur durch alle Untiefen, Stromschnellen und Kies-bänke gesteuert.[38] Als Transportmittel für die schweren Kisten kamen nur die landes-üblichen Keleks – flachgehende Flöße – in Betracht.[39] Sie werden bei Mossul zusam-mengebaut und nur flußabwärts verwendet. Das aus Baumstämmen gefügte Floß wird über luftgefüllten Ziegenbälgen gebaut, dadurch bleiben die Stämme oberhalb des Wasserspiegels und das Transportgut trocken, solange die Ziegenbälge dicht bleiben. Die Erfahrung der Kelekfahrer lehrte, daß Transportgut etwa bis Bagdad trocken transportiert werden könne. Andrae beschloß, jedem einzelnen Floß einen Aufseher oder einen seiner Mitarbeiter beizugeben. Er erinnerte sich, wie es im vorigen Jahrhun-dert Botta ergangen war, der die von ihm in Chorsabad ausgegrabenen großen Stein-plastiken von Mossul auf Keleks tigrisabwärts transportieren ließ: Die Funde ver-schlang der Tigris. Sie sind trotz verschiedener Bergungsversuche nie wieder gefunden worden.

Andrae glückte das Vorhaben. Erst in Bagdad waren die Keleks so weit abgesunken, daß am anderen Tage das Wasser die Kisten berührt hätte. In Bagdad konnte mit Hilfe des Dampfkranes die Fracht von den Keleks auf die Leichter der britischen Tigris-Schiffahrts-Gesellschaft umgeladen werden. Die Kisten kamen in Basra an, wo die Funde vom Hamburger Dampfer »Cheruskia« übernommen wurden. Der türkische Anteil konnte in Port Said auf ein nach Istanbul abgehendes Schiff verladen werden. Andrae selbst suchte so schnell wie möglich nach Europa zu gelangen.[40] Mit einer eng-lischen Linie ging es von Basra über Karatschi, Bombay, Aden (Nr. 112) nach Port Said, wo er umstieg auf ein britisches Torpedoboot, das Kurierdienst zwischen Ägyp-ten und Brindisi leistete und somit die schnellste Verbindung nach Europa war, wenn auch für die Reisenden eine unbequemere als die auf dem Passagierdampfer von Aden nach Neapel. Noch im Roten Meer hatte der Kapitän im Speisesaal den Funkspruch bekanntgegeben: Das österreichische Erzherzogpaar ist in Sarajewo ermordet worden. Auf dem Torpedoboot sprach man darüber: Quasi casus belli? Andrae war davon wenig berührt. Der Schnellzug von Brindisi nach Wien brachte ihn nach Villach, der Hochzeitstermin war festgesetzt. Drei Tage nach der Heirat waren Österreich-Ungarn und Serbien im Kriege. Die »Hochzeitsreise« führte stracks in den ersten Weltkrieg, nach Dresden, wohin Andrae als Hauptmann zu seinem Regiment beordert worden war.

Und der Dampfer mit den Assurfunden? Er befand sich bei Kriegsausbruch auf der Höhe von Lissabon, als der Kapitän mit Funktelegramm angewiesen wurde, den näch-sten Hafen eines neutralen Landes anzulaufen. Portugal trat 1916 in den Krieg ein. Schiff und Ladung wurden Kriegsbeute.[41]

---

38 Vgl. den ausführlichen Bericht MDOG 42, 1909, 63 ff.
39 Vgl. LE 218 f.
40 Vgl. LE 220 f.
41 Vgl. LE 219.

Der Krieg 1914–1918

Schon 1912 hatte Koldewey seinem ehemaligen Mitarbeiter vorausgesagt, dessen Ausgräbertätigkeit gehe dem Ende entgegen.[42] Anlaß war eine Postkarte aus dem schönen
Kärnten, die Andrae aus dem Urlaub nach Babylon geschrieben hatte. Koldewey antwortete fragend, was er denn in einer längst vermessenen Gegend zu tun habe, ob er
sich etwa verlobt habe? Eben das war geschehen. Daß ein guter Ausgräber verheiratet
sein könne, hielt Koldewey für eine Unmöglichkeit. Sein Ausspruch: »Mulier taceat in
excavationibus« wurde schon damals belächelt. Aber – er behielt recht: Andrae hat nach
1914 nicht wieder ausgegraben, sondern wieder aufgebaut, geordnet und dem Verständnis der Menschen das nahegebracht, was aus den Spuren der früheren Kulturen zu
erschließen war. Daran ist Andrae aber nach 1914 durch seine Teilnahme am Krieg verhindert worden bis 1920. Im Jahre 1915 war er Kompanieführer im Stellungskriege
nahe Laon. Andrae beschreibt die eigenen schrecklichen Kriegserlebnisse in Frankreich
in den »Lebenserinnerungen« nur knapp.[43] Gesprochen hat er nie darüber.

Im Laufe des Jahres 1915 wurde er (Nr. 2) zum Stabe des Feldmarschalls von der
Goltz[44] kommandiert, der beauftragt war, die türkische Mesopotamienfront zu stabili-
sieren. So wurde Andrae wieder in den Orient geführt und Teilnehmer an Ereignissen,
die für ihn, der jene Länder zu lieben gelernt hatte, sehr kummervoll gewesen sind.
Über Aleppo ging es auf einem Doppelkahn (Abb. 10) auf dem Euphrat nach Baghdad;
auch in Mossul hielt er sich auf (Nr. 167).

Seine Kriegstätigkeit konnte er nach den mühevollen, aber so ertragreichen Jahren
in Babylon und Assur nicht als sinnvoll ansehen. Auch aus dieser Zeit liegen Bilder von
ihm vor (Nr. 144–192. 194–198). In einigen aus den Jahren 1917 und 1918 (Türkei,
Irak, Syrien und Palästina) begegnet uns eine für Andrae neue Zeichentechnik, die

---

42 Vgl. LE 196.

43 Vgl. LE 223 f.

44 Wilhelm Leopold Colmar Freiherr von der Goltz, Generalfeldmarschall, Pascha, 12. 8. 1843–19. 4.
1916. LE 228 ff.: »Als die Türkei 1914 an der Seite der Mittelmächte in den Krieg eintrat, ging der alte Feldmarschall v. d. Goltz nach Konstantinopel, wo er viele Jahre als Instrukteur des türkischen Heeres gearbeitet
hatte. 1915 übernahm er das Kommando der türkischen Streitkräfte an der Irakfront und holte uns alte Ausgräber aus den verschiedenen Fronten in seinen Stab, denn er kannte die asiatische Türkei gar nicht und
brauchte Ratgeber. Sein Stab bestand aus allerlei bunten Rittmeistern, die keine Ahnung vom Orient hatten.
So wurden wir alten Koldewey-Leute nach Berlin beordert, diesem Stabe zugeteilt und noch 1915 in Marsch
gesetzt, über das verbündete Ungarn und Bulgarien in die Türkei. Mit der Zeit versammelten sich die ehemaligen Ausgräber in Syrien und Mesopotamien auf sehr verschiedenen Positionen gar nicht etwa alle in der
Nähe des greisen Feldmarschalls, dessen Armee aus den 12 Offizieren seines Stabes, deren Burschen, einem
Unterzahlmeister und Ordonnanzen bestand, während die türkischen Truppen von ihren Offizieren geführt
wurden.

Bei weitem die erfreulichste Persönlichkeit in Bagdad war der alte Generalfeldmarschall selbst, mehr Philo-
soph als Militär, gütiger Menschenkenner und -lenker, daher in der türkischen Armee und auch in der Bevöl-
kerung äußerst beliebt und verehrt.«

Vgl. auch Th. Wiegand, Halbmond im letzten Viertel (1970) 175.277; General Pertev Demirhan, Generalfeldmarschall Colmar Freiherr von der Goltz (1960); Hermann Teske in Neue Deutsche Biographie 6 (1964)
629 ff.

Abb. 10 Auf dem Euphrat von Meskene nach Baghdad: In der Kajüte, 20. 1./7. 2. 1916

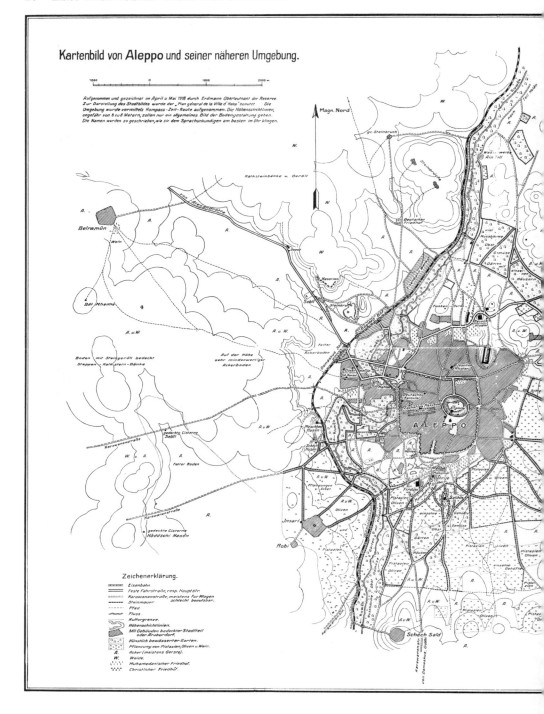

Kartenbild von **Aleppo** und seiner näheren Umgebung.

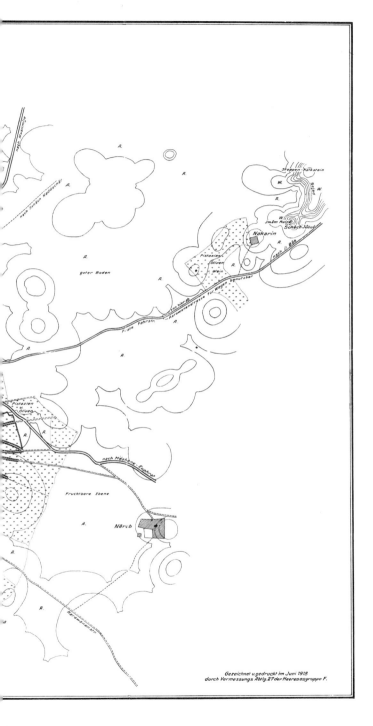

Abb. 11 Karte von Aleppo und
Umgebung, aufgenommen von
Olt. Erdmann unter der Leitung
von W. Andrae 1918

bekannte Impressionisten gebraucht haben. Der Zeichner will das Wirken des Lichtes durch die Farbgegensätze zwischen dem farbigen Papier und der Kreide zur Geltung bringen. Die Abbildungen Nr. 167 aus Mossul 1917 und Nr. 181. 182 aus Nazareth sind Beispiele für diese Versuche, von denen Andrae berichtet, daß sie entstanden sind aus der Begegnung mit Georg Lührig (dem späteren Direktor der Dresdener Kunstakademie)[45] in Baghdad und Aleppo.

Das deutsche Eingreifen war 1915 noch erfolgreich, was an der Persönlichkeit des alten Feldmarschalls lag. Er sprach türkisch, hatte jahrelang in der Westtürkei als Ausbilder der türkischen Armee gearbeitet. Die Türken verehrten ihn und taten auch in Bagdad, das er vorher nie gesehen hatte, alles für ihn. Einige ehemals in Mesopotamien tätige Archäologen waren ihm als Berater beigegeben. Andrae vergleicht die beiden Oberkommandierenden, mit denen er zu tun hatte: – Von der Goltz ließ sich beraten, informierte sich gründlich, überzeugte die Verbündeten und hatte Erfolg. Von Falkenhayn,[46] der 1917/18 in Syrien und Palästina kommandierte und durch Liman von Sanders[47] abgelöst wurde, tat das Gegenteil: Er wußte alles besser als sein Stab, die Verbündeten folgten nur widerwillig oder gar nicht.

In diesen Stäben galt Andrae als Sprachenkenner, obwohl er nur die Sprache der Bauern von Kuweiresch und Schergat aufgenommen hatte. So wurde er im Ostjordanland ein bescheidener Gegenspieler seines Kollegen Thomas Edward Lawrence,[48] der vor 1914 an der Ausgrabung in Karkemisch/Djerablus beteiligt gewesen war. Andrae hatte die Ausgrabung bei der Euphratbrücke der Bagdadbahn 1912 besucht ohne Lawrence zu treffen. Lawrence gelang es bekanntlich, die arabischen Stammesführer zum Aufstand gegen die türkische Staatsmacht zu bewegen. Die Bahnlinie Damaskus—Medina, die unter Meißner Pascha (Nr. 190)[49] gebaute sogenannte Hedschas-Bahn, für die Kriegführung der Türken von Bedeutung, wurde durch die von Lawrence geführten

---

45 * 26. 1. 1868. Vgl. Thieme-Becker 23 (1929) 449 f.

46 Erich Georg Anton Sebastian Reichsfreiherr von Falkenhayn, preußischer Generaloberst, 11. 11. 1861–8. 4. 1922. Vgl. Th. Wiegand a. O. 260 f. 263 f. 267.274; Friedrich Freiherr Hiller von Gaertringen in Neue Deutsche Biographie 5 (1961) 11 ff. s. v. Falkenhayn, v. 1.–LE 238 f.:
»Mit Sorgen im Herzen empfing ich die neue Beorderung nach Aleppo und später nach Nazareth zur Heeresgruppe Yıldırım (›Blitz‹), die General von Falkenhayn kommandierte. Er gehörte zu den seltenen Generälen, die alles schon selber im voraus wissen, und überdies war er das genaue Gegenteil zu von der Goltz hinsichtlich der Behandlung der türkischen Mentalität und stieß daher auf Widerstand, statt auf Gehorsam. Man munkelte schon, er sei auf den verlorenen Posten gesetzt, um abserviert zu werden, was denn auch 1918 geschah, als Liman von Sanders in sehr brüsker Weise das Kommando übernahm.«

47 Otto Liman von Sanders, preußischer General und türkischer Pascha, 18. 2. 1855–22. 8. 1929. Vgl. auch Th. Wiegand a. O. 167.204.274.279; Franz Menges, Neue Deutsche Biographie 14 (1985) 563 ff. s. v. Liman v. Sanders.

48 Thomas Edward Lawrence, Archäologe, Oberst, 15. 8. 1888–19. 5. 1935. – Vgl. auch Wiegand a. O. 213.263.278; T. E. Lawrence, Die sieben Säulen der Weisheit (The Seven Pillars of Wisdom); ders., Aufstand in der Wüste (Revolt in the Desert); A. W. Lawrence, Oberst Lawrence (Lawrence by his friends).

49 Heinrich August Meißner Pascha, Chefingenieur der Baghdad- und der Hedschasbahn und ihrer Verzweigungen im südlichen Palästina, Dozent an der Technischen Hochschule Ayas, 3. 1. 1892–14. 1. 1940. Vgl. auch MDOG 48, Juni 1912, 22; Wiegand a. O. 263.

Abb. 12 Der Schiffszimmermann der »Patmos«, März 1919

arabischen Sprengtrupps erheblich gestört. Auf dieser Bahn wurde Andrae 1918 einmal nach Süden in die Gegend von Ma'an geschickt.[50]

Andrae war schon nach Aleppo kommandiert, wo unter seiner Leitung von einem Oberleutnant Erdmann eine Karte des Stadtgebiets mit Umgebung angefertigt wurde (Abb. 11), als Nazareth von britischer Kavallerie am 20. September 1918 in kühnem Überraschungsangriff genommen wurde. Das deutsche Oberkommando Liman von Sanders mußte sich zurückziehen.[51] Im Oktober 1918 fuhr einer der letzten Züge mit deutschen Soldaten durch den eben fertiggestellten Taurus-Tunnel der Baghdad-Bahn unter Andraes Kommando. Im Marmara-Meer lagen schon britische Kriegsschiffe. Reste der deutschen Orient-Armee wurden auf leeren deutschen Schiffen, die seit 1914 im Bosporus ankerten, interniert, Andrae mit 960 Mann auf dem 3000 t großen Kohlendampfer »Patmos« (Nr. 198 Abb. 12). Dieser verließ Anfang Februar 1919 Konstantinopel unter Führung des englischen Kapitäns Moses (Nr. 197) und traf im März in Cuxhaven ein.

Bodensee 1919–1921; Berlin 1921–1956

Während eines Urlaubs in Europa hatte Andrae 1918 in Hemmenhofen am Untersee, Kreis Konstanz, ein altes, etwas morsches Bauernhaus gekauft. Dort lebten Frau und Sohn. Zunächst ohne Stellung überlegte Andrae, ob er Maler werden solle, begann jedoch seine Ausarbeitung über Assur. 1921 wurde er Koldeweys Nachfolger als Kustos bei der Vorderasiatischen Abteilung der Staatlichen Museen in Berlin und nahm nach seiner Habilitation für das Fach Vorderasiatische, Ägyptische und Byzantinische Baukunst an der Technischen Hochschule in Berlin-Charlottenburg seine Vorlesungen als Privatdozent auf.[52] Im Museum begann die Bearbeitung der Funde aus Mesopotamien.

Im Jahre 1925 konnte Andrae in »auswärtigen Angelegenheiten« für das Museum tätig werden.[53] Herr Dr. Stüwe, der deutsche Konsul in Lissabon, hatte die portugiesi-

---

50 Vgl. LE 245 f.:

»Ich erhielt Befehl, eine Kiste voll türkischer, in Deutschland geprägter Goldpfunde ins Ostjordanland zu schaffen, wo der sogenannte ›Kleine Dschemal Pascha‹ ein türkisches Truppenkontingent gegen aufsässige Araber östlich des Toten Meeres führen sollte, den ich mit dem nötigen Kleingeld zu versorgen hatte, zugleich mit der Anweisung, das Geld möglichst lange zurückzuhalten! Der Grad des bundesgenössischen Vertrauens war daran zu ermessen. Ich sah auf dieser sonst etwas einsamen Reise von ferne aus dem Zuge von Meißner Paschas Mekkabahn die Ruinen von Mschatta ›in plena solitudine‹, aber fassadelos, denn diese Fassade hatte der Sultan Abdulhamid bereits dem Kaiser Wilhelm geschenkt, und sie war von Bruno Schulz ins Kaiser-Friedrich-Museum zu Berlin gebracht worden. Ich aber konnte von Glück sagen, daß ich auf meiner Mekkabahn nicht von einem der vielen Sprengattentate des ›Aufstands in der Wüste‹, d. h. meines Gegenspielers bei den Arabern, T. Lawrence, erwischt wurde, deren Spuren sich verschiedentlich zeigten und viel Blut gekostet haben.«

51 Liman von Sanders, Fünf Jahre Türkei (1920) 354 ff.

52 J. Renger a. O. (vgl. Anm. 24) 187.

53 LE 252.

Abb. 13 Getrude Bell 1909 vor ihrem Zelt in Babylon

sche Regierung dazu bewegen können, die beschlagnahmten Assurfunde herauszugeben. Als Andrae in Portugal eintraf, um sie zu übernehmen, war die Regierung gestürzt. Erst im Frühjahr 1926 hatten weitere Verhandlungen des deutschen Gesandten, Herrn von Voretzsch, Erfolg. Andrae konnte die Fundkisten auf ein deutsches Schiff verladen lassen.[54] Über Hamburg kamen die Kisten aus Portugal auf dem Wasserwege bis zur Museumsinsel in Berlin. Andere Kisten waren im Kriege in Basra den englischen Truppen in die Hände gefallen und ins Britische Museum überführt worden. Weniges davon erhielt Andrae 1923 zurück.[55]

In der Mitte des Jahres 1926 traf eine Botschaft von Miss Gertrude Bell in Berlin ein,

54 Vgl. W. Andrae, MDOG 65, 1927, 1 ff. mit Abb. 2; LE 219.258.260 f.
55 LE 255 f.

die irakische Regierung gebe die in Babylon lagernden, seit 1917 beschlagnahmten Kisten frei, die u. a. etwa 300 000 emaillierte Ziegelbrocken von Kasr-Hügel enthielten,[56] Berlin möge eine Delegation zur Übergabe schicken.

Kurz vorher war in Berlin eine wichtige Entscheidung gefallen: Im großen Museumsneubau, begonnen von Messel,[57] von Stadtbaurat Hoffmann[58] weitergeführt, stand der Südflügel der Vorderasiatischen Abteilung zur Verfügung, weil Heinrich Schäfer[59] seine Ägyptische Abteilung lieber im Stühlerbau (er wurde im Kriege 1939–1945 zerstört und nicht wieder aufgebaut) lassen wollte. Mit den Funden von Assur und Babylon, letztere nun von Miss Bell angeboten, eröffnete sich die Aussicht, altmesopotamische Architekturteile in großem Stile, teilweise in Originalgröße wieder aufzubauen. Das ist um 1930 unter Andraes Leitung geschehen (vgl. die Entwürfe Nr. 81–84), etwa gleichzeitig mit dem Aufbau der anschließenden hellenistischen Architektur-Säle im Museumsneubau, der dann allgemein bekannt wurde unter dem Namen Pergamon-Museum.

Weil die Entscheidung von Miss Bell, einer außergewöhnlichen Frau, eine Rolle gepielt hat, sei hier über ihre Begegnung mit Walter Andrae berichtet. Im Gästebuch der Babylon-Expedition befindet sich der Namenszug von Gertrude Lowthian Bell vom 1. 4. 1909 (Abb. 13). Sie setzte dazu einen einzeiligen Spruch in arabischer Schrift. In jenen Tagen war Miss Lowthian Bell[60] auch in Assur.[61] Zweimal kam sie dorthin und

---

56 LE 258.261.

57 Dr.-Ing. Alfred Messel, Geheimer Regierungsrat, Architekt der Berliner Museen, 22. 7. 1853–24. 3. 1904.

58 Ludwig Hoffmann, Dr.-Ing. Geheimer Baurat, Stadtbaumeister Berlin 1896–1928, 30. 7. 1852–11. 11. 1932.

59 Prof. Dr. Heinrich Schäfer, Direktor der Ägyptischen Abteilung der Berliner Museen, 29. 10. 1868–6. 4. 1957.

60 A. J. Arberry (Professor an der Universität Cambridge) in: Gertrude Bell, Persische Reisebilder (Hamburg, 1949; Titel der Originalausgabe »Persian Pictures«, London 1947) 178 ff.:

»Gertrude Lowthian Bell, Tochter von Sir Hugh Bell und Enkelin von Sir Lowthian Bell, Baronet, wurde am 14. Juli 1868 auf dem Wohnsitz ihres Großvaters in Durham geboren. 1885 belegte sie Vorlesungen in Lady Margaret Hall in Oxford und schloß zwei Jahre später mit einer glänzenden Eins in Geschichte ab. 1891 begann sie persisch zu lernen, nachdem ihr Onkel, Sir Frank Lascelles, zum britischen Gesandten in Teheran ernannt worden war; und als sie im folgenden Frühjahr Lady Lascelles nach Persien begleitete, hatte sie den großen Vorteil, die Sprache dieses Landes sprechen und lesen zu können. Sie hielt ihre Erfahrungen und Eindrücke während dieses Besuches in ihrem Tagebuch fest, ohne jeden Gedanken daran, sie der Öffentlichkeit zugänglich zu machen; doch Mr. Bentley, der Verleger, war sehr daran interessiert, sie zu drucken, und ihre Familie unterstützte diesen Plan, so daß sie schließlich, mit einiger Schüchternheit, in eine Veröffentlichung einwilligte; wohl aber bestand sie darauf, daß ihr Name nicht erwähnt werden sollte. So erschienen diese Skizzen 1894 unter dem Titel *Safar Nameh. Persische Bilder. Ein Reisebuch.* Das Buch wurde damals sehr gut aufgenommen, dann aber vergessen. Es wurde erst 1928 neu aufgelegt, als Messrs. Ernest Benn es mit seinem kürzeren Titel *Persische Reisebilder* und einem Vorwort von dem verstorbenen Sir Denison Roß herausbrachten.

Die Generation, die die Erstauflage zu lesen bekam, kannte Gertrude Bell als eine vollendete junge Dame aus guter Familie und von glänzenden Geistesgaben. Die zweite Auflage erschien kurz nach dem unerwartet frühen Ende eines Lebens hervorragender Dienste, die Gertrude Bell nicht nur ihrem Lande, sondern der ganzen Menschheit erwies. Zwanzig Jahre später, als das Buch ein drittes Mal veröffentlicht wird, ist Gertrude Bell für die jüngere Generation ein Name und eine Legende und ihr am besten bekannt als die Schreiberin bezaubernder intimer Briefe. Sie war jedoch unendlich mehr als das; denn von ihr darf man ehrlich sagen, was selbst unter den Berühmtheiten nur von wenigen gesagt werden kann, daß sie in einem wichtigen Teil der Welt tätigen Einfluß auf die Geschicke der Menschen hatte.

Nach ihrem Besuch in Persien kam Gertrude Bell nie wieder mit diesem Land in Berührung; ihre persische Episode fand im Jahre 1897 mit der Veröffentlichung von *Gedichten aus dem Divan des Hafis* ihren Abschluß, ein bemerkenswertes Denkmal ihrer Bildung und literarischen Begabung; obwohl einige zwanzig andere Menschen Hafis ins Englische übersetzten, bleiben ihre Übertragungen die besten. Es war die arabische Welt, die seitdem ihr Hauptinteresse und ihre ganze Hingabe beanspruchte; angefangen von ihrem ersten Aufenthalt in Jerusalem im Jahre 1899 bis zu ihrem Tode in Bagdad im Jahre 1926, verbrachte sie den größeren Teil ihres Lebens unter den Arabern.

Die Archäologie war der ursprüngliche Anlaß zu ihren ausgedehnten Reisen in der Wüste und in den fruchtbaren Landstrichen; diese Reisen vermittelten ihr eine umfassende und genaue Kenntnis der arabischen Stämme und der arabischen Politik und führten dazu, daß David Hogarth sie 1915 aufforderte, in seine Geschäftsstelle für Arabien in Kairo einzutreten. Von der Zeit an war sie die enge Mitarbeiterin und geschätzte Kollegin von Männern, deren Namen in der Geschichte des Nahen Ostens fortleben werden, Männern wie T. E. Lawrence, Cox, Wilson, Dobbs, Philby, Storrs. Im Jahre 1916 schloß sie sich dem Stab von Sir Percy Cox beim Generalhauptquartier in Basrah an und begleitete Cox im folgenden Frühjahr nach Bagdad; sie war seine Sekretärin für orientalische Angelegenheiten und auch die seines Nachfolgers als Hoher Kommissar für den Irak, Sir Henry Dobbs; abgesehen von ihrer Teilnahme an der Friedenskonferenz in Paris im Jahre 1919, verblieb sie bis zu ihrem Lebensende auf ihrem Posten. Obwohl sie hauptsächlich mit politischen Angelegenheiten beschäftigt war, vernachlässigte sie ihre erste Liebe nicht: 1921 wurde sie ehrenhalber zum Direktor für Altertumsforschung ernannt und gründete das Irak-Museum. Sie starb auf der Höhe ihres Ruhms und in der vollen Reife ihrer Kräfte am 12. Juli 1926; in Bagdad wurde sie beerdigt.

Ihr vorzeitiger Tod, zwei Tage vor ihrem achtundfünfzigsten Geburtstag, wurde geradezu als ein Verhängnis betrachtet; er war der Anlaß zu einer seltenen ministeriellen Ehrung im Unterhaus durch den Kolonialsekretär, Mr. L. S. Amery ...

Das vielleicht denkwürdigste Porträt von Gertrude Bell auf dem Höhepunkt ihres Lebens verdanken wir V. Sackville-West in *Eine Fahrt nach Teheran:*

»Ich spürte, daß es ihre Persönlichkeit war, die alle die in der Fremde lebenden Engländer zusammenhielt und einen Mittelpunkt für sie bildete, deren anderes gemeinsames Band ihr Dienst für den Irak war ... Was immer für ein Thema sie berührte, sie belebte es; diese Vitalität war unwiderstehlich.«

61 Gertrude Lowthian Bell, Amurath to Amurath (1911) 221 ff.:

»We rode down into the ruin-field and found one of Dr. Andrae's colleagues at work in the trial trenches. He directed us to the house set round with flowers, as I had predicted, wherein the excavators are lodged. There Dr. Andrae and Mr. Jordan made me so warmly welcome that I felt like one returning after absence into a circle of life-long friends. They had grave news to give me, news which was all the more disquieting because it was as yet nothing but a rumour. Constitutional government had foundered suddenly, and it might be for ever. The members of the Committee had fled from Constantinople, the Liberals were fugitive upon their heels, and once more 'Abdu'l Hamîd had set his foot upon the neck of Turkey. So we interpreted the report that had reached Asshur, but since there was no means of allaying on of confirming our anxieties we turned our minds to more profitable fields, and went out to see the ruins.

A site better favoured than Kal'at Shergât for excavations such as those undertaken by Dr. Andrae and his colleagues could scarcely have been selected. It has not given them the storied slabs and huge stone guardians of the gates of kings with which Layard enriched the British Museum; they have disappeared during the many periods of reconstruction which the town has witnessed; but those very reconstructions add to the historic interest of the excavations. Asshur was in existence in the oldest Assyrian period, and down to the latest days of the empire it was an honoured shrine of the gods; there are traces of Persian occupation; in Parthian times the city was re-built, walls and gates were set up anew, and the whole area within the ancient fortifications was re-inhabited. Valuable as are the contributions which Dr. Andrae has been able to make to the history of Assyria, the fact that he is bringing into the region of critical study a culture so shadowy as that of the Parthians has remained to us, in spite of its four hundred years of domination, adds greatly to the magnitude of his achievement. His researches in this direction have been pursued not only at *Asshur,* but at the Parthian city of Hatra, a long day's journey to the west of the Tigris, where the famous palace is at last receiving the attention it merits ...

As Dr. Andrae led me about the city, drawing forth its long story with infinite skill from wall and trench and cuneiform inscription, the lavish cruel past rushed in upon us. The myriad soldiers of the Great King, transported from the reliefs in the British Museum, marched through the gates of Asshur; the captives, roped

wurde dort gerne gesehen. Andrae beschreibt ihren Besuch:[62] »Eine der bedeutendsten Persönlichkeiten unter den Besuchern aber war zweifellos Miss Gertrude Lowthian Bell, die zweimal nach Assur kam. Sie wollte *alles* wissen und kroch unermüdlich mit mir in alle Winkel und Gruben der Grabung. Ihr selbständiges mutiges Reiten in der asiatischen Türkei hatte nicht n u r politische Absichten und Hintergründe, sondern wurde auch aus einem flammenden archäologischen Interesse heraus unternommen. Wir haben lange Gespräche über beide Themen geführt, auf die sie sehr offenherzig einging. Ihre Verwandtschaft in diplomatischen Kreisen Englands und ihre vielen Reisen hatten ihr eine ungewöhnliche Übersicht über Länder und Leute verschafft und machten sie geeignet, später im ersten Kriege eine führende Rolle in der englischen Orientpolitik zu spielen. Zur Zeit ihres Assurbesuches hatte sie das arabische Wüstenschloß Ocheidr (nordwestlich von Kerbela) aufgenommen. Den schönen Band darüber hat sie mir mit freundschaftlichen Worten gewidmet. Ihr sprachliches Können war bewundernswert, wenn es auch durch ihre Lebensmöglichkeiten besonders begünstigt war. Ihre nächsten Verwandten fungierten in hohen britischen Ämtern im Ausland, z. B. in Berlin, Teheran, Indien und sie konnte sich als deren Gast in der Jugend die verschiedenen Landessprachen aneignen. Sie sprach daher gern mit uns deutsch und sagte nur kritische Dinge auf englisch. Beim zweiten Besuch hatte sie vermutlich schon einen diplomatischen Auftrag nach Mesopotamien mitgebracht und befreundete sich mit allerlei Scheichs, was die normalen britischen Beamten nicht konnten. Man hat es nachher im Kriege gespürt. Da tanzten die mesopotamischen Scheichs nach dem Willen der ›Weißen Königin‹, die Emir Feisal zum König machte – und die hieß Miss Bell«!

Gertrude Lowthian Bell ihrerseits schildert in einem Briefe (1913 oder 1914) die Begegnung mit Andrae in Assur: »Er ist ein großer, kräftiger, stiller Mann, welcher den größten Teil von 15 Jahren als Ausgräber in Mesopotamien verbracht hat, und Du kannst kaum begreifen, wieviel Arbeit und Selbstverleugnung dies bedeutet, solange Du dies nicht gesehen hast. Hier in Assur gibt es keine Vermutungen und kein Hetzen, sondern so genaue Beobachtung, daß nichts der Aufmerksamkeit entgeht.«[63]

---

and bound, crowded the streets; defeated princes bowed themselves before the victor and subject races piled up their tribute in his courts. We saw the monarch go out to the chase, and heard the roaring of the lion, half paralyzed by the dart in its spine, which animates the stone with its wild anguish. Human victims cried out under nameless tortures; the tide of battle raged against the walls, and, red with carnage, rose into the palaces. Splendour and misery, triumph and despair, lifted their head out of the dust.

One hot night I sat with my hosts upon the roof of their house. The Tigris, in unprecedented flood, swirled against the mound, a waste of angry waters. Above us rose the zigurrat of the god Asshur. It had witnessed for four thousand years the melting of the Kurdish snows, flood-time and the harvest that follows; gigantic, ugly, intolerably mysterious, it dominated us, children of an hour. ›What did they watch from its summit?‹ I asked, stung into a sharp consciousness of the unknown by a scene almost as old as recorded life. ›They watched the moon‹, said Dr. Andrae, ›as we do. Who knows? they watched for the god.‹ I have left few places so unwillingly as I left Kal'at Shergât.«

62 LE 174; Erwähnung im Bericht vom 27. April 1909: MDOG 42, 1909, 34.

63 Elizabeth Burgoyne, Gertrude Bell from her Personal Papers 1889–1914 [London 1958] 267 in: Deutsche Orient Gesellschaft (1984) 21; vgl. ferner Anm. 60 bes. Anfang und Ende bezüglich der gegenseitigen Wertschätzung dieser in vielem wesensverwandten Menschen.

Andraes Hinweis auf die Einsetzung König Feisals I. (Sohn des Emirs von Hed-schas, der den Aufstand der Araber im Weltkrieg 1914–18 anführte und von T. E. Lawrence beraten wurde), bezieht sich auf die Tatsache, daß es Miss Lowthian Bell gelang, im August 1921 die einflußreichsten Scheichs und Notabeln des neu entstande-nen Irak-Staates zu bewegen, Feisal zum König zu erheben. Feisal war 1920 in Syrien zum König ausgerufen, aber von der französischen Mandatsmacht vertrieben worden. Im Irak hatten die Engländer schrittweise zunehmend Selbständigkeit zugesagt. Neben den arabischen Behördenspitzen gab es britische Berater. Miss Lowthian Bell war als ausgezeichnete und kluge Landeskennerin wichtigste Beraterin – auch ihrer Landsleute, hielt sich aber im Hintergrund. Sie hat am Anfang der zwanziger Jahre das Iraq-Mu-seum begründet und leitete es bis zu ihrem Tode 1926 (vgl. Anm. 53). Nach der Beset-zung Baghdads 1917 hatte sie sogleich das ihr bekannte Haus der Babylon-Expedition mit den dort noch lagernden Funden und Einrichtungen unter ihre Obhut genommen. Sie hat in großartiger, beispielhafter wissenschaftlicher Kollegialität die Zugänge zumauern[64] und den Gebäudekomplex unter Bewachung stellen lassen. Ein neues Anti-kengesetz des Staates Irak regelte den Verbleib von Funden, die ausländische Forscher ans Licht fördern sollten. Außer Duplikaten, die nach besonderer Genehmigung der Antikenverwaltung hätten ausgeführt werden können, mußten nun grundsätzlich alle Funde im Lande bleiben. Miss Bell kannte die Ziegelbrocken von Babylon. Sie sah keine Möglichkeit, sie in Baghdad zu entsalzen, sie konservieren und zusammensetzen zu lassen und befand, sie sollten nach Berlin geliefert werden.[65] Diese Entscheidung war die einzig richtige, da sonst das Material vom Salz zerfressen, zerfallen und für alle Zei-ten verloren gewesen wäre. Walter Andrae schreibt dazu in seinen Lebenserinnerun-gen: So ist »die Fertigstellung der Babylon-Säle des Berliner Museums zum Teil Miss Bell zu verdanken« (LE 175). Dafür sollten nachher ein zusammengesetzter Löwe und eine Auswahl gebrannter Tontafeln an das Iraq-Museum gehen (LE 263).

Die preußische Regierung bestimmte Andrae, die Übergabeverhandlungen in Bagh-dad zu führen und den Abtransport in Babylon zu leiten. Andrae wählte sich als Assi-stenten Dr. Julius Jordan, den einstigen Mitarbeiter in Assur und Ausgräber in Uruk. Noch in Lissabon erreichte Andrae die Nachricht, Miss Gertrude Lowthian Bell sei plötzlich gestorben.[66] Bleibt die Zusage gültig? Das war die Frage. Andrae entschied zu fahren. Miss Bells Wort galt über ihren Tod hinaus – die Verhandlungen in Baghdad verliefen glatt.[67] Schwieriger war es, die inzwischen morschen Kisten in Babylon zu

64 LE 263 und hier Anm. 66.

65 LE 175 »Kurz vor ihrem Tode – sie leitete damals das Museum des neu gegründeten Staates Irak – hatte sie die Anordnung getroffen, daß die immer noch in Babylon lagernden Kisten mit Bruchstücken der Relief-Tiere der Prozessionsstraße an das Berliner Museum zurückgegeben werden sollten.«

66 Vgl. Anm. 52, LE 174. 261.

67 LE 262. – Vgl. zum ganzen Komplex W. Andrae, MDOG 65, April 1927, 7 ff.:
»Reise nach Babylon zur Teilung der Babylon-Funde:
Die von Koldewey in Babylon gelassenen Funde aus den Ausgrabungen der Deutschen Orient-Gesell-schaft und der Berliner Museen sollten nach einer Korrespondenz der als Honorary Director of Antiquities des Iraq-Staates fungierenden Miss Gertrude Bell mit der Deutschen Orient-Gesellschaft auf Grund des

ersetzen.[68] Die ganze alte Belegschaft des Expeditionshauses, ehemalige Aufseher, der Wasserträger Ali Dschamus »Ali der Wasserbüffel« (Abb. 14) und die Handwerker (Abb. 15) aus Kuweiresch und Hille waren wieder da und halfen.[69] Eine kleine Flotte von Booten wurde herangetreidelt, kurdische Lastträger schafften die Kisten aus dem

---

neuen Antiken-Gesetzes des Iraq-Staates so geteilt werden, als seien die Ausgrabungen erst jetzt, seit dem Bestehen dieses Gesetzes erfolgt. Die D. O.-G. schlug mich als Delegierten vor, der Herr Generaldirektor der Staatlichen Museen erteilte sein Einverständnis hierzu und die Iraq-Regierung nahm durch Miss Bell den Vorschlag an. Als Zeit für die Arbeiten wurde Herbst 1926 festgesetzt. Auf Grund meiner beim Transport der Assur-Funde aus Porto gemachten Erfahrungen hatte ich die Mitnahme eines Assistenten beantragt; sie fand auch bei der Iraq-Regierung keinen Widerspruch. Der Herr Minister für Wissenschaft, Kunst und Volksbildung bewilligte die Mittel für die Rückgewinnung von Babylon-Funden. Die Deutsche Orient-Gesellschaft stellte Dr. Jordan für die Beteiligung an den Arbeiten zur Verfügung. Das Ende Juni erfolgte unerwartete Ableben von Miss Gertrude Bell änderte nichts an dem Vorhaben. Ihre Anordnungen waren, wie sich später herausstellte, von den Behörden in Bagdad unverändert beibehalten worden.«

Vgl. auch LE 262 f.:

»Sonntag, den 15. Oktober 1926 meldeten wir uns durch den Adjutanten, Captain Holt, beim High Commissioner Sir Henry Dobbs, der uns nach kurzer freundlicher Begrüßung an Mr. Cooke, den Honorary Director of Antiquities, Miss Bells Nachfolger in dieser Funktion, verwies. Wir verabredeten mit diesem für den nächsten Tag, den 16., die gemeinsame Fahrt nach Babylon und den Beginn unserer Arbeiten und warfen einen Blick in das von Miss Bell neu installierte Iraq-Museum im Gebäude der Government Press an der Straße zur alten Brücke, in dem Abd el Kadr Patschatschi, unser alter Kommissar bei den Ausgrabungen in Assur, als Kurator fungiert. Dessen Gehilfe Selim Levi fuhr mit nach Babylon.

Am 16. Oktober legten wir auf dem Grabe von Miss Bell einen Kranz nieder. Wir fuhren um 8 Uhr ab und waren um 11 Uhr in Babylon, besprachen mit Mr. Cooke das Notwendigste über die Arbeit an Ort und Stelle und bekamen schon jetzt seine Zusicherung, daß wir die gesammelten Emailziegelbrocken nach Berlin schaffen dürften. Ebenso die ungebrannten Tonsachen. Ein zusammengesetzter Löwe und eine Auswahl gebrannter Tontafeln sollen nachher an das Iraq-Museum gehen. Das Expeditionshaus wurde uns zur Verfügung gestellt, ebenso die von der Regierung angestellten Wächter und der Rest der Möbel. Betten brachte Mr. Cooke für uns mit.«

68 MDOG 65, 1927, 12 ff.; LE 263 ff.:

»Das Expeditionshaus wurde uns zur Verfügung gestellt, ebenso die von der Regierung angestellten Wächter und der Rest der Möbel.

Das alte Haus, welches die Funde enthielt, war auf Veranlassung von Miss Bell zugemauert worden, doch über eine primitive Leiter zugänglich. Wir hackten die eine »Museums«-Tür auf und stellten den verzweifelten Zustand der unverpackten Funde fest; sie waren durchwühlt, verstreut und zum Teil vom undichten Dach her durchnäßt. Einiges andere lag in anderen Räumen wüst durcheinander. Viele unfreundliche oder unverständige Hände schienen hier am Werke gewesen zu sein. Die Bücherbestände waren im Speisezimmer untergebracht, dem einzigen noch trockenen Raum. Koldeweys Zimmer war ausgeräumt, seine Decke eingestürzt. Die offene Halle im Hofe enthielt ca. 500 verpackte Kisten, meist Emailziegelstücke. Das eingestürzte Dach über ihnen hatten die Engländer dankenswerterweise mit Wellblech neu decken lassen. Unzählige Fledermäuse, Tauben, Spatzen, Hornissen und weiße Ameisen nisteten in den verlassenen Räumen. Im Hofe wuchsen junge Palmen, die bei Koldeweys Auszug 1917 noch nicht dastanden und weggeworfenen Dattelkernen ihr Dasein verdankten, darunter eine, deren Krone bereits das 8 m hohe Dach erreicht hatte und mit ihren mächtigen Wedeln schon einen großen Teil des Hofes ausfüllte. Dicke Staubschichten lagerten über allem, und wie in einem Naturschutzpark sah man wenige Spuren von Menschen, welche die idyllische Ruhe dieses zugemauerten Schlosses in den letzten Jahren gestört haben mochten. Der Eindruck war nicht viel verschieden von dem, den man haben mag, wenn man ein »intaktes« ägyptisches Königsgrab öffnet und findet, daß doch schon jemand drin gewesen ist.

LE 266:

»Gegen Ende der Arbeit erschien Abd el Kadr Patschatschi, der Kurator des Irak-Museums in Babylon, um Teilung und Transport zu überwachen und durch Dokumente zu erleichtern.«

69 LE 264 f. = MDOG 65, 13 ff.

Abb. 14 Ali Dschamus, der einäugige Wasserträger
der Babylon-Grabung, 1926

Hause auf die Schiffe, die aber im Schlamm des sich absenkenden Flusses festlagen.
Eine eilige Autofahrt zum Hindije-Stauwerk, und die Verhandlung mit dem britischen
Wasserdirektor gab dem Hille-Arm des Euphrat das nötige Wasser,[70] die Boote wurden
flott, brachten die Kisten nach Hille zum Kran der Schmalspurbahn Baghdad—Basra.
Dort waren die nötigen Güterwaggons zur Stelle. Bald gingen sie nach Basra, wurden
am Hafen noch einige Zeit in einer Lagerhalle verstaut und schließlich von einem deut-

Abb. 15 Tischler beim Vernageln
einer Transportkiste, Babylon 1926

70 LE 267 f. = MDOG 65, 17 ff.

schen Schiff – der »Trautenfels« – aus dem Schatt el Arab nach Hamburg, von dort auf Elbe, Havel und Spree nach Berlin gebracht, wo am 20. Januar 1927 insgesamt 536 Kisten aus Babylon eintrafen, von denen ca. 400 allein mit emaillierten Ziegelbrokken gefüllt waren.[71]

Andraes Verhandlungen in Baghdad hatten dazu geführt, daß die Entsendung einer deutschen Forschungsexpedition nach Uruk-Warka möglich wurde. 1928 wurde die 1913 eingestellte Arbeit in Uruk wiederaufgenommen, Andrae betreute sie von Berlin aus.

1928 nach dem frühen Tode von Otto Weber wurde Andrae Direktor der Vorderasiatischen Abteilung der Staatlichen Museen (Abb. 16), ein Amt, das er bis 1951 innehatte. Er kam damit auf einen Posten, der traditionsgemäß stets einem Philologen übergeben worden war. Den Wahlvorschlag gegenüber dem preußischen Kultusministerium hatte das Direktoren-Kollegium der Staatlichen Museen zu machen. Kurt Regling, Direktor des Münzkabinetts, schlug vor, in Anbetracht der bevorstehenden Einrichtung der Vorderasiatischen Abteilung im Museumsneubau, diesmal einen Architekten zu wählen, der noch dazu seine Ausstellungsobjekte vom Augenblick ihrer Entdeckung kenne. Kollegium und Minister folgten dem Vorschlag.[72]

Im folgenden Lebensabschnitt übernahm Andrae Lasten, die ihn mit noch größeren Sorgen beladen haben als einst die Grabung. Seit dem Tode Koldeweys am 4. 2. 1925 hatte er neben der Bearbeitung der Funde von Assur auch die Veröffentlichung Babylons zu übernehmen. Ende 1927 begann die intensive Arbeit an der Zusammensetzung der babylonischen Reliefbilder. Andrae erwirkte als Arbeitsraum die Säulenkolonnaden an der Nationalgalerie auf der Museumsinsel. Zwischen den Säulen wurde eine Mauer hochgezogen, in die oben verglaste Fenster eingesetzt wurden. Folgerichtig organisiert konnte der Arbeitsprozeß ablaufen: Reinigung und Entsalzung, Konservierung und Zuordnung zu den jeweiligen Tier-, Pflanzen- oder Ornamentformen, schließlich das Zusammensetzen nach den vorgegebenen babylonischen Ziegelmarken.[73] Um die zu

---

71 LE 268 f.:
»Insgesamt wurden acht Waggons nach Basra und vier nach Bagdad verladen. 536 Kisten waren für Berlin, 93 für Bagdad bestimmt; das Mengenverhältnis ist natürlich keinerlei Maßstab für die stattgehabte Teilung. Koldewey hatte im Laufe der letzten 14 Arbeitsjahre ungefähr 400 Kisten voll emaillierter Ziegelbrocken sammeln lassen, deren Schicksal damit stand und fiel, ob sie nach Berlin gehen durften oder nicht, wo man den ersten Teil bereits bearbeitet und zu Ornamenten und Relieftieren zusammengesetzt hat. Es ist zweifellos dankbar zu begrüßen, daß uns die Antiken-Verwaltung des Iraq instand gesetzt hat, dieses Werk zu vollenden – die einzige vernünftige Lösung, die es hierfür gab! Die übrigen Gegenstände sind teils der Zahl, teils dem Werte nach mit dem Iraq-Museum geteilt worden, wie es das neue Antikengesetz des Landes verlangt.« = MDOG 65, 20 f.
72 LE 258 f.
73 W. Andrae, MDOG 13, 1902, 1 ff. und MDOG 66, 1928, 20 ff.:
»Eine erste Sendung, die Koldewey schon 1903 nach Berlin spediert hatte, war inzwischen unter der Leitung der Vorderasiatischen Abteilung durch den Bildhauer Scheschonka und den Inspektor Otto nahezu aufgearbeitet worden. Nach einem Abkommen mit dem Generaldirektor des Stambuler Antiken-Museums mußte die Hälfte jenes Zusammensetzungsergebnisses nach Konstantinopel geliefert werden, es sind dies je zwei Löwen, Stiere und Drachen, welche jetzt die Wände des altorientalischen Saales im dortigen Museum zieren. Ende 1927 wurde mir dann die Verantwortung für die neue Sendung aus Babylon, die im Frühjahr

rekonstruierenden Architekturteile auszuführen, bedurfte es der Ergänzung der bildlosen emaillierten Ziegelflächen und einfachen Ornamente. In drei Keramikfirmen Berlins ließ Andrae Versuche ausführen, die schließlich in der Wiederfindung einer der

1927 eingetroffen war, übertragen. Sie war inzwischen nach dem von Prof. Rathgen im chemischen Laboratorium der Museen ausgearbeiteten Verfahren schon zu einem guten Teil entsalzt und paraffiniert und somit für die Zusammensetzung reif gemacht worden. Diese Arbeit begann Anfang 1928 und ist dem tüchtigen Bildhauer und Formermeister Struck übertragen, der mit 6 bis 8 Gehilfen und größter Engelsgeduld die Hunderttausende von Brocken nach Fundorten und Tier- bzw. Ornamentgattungen ordnet, dann Zusammensetzungsversuche an den einzelnen Ziegeln macht, bis er endlich zur Zusammensetzung ganzer Tiere, d. h. also wieder: der Löwen, Stiere und Drachen, und dann auch verschiedener Ornamente schreiten kann, die jetzt ebenfalls mit eingetroffen sind. Was das bedeutet, kann man an der Tatsache ermessen, daß die Löwenstraße in Babylon nach Koldeweys Berechnung beiderseits je mindestens 60 Löwen in den Wandschmuckstreifen aufwies, also 120 Löwen im ganzen. Man kann natürlich nicht erwarten, daß diese ungeheure Zahl auch nur annähernd wieder zusammenkommt. Die aufmerksamen Leser von Koldeweys Grabungsberichten in diesen Mitteilungen und vor allem in seinem Buche über das wiedererstehende Babylon werden sich erinnern, in welch trostlosem Zustande die arabischen Ziegelräuber die Straßenmauern wie überhaupt den ganzen großen Ziegelpalast Nebukadnezars, dem wir ja diesen Farbenschmuck verdanken, hinterlassen haben. Beim Zusammensuchen der Stücke finden wir Zusammengehöriges nach den Fundortangaben oft bis zu 100 m auseinandergerissen, was sich durch das häufige Durchwühlen der Schutthalden nach größeren und kleineren Ziegelstücken durch die späteren Ziegelräuber leicht erklärt.

Welch mühselige Arbeit dieses Zusammensuchen ist, lehrt ein Blick auf die unendlich langen Arbeitstische bei Struck, auf denen wohlgeordnet alles, was zu einer und derselben Ziegelform gehört, zusammenliegt, also z. B. alle Stücke mit dem Löwenauge oder mit der rechten Vordertatze des linksschreitenden Löwen. Wir wissen ja, daß alle 60 Löwen einer Straßenseite aus einer und derselben Form stammen, d. h. jeder der etwa fünfzig Ziegel von etwa 33 cm Seitenlänge und etwa 10 cm Höhe, die einen Löwen zusammensetzen, aus je einer Form, ebenso die 60 anderen Löwen, die sich von jenen dadurch unterscheiden, daß sie in der anderen Richtung marschieren und in einer anderen Fugenteilung stehen. Ebenso aber auch die zwei Arten von Stieren und von Drachen. Dazu kommen Farbenunterschiede aller dieser 6 Tiergattungen. Nun muß man außerdem noch berücksichtigen, daß die Ziegel bei der Ausraubung der Mauern nicht gerade glimpflich behandelt worden sind und zerborsten auf uns kamen. Dieses Zerbersten geschah in gewisser Weise gesetzmäßig an den Stellen, wo bei der Herstellung in Nebukadnezars Fabriken die Former ihre Tonbatzen beim Eindrücken in die Form zusammenstoßen ließen. Ihre Fingerabdrücke zeigen es deutlich, wie sie sich bemühten, den Ton in sechs oder sieben kleineren Batzen besonders sorgfältig in das Relief hineinzudrücken. Dabei sind anscheinend auch Kinder und Frauen tätig gewesen, denn die Finger sind oft recht zart. Ganz innig haben sich diese Batzen nicht miteinander verbunden. Beim Brennen blieb da immer ein feiner Haarriß, und an diesen Stellen ist dann die Relieffläche fast immer geborsten. Wir bekommen daher eine immer etwa 6–7 Bruchstücke von jeder Relieffläche eines Ziegels, und nun muß der Zusammensetzer aus den oft in die Hunderte gehenden Möglichkeiten zwei zusammenpassende Bruchflächen herauszufinden suchen. Das gelingt in der Tat, und erst, wenn alles Suchen vergeblich ist, geht es an die Ergänzung, bei der die absolute Nachahmung des Antiken natürlich vermieden wird.

Über die Berechtigung dieses ungeheuren Aufwandes an Arbeit und Kosten brauche ich den Lesern dieser Mitteilungen kaum ein Wort zu sagen. Wir getrauen uns, das Ergebnis neben die großen Skulpturen von Pergamon und neben die Mschattafassade zu stellen, und fühlen uns als verantwortliche Hüter eines großen geschichtlichen Wertes, dem wir die größte Sorgfalt zuzuwenden verpflichtet sind. Das Ergebnis wird für sich selber sprechen und uns jeder Rechtfertigung überheben.«

Vgl. ergänzend dazu die diesbezüglichen Arbeiten des chemischen Laboratoriums der Berliner Museen und Friedrich Rathgen (2. 6. 1862–19. 11. 1942) in: H. Otto, Das chemische Laboratorium der Königlichen Museen in Berlin, Berliner Beiträge zur Archäometrie 4, 1979, 55:

»Noch größer war der Arbeitsaufwand zur Rettung der vielen glasierten Ziegel von der bekannten Prozessionsstraße und des Ischtartores in Babylon, die etwa 1% Kochsalz enthielten und bei deren Trocknung die Gefahr bestand, daß die Glasuren abbröckeln würden. Die Auslaugung zur Entfernung des Salzgehaltes wurde in 200 großen Bottichen vorgenommen, für deren Unterbringung sogar eine Baracke errichtet werden mußte. Sie konnte nach eineinhalb Jahren beendet werden.« 64 ff. 76 f. – Vgl. auch L. Jakob-Rost – E. Klengel – R.-B. Wartke – J. Marzahn, Das Vorderasiatische Museum (1987) Abb. 141.

babylonischen Email-Technik gleichkommenden gipfelten.[74] Als Andraes Pläne
Gestalt auf dem Papier annahmen, sahen die Beamten der Baubehörden noch die ungeheure Menge an Ziegelbrocken auf den langen Tischen in den Kolonnaden.[75] Es war
nicht leicht, die Beamten dazu zu bringen, sich das noch nicht sichtbare Ergebnis vor-
zustellen. Wie es gelang, beschreibt Andrae in seinen Lebenserinnerungen p. 274 f.: »Es
mußte mit der Bauleitung eine vernünftige Abänderung des ohne unsere Mitwirkung
errichteten Rohbaues des Ausstellungsgeschosses erreicht werden. Der ganze Südflügel
wurde uns gewissermaßen als Konfektionsfrack geliefert, der nicht vorn und nicht hinten paßte. Man mußte versuchen, aus den überdimensionalen Wänden und Räumen das
beste noch Mögliche zu gestalten. Mit einigen Aquarellen hatte ich versucht, der gerin-
gen Vorstellungskraft der Museumsarchitekten perspektivisch und farbig nachzuhel-
fen. Auch dem geldbewilligenden Ministerium mußte nachgeholfen werden, und zwar
auf die allerverständlichste Weise: in Naturgröße! Dem Baurat Wille hatte meine Per-
spektive vom Ischtar-Tor so sehr imponiert, daß er dasselbe in Naturgröße in Holz auf-
zimmern und mit Papier bespannen ließ, auf dem die Kulissenmaler der Staatsoper
meine Stiere und Drachen naturgetreu und mit Schlagschatten aufmalen mußten – es
war eine Lust, das anzuschauen.[76] Die Ministerialräte, welche vorher von jedem Tier
nur *ein* Paar bewilligen wollten, weil sie doch alle »gleich« seien, waren von diesem
Theater-Modell so ergriffen, daß sie gleich alles bewilligten. Ich pries den Baurat, er
hieß Wille, nannte ihn hinfort ›Der gute Wille‹, und pries die Kulissenmaler und ihre
großen Pinsel.

Beinahe hätte es noch eine Panne gegeben: Das Ischtar-Tor ›stand nicht auf Achse‹,
was in einem preußischen Staatsbau doch nicht vorkommen darf. Dies konnte aber
nicht geändert werden, weil im nächsten Saale das berühmte Milet-Tor schon aufgebaut
war und sein Durchgang offen bleiben mußte, eben durch das Ischtar-Tor, das Rücken
an Rücken hinter ihm stand. Um den Grundriß ›interessanter‹ zu machen, hatte Ludwig
Hoffmann, der Nachfolger Alfred Messels, als der Schöpfer des Neubaues, dem Milet-
saal eine andere Mittelachse zu geben geruht als dem Ischtar-Tor-Saal. Also – hieß es –
geht nicht! Ich sprang mit der trockenen Bemerkung ein: ›Unser König Nebukadnezar
hat sein Ischtar-Tor in Babylon auch nicht auf Achse gestellt!‹ – Der Bau war gerettet,
und ›für alle Zeiten‹ wird man als Prozessionsteilnehmer auf der Löwenstraße ein biß-
chen schief auf das Ischtar-Tor blicken.«[77]

Der Aufbau der Abteilung war in jenen Jahren vor und nach 1930 immer wieder
gefährdet durch die wirtschaftlichen Schwierigkeiten, die Andrae stets erneut bei Verhandlungen im preußischen Finanzministerium zu überwinden hatte.

---

74 LE 274: »Dazu gewann ich drei Berliner keramische Werkstätten, die jede nach ihrer Art Versuche
anstellten, die sechs babylonischen Schmelzfarben möglichst getreu nachzuahmen, was derjenigen von Frau
Helene Körting weitaus am besten gelang.«
75 Vgl. Foto-Abb. bei W. Andrae, MDOG 66, April 1928, 19 ff.; J. Renger a. O. (s. Anm. 24) 161
Abb. 17; H. Otto, Berliner Beiträge zur Archäometrie 4, 1979, Abb. auf p. 64–66.
76 MDOG 66, April 1928, 23 Abb. 9.
77 Vgl. seine Entwürfe Nr. 81–84 mit dazugehörigem Text.

Abb. 16 Walter Andrae, 1952. Portrait von I. Grashey-Straub

Aus dem Bestand der emaillierten Ziegelbrocken von Ischtar-Tor und Prozessionsstraße ließen sich mehr Tierbilder zusammensetzen als für die Rekonstruktion nötig waren. So erhielt das Irak-Museum einige Exemplare geschenkt, die übrigen aber konnte Andrae an Museen in Europa und Amerika verkaufen.[78] Nach dem Gesetz hätten die Einnahmen aus dem Verkauf von Staatseigentum dem stets einnehmenden Finanzministerium gehört. Andrae durfte die nicht unerheblichen Beträge für den völligen Ausbau der Abteilung verwenden, dank kunstsachverständiger Beamter im Finanzministerium. In einer Zeit der schärfsten Finanzkrise Deutschlands war das keine Selbstverständlichkeit.

Andrae hätte die Verantwortung für die nach vielen Richtungen verzweigte Museumsarbeit, für die Fundbearbeitungen, zu denen ab 1928 auch Uruk-Warka hinzukam, für die Publikationen, für den Ausbau der Abteilung im Museum, für die Lehrtätigkeit an der Technischen Hochschule Berlin nicht ohne die zahlreichen Helfer, die er fand oder an sich zog, bewältigen können.

In den Orient kam Andrae nach 1926/27 noch zweimal. 1932 konnte er bei einer Reise durch den Irak und durch Syrien die Ausgrabungsstätten in diesen Ländern aufsuchen, insbesondere aber die Fortschritte der Grabung in Uruk sehen. Ein Archäologenkongreß in der Türkei ermöglichte einen Besuch in Boğazköy-Ḫattuša, wo Kurt Bittel seine Grabungen aufgenommen hatte. Zur Aufzählung der äußeren Lebensdaten gehört, daß Andrae seit 1923 als außerplanmäßiger Professor an der Technischen Hochschule, Berlin, lehrte. 1946 bis 1951, als über Siebzigjähriger (Nr. 3) wirkte er als Ordinarius für Baugeschichte und Bauaufnahme an derselben Institution, die mittlerweile zur Technischen Universität geworden war. Bei seiner Emeritierung im Jahre 1952 wurde er Ehrensenator dieser Universität (Abb. 16). 1914 erhielt er die silberne Leibniz-Medaille der Preußischen Akademie der Wissenschaften, 1951 das Großkreuz des Verdienstordens der Bundesrepublik.

Deutlicher als durch eine solche Aufzählung kann ein Bericht von persönlichem Erleben das Wesen einer Individualität schildern. Deshalb sei hier die Erinnerung seines Schülers, Mitarbeiters und Nachfolgers, Professor Dr. Ernst Heinrich[79] auszugsweise angefügt[80], weil über Walter Andrae Zutreffenderes bisher nirgendwo gesagt oder geschrieben worden ist. Ernst Heinrich sprach zum Gedenken an Walter Andrae bei der Tagung der Koldewey-Gesellschaft im Jahre 1957. Andrae gehörte zu den Mitbegründern dieser Gesellschaft der Bauforscher.

---

78 LE 277 f.
79 15. 12. 1899–28. 3. 1984.
80 E. Heinrich, in: Neue Ausgrabungen im Nahen Osten, Mittelmeerraum und in Deutschland, in: Bericht über die Tagung der Koldewey-Gesellschaft in Regensburg vom 23.–27. 4. 1957, 7 ff.

Gedenkrede von Ernst Heinrich über

LEBEN UND WIRKEN WALTER ANDRAES

Als junger Student hörte ich zuerst von ihm durch meinen Lehrer Daniel Krencker, der uns, begeistert und begeisternd, von dem Mann und von seiner Arbeit in Babylon und Assur erzählte und uns aufforderte, mit ihm Zeichnungen von Andrae anzusehen, die damals gerade in einem Raum des Alten Museums ausgestellt waren. Da sah ich zum ersten Mal die naturgroßen Aquarelle der Ziegelreliefs aus Babylon und die liebevoll gezeichneten Rekonstruktionen der Bauwerke aus Assur, Bilder aus einer fremden und für uns schwer verständlichen Welt. Dann trat Andrae selbst zu uns. Er war damals nach den zehn Jahren seines Ausgräberlebens, nach den Kriegsereignissen, die er zum großen Teil wieder im Orient als Offizier miterlebt hatte, und nach einer kurzen Zeit beschaulicher Ruhe auf seinem Gütchen in Hemmenhofen am Untersee gerade in Berlin ansässig geworden. Von ungewöhnlich großer und achtunggebietender Gestalt, sah er robust und gesund aus. Ohne daß er im geringsten posierte, machte er auf uns den Eindruck eines bedeutenden und vor allem eines in sich ruhenden, seiner selbst sicheren Mannes: Er sprach nicht viel, gab eigentlich nur auf Krenckers Fragen die notwendigen Antworten, aber das wenige, was er uns sagte, machte seine Bilder so lebendig, daß wir alle davon gepackt wurden. Er war sehr ernst und sprach sehr sachlich, und dieser erste Eindruck von ihm, der lange bei mir haften blieb, erweckte tiefen Respekt, ohne daß sich zunächst der Reichtum seines Herzens ahnen ließ.

Ganz ähnlich – fast möchte ich sagen: fremd und kühl – war zunächst mein Verhältnis zu ihm, als ich unter seiner Leitung zu arbeiten begann. Es war durchaus nicht sehr leicht, an ihn heranzukommen. Heinrich Lenzen und ich waren im Sommer 1928 fast zu gleicher Zeit für die Bearbeitung der Babylon- und Assurfunde eingestellt worden, und es ist sehr bezeichnend für ihn, in welcher Weise er uns anleitete. Er tat das nämlich eigentlich gar nicht. Wir hatten jeder ein recht schwieriges Thema zugewiesen erhalten, für dessen Behandlung uns zunächst die einfachsten Kenntnisse fehlten. Dazu wurden uns die Grabungszeichnungen und Inventare in die Hand gegeben und gezeigt, wo im Magazin des Museums die zugehörigen Funde aufbewahrt wurden. Dann wurde uns überlassen, mit der gestellten Aufgabe fertig zu werden. Ich bin heute davon überzeugt, daß Andrae nicht aus mangelndem Interesse für uns, sondern ganz bewußt so gehandelt hat. Literaturkenntnisse und Methodik waren für ihn gewiß nicht Nebensachen, aber er sah derartiges als Handwerkszeug an, das ein jeder sich selbst erwerben mußte. Wer dazu nicht den Willen, die Ausdauer und den Fleiß mitbrachte, der mußte sehr bald steckenbleiben und ging von selbst, und das war Andrae dann ganz recht. Seine Korrekturen setzten erst ein, als unsere Arbeiten in die letzte Form gegossen wurden. Natürlich haben wir bei dieser Arbeitsweise erhebliche Umwege gehen müssen, wenigstens bei mir war das so, und wir haben, wie man gewöhnlich sagt, »viel Zeit verloren«. In Wirklichkeit kam dabei doch wohl für das, was wir später tun sollten, ein Gewinn heraus, und Andrae hatte eine Charaktereigenschaft, die heute eine Seltenheit geworden ist: Er konnte warten und alle Dinge reif werden lassen. Nie habe ich ihn ungeduldig gesehen, und während der Zeit, als der Museumsneubau, die Neuaufstellung der Vorderasiatischen Abteilung, die Publikationen, seine Lehrtätigkeit an der Technischen Hochschule und im Museum, die Sorge für die Expeditionen im Vorderen Orient und seine Tätigkeit im Vorstand unserer Fachgesellschaften ihm wirklich ungewöhnliche Lasten aufbürdeten, machte er nicht einen Augenblick einen gehetzten Eindruck, obwohl er so gut wie andere Termine einzuhalten hatte. Nie habe ich von ihm die beliebte Floskel gehört: Ich habe keine Zeit. Wo Verwirrung herrschte, da stellte seine überlegene Ruhe die Ordnung sogleich wieder her. Wir haben ihn auch nie erregt sprechen hören, niemals erlebt, daß er »aus dem Häuschen geriet«, wie man in Berlin sagt. Fehler korrigierte er in Ruhe, über kleine Entgleisungen, die andere als Kränkung empfinden und übelnehmen würden, ging er hinweg oder strafte sie mit treffendem, aber nicht vernichtendem Spott. Dem Übeltäter trug er schon deshalb nichts nach, weil ihm derartiges viel zu unwichtig war und er es sofort vergaß. Fühlte er sich allerdings an einer empfindlichen Stelle durch Leichtfertigkeit oder Übelwollen verletzt oder glaubte er sein Vertrauen mißbraucht, so zog er zwischen sich und dem anderen einen endgültigen Strich. Ein derartiger Bruch war dann nicht mehr zu reparieren.

Nur eins hat Andrae von vornherein von uns verlangt, und er hat sich auch überzeugt, daß wir ihm in dieser Hinsicht folgten: Bei allem, was wir arbeiteten, mußte die größte Genauigkeit und Akkuratesse angewandt werden, ganz gleich, ob es sich dabei um einen wichtigen oder dem Anschein nach weniger wichtigen Gegenstand handelte. Auch er selbst arbeitete in dieser Weise. Ich glaube, es ist notwendig, das hervorzuheben, weil viele ihn hauptsächlich aus seinen letzten Werken kennen, in denen er stets sehr weitgespannte Zusammenhänge zu erkennen und zu schildern suchte, wobei manche Einzelheiten zu kurz kommen mochten. Dabei wird leicht übersehen, daß er auch, in den Anfängen sogar hauptsächlich, ein Meister der peinlich genauen, geduldigen, entsagungsvollen Kleinarbeit war. Schon die Zusammensetzung der Ziegelreliefs aus Babylon, ganz im Anfang seiner Laufbahn, war ein Beweis dafür. Im Jahre 1922 sind seine »Archaischen Ischtartempel in Assur« erschienen, und sie waren auf unserem Gebiet epochemachend, weil da zum ersten Mal sorgfältige Schichtuntersuchungen veröffentlicht wurden; sie gaben die ersten sicheren Beiträge der Grabungstechnik zur Aufstellung der altmesopotamischen Chronologie und Kunstgeschichte, und ihre Ergebnisse sind bis heute unentbehrlich. Bei solchen minutiösen Arbeiten habe ich ihn damals, als die aus Lissabon heimgeholten Funde aus Assur und Babylon für die Publikationen und für die Aufstellung vorbereitet wurden, oft beobachtet. Er unterzog sich ihnen mit der gleichen Geduld, ob es sich um die Zusammensetzung eines einfachen Vorratsgefäßes oder um die Wiedergewinnung einer großen Skulptur aus unzähligen Bruchstücken handelte. Wochenlang hat er zusammen mit unserem Formermeister probiert, bis er die Stellung der Figuren an dem großen Wasserbecken aus Assur erkannt und die größtmögliche Sicherheit für dessen Rekonstruktion erreicht hatte. Mit derselben Sorgfalt und Ruhe, niemals etwas überhastend, ging er bei der Planung der neuen Museumsräume und der Aufstellung der Funde vor, dabei jede Einzelheit, auch die technischen Fragen, bis zur Form der einzelnen Vitrine, im voraus bedenkend. Die gute, ehrliche Kärrnerarbeit kannte er, und er wußte sie zu schätzen. Nur warnte er immer davor, beim Sammeln von Einzelheiten und selbst beim Erkennen historischer, kunstgeschichtlicher und kulturgeschichtlicher Zusammenhänge stehenzubleiben. Für ihn waren dies alles nur Etappen auf dem Wege zu einem Ziel, von dem gleich noch zu reden sein wird. Die Genauigkeit in der Arbeit, die er übte und verlangte, war bei ihm nicht einfach eine Forderung der Arbeitsmethode, ohne die alle Ergebnisse zweifelhaft bleiben müssen, sondern sie kam aus einem ungewöhnlich ausgebildeten Respekt vor der Hinterlassenschaft der alten Völker, mochte es sich dabei um die einfachste Keramik oder um Beispiele der großen Kunst handeln. Auch das unscheinbarste Stück faßte er so zart an, als ob es sich um die größte Seltenheit handelte, und nie begnügte er sich unbekannten, rätselhaften Erscheinungen gegenüber mit trivialen Erklärungen. Auch in ihnen sah er Zeugen eines vergangenen Lebens, das ihm nicht tot und isoliert erschien, sondern das als Vorstufe und Teil unseres eigenen Lebens die höchste Ehrfurcht verdiente. Ehrfurcht: das war ein Gefühl, das ihn ganz erfüllte. Daß man nur mit ehrfürchtigem Sinn Hand an die Überreste der alten Kulturen legen dürfe, hört man oft, aber es wird nicht immer danach gehandelt. Bei ihm aber war die Praxis seiner Arbeit bis ins kleinste davon bestimmt, und diese Einstellung bei seinen Schülern und Mitarbeitern wachzurufen, war das erste Anliegen seiner Lehre.

Die Art und Weise, wie er uns zu Beginn unserer Tätigkeit bei ihm uns selbst überließ, könnte fast den Eindruck erwecken, als ob er kein Talent und keine Neigung zur Tätigkeit eines Lehrers gehabt habe. Aber gerade das Gegenteil war der Fall, denn alles, was er tat, war letzten Endes darauf ausgerichtet, auf die Menschen seiner Umgebung zu wirken, sie im eigentlichen Sinne des Wortes zu bilden, nur tat er das in einer sehr ungewöhnlichen und unsystematischen Weise. Zuerst wirkte auf uns nur sein Beispiel. Das änderte sich, als wir ihm näher gekommen waren. Die Zahl seiner Mitarbeiter hatte sich vermehrt, und fast an jedem Mittag kam er aus seinem Amtszimmer zu uns hinunter in den Zeichensaal, um eine Stunde mit uns zu verbringen. Da begann dann eine Unterhaltung, in der Andrae selbstverständlich das Wort führte. Er konnte wundervoll erzählen, und natürlich drehte sich das Gespräch zumeist um den Orient und was er dort erlebt und erfahren hatte. Das Land mit seinen Steppen und Wüsten, mit den beiden Flüssen und den begleitenden Gebirgen, mit seinen Städten und ihren kurdischen und arabischen Bewohnern haben wir da mit seinen Augen sehen und lieben gelernt, so daß, als wir dann selbst hinauskamen, uns eigentlich nichts mehr ganz fremd war. Dem schlossen sich Schilderungen des Alltags im Grabungsleben mit seinen Leiden und Freuden an. Andrae hatte einen ausgesprochenen Sinn für das Komische, und manches, was ihm vielleicht da draußen Kummer und Sorge gemacht hatte, wurde nun in einer Form wiedergegeben, die wahre Lachstürme hervorrief. Auf diese Weise lernten wir das Drum und Dran einer Grabung in der Theorie gründlich kennen, und nebenbei stellten sich uns eine Menge von Persönlichkeiten höchst lebendig vor, Gurlitt und Koldewey, Andraes Lehrer, für die er Zeit seines Lebens ein dankbares Herz und eine fast schwärmerische Verehrung bewahrte, die Mitarbeiter in Babylon und Assur bis zu den damals maßgebenden Persönlichkeiten in der Wissenschaft, in den Behörden und in der Wirtschaft. Auch die auf diese Weise gewonnene Kenntnis von Personen und Charakteren hat uns später viel genutzt. Aber Andrae blieb dabei nicht stehen, und selbstverständlich kam die Rede bald auf das, was ihn und uns im Augenblick persönlich beschäftigte. Für ihn standen damals neben der Aufstellung der Sammlungen die Vorarbeiten für die »Urformen des Bauens im Alten Orient« und später für »Die Ionische Säule, Bauform oder Symbol« im Vordergrund. Andrae erlebte damals den Übergang zu einer neuen Arbeitsweise. Gegen Ende seines Lebens hat er diesen Vorgang, den er nicht nur für seine Person für richtig hielt, sondern als eine ganz allgemein berechtigte Endstufe jeder wissenschaftlichen Tätigkeit ansah, etwa so formuliert: »Was im materiellen Pol erarbeitet worden ist und emotionell, also auch psychologisch einigermaßen erfaßt wurde, müßte nun ebenso energisch am spirituellen Pol aufgesucht und ergänzt werden.« Viele von Ihnen kennen wohl das Zitat aus unserer Festschrift zu seinem 80. Geburtstag, Andrae hat in den folgenden Sätzen noch deutlicher ausgeführt, was er meinte. Für unsere Unterhaltungen hatte das die Folge, daß Fragen wie etwa die nach der zeitlichen Zuordnung von Funden oder nach ihrer Ergänzung und alles ähnliche eine untergeordnete Rolle spielten. Ihre Beantwortung war für ihn eine Voraussetzung, die durch die gute, ehrliche Kärrnerarbeit immer wieder geschaffen werden mußte und sollte, die er aber für den Augenblick als geschaffen und abgetan ansah. Das Ziel war, hinter der Form, der Erscheinung der Dinge ihren ursprünglichen Sinn, ihren Geistgehalt zu erkennen. War eine solche Erkenntnis gelungen, so hatte sie für Andrae nicht mehr antiquarischen Wert, sondern als Zeuge einer bestimmten Stufe physischer Existenz und ihrer Beziehung zur Metaphysik war sie ihm ein Mittel zur Erkenntnis und zur Fortbildung des eigenen Wesens. Ich weiß, daß Andrae selbst mit den Formulierungen, mit denen ich diese für ihn so wichtigen Anliegen zu umschreiben versuche, sehr wenig einverstanden wäre, aber ich kann eben nur mit meinen Worten sagen, was wir damals erlebten. Mir erschien es, als setzten sich bei Andrae wissenschaftliche Erkenntnisse um in ethische, für jede Zeit und auch für die Gegenwart gültige Qualitäten. Das »Erkenne dich selbst in dem, was du im Alten erkennst« und das »Wachse an deiner Erkenntnis und lebe danach« war der eigentliche Inhalt seiner Lehre. Ich weiß noch, wie ich erstaunte, als er mich im Jahre 1928 bat, ihm bei seinen Vorlesungen und Übungen in der Technischen Hochschule zu helfen, und ich seine ersten Vorlesungen hörte. Da wurde so gut wie kein Stoff vorgelegt, – das blieb mir in den Übungen überlassen – aber vom Wesen der Dinge ausgehend führte er seine Hörer zum Wesen des Menschen, wie er es sah, und darüber hinaus bis zu den dunkelsten Geheimnissen der Metaphysik. Auch nach dem zweiten Weltkrieg, als er Ordinarius für Baugeschichte war, lehrte er in dieser Weise. Ein anderer hätte sich das kaum erlauben dürfen, ihm aber folgten die Studenten mit Spannung, und seine Schüler sprechen noch heute von diesen ungewöhnlichen Kollegs, und zwar die meisten mit großer Dankbarkeit. Dies Anliegen der Menschenführung stand bei fast allem, was er tat, im Vordergrund. Es sprach auch aus seinen Vorträgen im Museum, und sogar die Aufstellung der Funde diente diesem Ziel. Ein flüchtiger Besucher sah nur eine Ordnung nach dem Zeitablauf, wie das üblich ist, und bewunderte vor allem die großen Architekturen aus Babylon und Assur, die ja neben dem Pergamonaltar eine besondere Berühmtheit der Berliner Museen bildeten und noch bilden. Aber Andrae sah darin eine Darstellung von Stufen der Menschheitsentwicklung, die man erkennen und in sich wirken lassen sollte, und wir wissen, daß darauf die Reihenfolge, die Auswahl der Fundstücke, die Bilder an den Wänden, die nach eigenen Bildern von ihm gemalt waren, ja sogar die Farben der Wände, der Decken und einzelner Verzierungen bis ins kleinste zugeschnitten waren.

Es war nicht immer leicht, Andraes Gedankengängen zu folgen, und was er in den letzten 25 Jahren seines Lebens gesagt und geschrieben hat, blieb nicht immer ohne Widerspruch. Selbst bei unseren Gesprächen im Museum ging es manchmal lebhaft zu, und ich habe erlebt, daß in seinen Vorträgen Männer von wissenschaftlichem Rang, die durchaus nicht eng dachten und nebenbei seine guten Freunde waren, geradezu leidenschaftlich protestierten. Andraes Grundhaltung war bestimmt durch gewisse, sehr eigentümlich ausgeprägte Vorstellungen religiös-philosophischer Art. Man hat gelegentlich gemeint, daß er Begriffe aus diesem Vorstellungskreis bei der Deutung seiner Funde in diese hineinprojiziert habe, statt, wie es die exakte Forschung sonst tut, den Dingen ihren Gehalt abzufragen. Andrae hätte in einer solchen Unterstellung vielleicht nicht einmal einen Vorwurf gesehen, weil er beide Gebiete nicht trennte und weil bei ihm neben die Anschauung, das, was er »Die Schau« nannte, mit dem gleichen Anspruch auf die Realität ihrer Ergebnisse trat. Man dürfte eine solche Arbeitsweise kaum zu allgemeinem Gebrauch empfehlen, jeder andere würde dabei scheitern, selbst wenn er im übrigen dieselbe jahrzehntelange Übung im sachlichen, unvoreingenommenen Beobachten und die gleiche gründliche klassische Bildung besäße wie Andrae. Bei ihm aber führte das Zusammenspiel von Anschauung des Forschers und der Schau des Dichters – denn darum scheint es sich mir im Grunde zu handeln – zu Ergebnissen, die ganz ihm eigentümlich und von unschätzbarem grundsätzlichen Wert sind, selbst wenn einzelnes davon sich als überholt erweist oder erweisen wird. Und ebenso hat er in dem Sinne, den er anstrebte, erziehend gewirkt, auch bei solchen, die ihm auf seinen besonderen Wegen nicht folgen konnten und wollten. Er war weitherzig genug, auch eine andere Denkart neben sich zu dulden, wenn nur die Hingebung zur Sache, der Wille zur Ehrlichkeit und Treue vorhanden zu sein schien, die er verlangte und die er vorlebte.

Wer Andrae ganz kennen wollte, der mußte ihn bei sich zu Hause sehen, bei seiner Frau, die nicht nur für sein leibliches Wohl sorgte, sondern ihn auch auf allen seinen Gedankengängen begleitete, und bei seinen Kindern. Er war ein rechter Kinderpapa, hatte für seine Kinder Zeit, zeichnete ihnen die entzückendsten Bilderbücher und zog im Sommer fast an jedem schönen Sonntag mit der ganzen Familie hinaus zu einem stillen märkischen See, wo der Tag in Licht, Sonne und Wasser zugebracht wurde. Übrigens unterbrach auch das seine Gedankenarbeit nicht. Freude an der Natur, an den Kindern, an den Freunden, an der Arbeit vereinigten sich bei ihm zu einem einzigen Klang. An den Sonntagen da draußen auf der Wiese oder im Schiff liegend, hat er seine »Urformen« auf hundert Zettelchen zu Papier gebracht. Seine väterliche Fürsorge beschränkte sich nun durchaus nicht auf seine Familie. Wer immer in seinem Bannkreis Sorgen hatte, der durfte zu ihm kommen und fand bei ihm Rat, und, wenn es notwendig war, auch Hilfe, die er, wie ich vermute, oft unter erheblichen persönlichen Opfern leistete. Sein Bannkreis reichte weit. Seine Vorträge und Führungen waren in Berlin berühmt, und mit der Zeit bildete sich ein Stamm von Besuchern, die sich untereinander kannten und sogar zu Freunden wurden. Außerhalb unserer Museumsphäre bestand ein anderer Kreis, zu dem Andrae durch seine Religionsgemeinschaft Verbindung hatte, und darum legten sich im weiten Ring die Beziehungen zu seinen Kollegen und Fachgenossen zu Haus und in der weiten Welt, die zum großen Teil auch ausgesprochen freundschaftlicher Natur waren. Den Mittelpunkt seines Lebens aber bildete doch wohl unser Kreis, der im Museum, den er selbst gesammelt und deren wirtschaftliche Grundlagen er fast aus dem Nichts geschaffen hatte und auf rätselhafte Weise erhielt. Er konnte wohl stolz sein, wenn er, wie es bisweilen geschah, von einem seiner Mitarbeiter zum anderen ging und die Tagesarbeit mit ihnen besprach: von seinen beiden getreuen Sekretärinnen zu seinen alten Freunden und Mitarbeitern aus Assur und Babylon und zu uns jungen Architekten, zu den Philologen, dem Archäologen und zur Bibliothek, zu den beiden Photographinnen, dem alten Abteilungsinspektor, zu den Meistern und Arbeitern in den Magazinen, in der Formerei, in der Stein- und der Tischlerwerkstatt. Es war allein seine Energie, sein Sorgen und sein Wille, die dies zusammenhielten. Das Schönste daran war, daß dabei niemand einen Zwang empfand. Wo er erschien, da wurde nicht etwa besonderer Eifer gezeigt, das eben begonnene Frühstück unterbrochen oder die Nebenarbeit beiseite gelegt. Obwohl er den allergrößten Respekt genoß, fürchtete niemand in ihm den Vorgesetzten, und die Augen wurden hell und die Gesichter froh, wohin er kam. Durch ihn waren wir alle eine große Familie und gaben ihm, wenn wir unter uns von ihm sprachen, den Namen eines Vaters.

Der Krieg hat Andrae so gut wie anderen schwere Verluste gebracht, in der Familie sowohl wie im Amt. Die Kreise seiner Freunde waren zerstreut, das Museum schwer beschädigt und beraubt. Er hat sich sofort an die Arbeit gemacht, hat in vielem noch einmal von vorn angefangen, ja an der Technischen Universität übernahm er mit dem Ordinariat für Baugeschichte und Bauaufnahme noch schwerere Lasten als früher. Dann begann sein Augenleiden, und wie es ihn in zunehmendem Maße behinderte, zog er sich langsam aus seinen Ämtern und Verpflichtungen zurück. Trotzdem blieb er, solange er lebte, der Mittelpunkt aller unserer Bestrebungen. Uneigennützig half er dem neuen Direktor der Vorderasiatischen Abteilung, seiner Fakultät stand er auch noch als Emeritus zur Verfügung, mit Überlegenheit und Weisheit präsidierte er in den Sitzungen der DOG, den Vorstand der Koldeweygesellschaft beriet er und sorgte vor allem für die noch ausstehenden Bände der Publikationen der Deutschen Orient-Gesellschaft. Als der letzte Band der Architekturpublikationen aus Assur erschien und damit sein Lebenswerk gesichert war, ist er gestorben. Ich habe an der Aussegnung teilnehmen dürfen, die nach dem Ritus seiner Glaubensgemeinschaft stattfand, am Tage vor der offiziellen Trauerfeier mit ihrem Gepränge und den üblichen Laudationes. Doch in seinem Hause war es keine Trauerfeier. Es wurde keine Träne geweint und kein Wort gesagt außer denen der Liturgie. Es war ein dankbares Abschiednehmen von einem wahrhaft Vollendeten, der seine Arbeit redlich getan hat, der ein Segen war für viele, der Liebe gegeben und sehr viel Liebe zurückerhalten hat, und der uns nun voraufgegangen ist in die Wandlung. Und mit Dank, daß er lebt und daß er der unsere war, wollen wir sein Andenken in Ehren halten.

KATALOG DER TAFELN 1–128 (NR. 1–198)

(Wenn nicht anders vermerkt ist als Untergrund helles Zeichenpapier
oder heller Zeichenkarton verwendet worden)

1 1908 – farb. Kreiden auf getöntem Papier – 23,0 × 18,8
Selbstportrait, Assur.

2 1915 – Ölgemälde von Johann Walter-Kurau – 87,0 × 79,0
Walter Andrae als Hauptmann vor einem seiner ersten Entwürfe für einen Löwen der Prozessionsstraße zu Babylon, vgl. die Signatur AW 1899 neben rechter Löwenpranke und Nr. 80.
Deutsches Archäologisches Institut, Abt. Baghdad.
Zum Maler: Thieme-Becker 35 (1942) 133: Walter-Kurau, Johann, Maler, 4. 2. 1869–1932. Vom selben Maler stammt u. a. auch das große Wandbild vom Kasr in Babylon im Vorderasiatischen Museum zu Berlin, vgl. L. Jakob-Rost – E. Klengel – R. B. Wartke – J. Marzahn, Das Vorderasiatische Museum (1987) 91.

3 1948 – Ölgemälde von Otto Jäger – 63,4 × 50,0
Walter Andrae.
Deutsches Archäologisches Institut, Abt. Baghdad.
Zum Maler: H. Vollmer, Allgemeines Lexikon der bildenden Künstler des XX. Jahrhunderts 2 (1955) 522: Jäger, Otto, Dr. phil. und Arzt, dtsch. Bildnismaler, *21. 8. 1900.

4 18. 12. 1898 – Aquarell – 17,6 × 25,3
Im Hafen von Alexandria.
Vgl. RK 97 ff.

5 21. 12. 1898 – Aquarell – 18,8 × 25,5
Port Said.
Vgl. RK 100 f.

6 22. 12. 1898 – Bleistift – 18,5 × 27,5
Der »Nettuno« vor Jaffa (Bildbeschriftung »Saturno« nachträglich und falsch).
Berlin, Staatsbibliothek, SPK, Nachlaß Andrae 15/2.

vgl. RK 101 ff.:

»An der hafenlosen palästinisch-syrischen Küste entlang zu fahren, weckt andere Gefühle als die Fahrt längs der Nordafrikaküste. Man muß sich die Küstenschiffahrt der alten Phöniker vorstellen, die sich an den Gestaden des Mittelmeers bis zu den Säulen des Herkules handeltreibend entlangtasteten, ohne eigentliches Heimatemporium. Was man hier Hafen nennt, kann nur Kähne und Fischerboote notdürftig gegen die Brandung schützen, die westliche Stürme gegen diese Nordsüdküste werfen. Der alte ›Nettuno‹ war wie ein dampfender, etwas schmierig gewordener Phöniker und hielt sich, wie die Alten und auch wie die gelehrigen Schüler der Phöniker, die Hellenen, immer hübsch nahe an der Küste. Aber in die ›Häfen‹, außer in den von Beirut, getraute er sich nicht einzulaufen.«

7 22. 12. 1898 – Aquarell und Bleistift – 18,0 × 26,9
Jaffa, vom Schiff aus gesehen.
RK 102:
»Die Palästina-Küste hat etwas Abweisendes. Ein gleichmäßiger niedriger Höhenzug verwehrt einem, wenn man von Port Said herankommt, den Blick in das höher steigende Binnenland. Bräunlich gefärbt, zieht er sich genau von Süd nach Nord. Das große geschichtliche Geheimnis des Landes bleibt dem Seefahrer stumm verschlossen. Auch in Jaffa, dem alten Joppe, bemerkt man vom Innern nicht viel, wenn die Dampfer auf der Rheede liegen. Es geschieht oft genug, daß der Dampfer nicht leichtern und keine Passagiere absetzen kann, die dann nach Cypern oder zurück nach Port Said zur See spazieren geführt werden, unter Umständen mehrere Male, bis ihnen das Aussteigen gelingt.«

8 22. 12. 1898 – Bleistift – 27,2 × 18,4
Auf der »Nettuno« vor Jaffa (vgl. Nr. 6.7). Robert Koldewey mit dem Arabisten Dr. Bernhard Moritz (vgl. LE 32). Bruno Moritz war bereits 1886/87 Begleiter R. Koldeweys bei dessen erster Reise nach Mesopotamien (Surghul und el Hibba), vgl. RK 38.96. Als Direktor der khedivialen Bibliothek in Kairo nahm er an der Baalbek-Untersuchung teil, allerdings nur acht Tage lang, da die ihn interessierenden arabischen Inschriften zu hoch angebracht waren. Vgl. RK 101.

9 23. 12. 1898 – Bleistift – 27,5 × 19,0
Blick auf Beirut.
Berlin, Staatsbibilothek, SPK, Nachlaß Andrae 15/3.
Vgl. RK 104.

10 23./26. 12. 1898 – Aquarell – 34,7 × 24,8
Beirut, Blick aus dem Hotel Bassoul.

11 28. 12. 1898 – Aquarell – 17,0 × 25,0
Baalbek, Übersicht (Tempelbezirk) Berlin, Staatsbibliothek, SPK, Nachlaß Andrae 15/4.
Vgl. RK 96. 106 ff. und LE 29 f.:
»Nach der Seereise, der Landung in Alexandrien und dem Aufenthalt in Damaskus über die Weihnachtszeit 1898 wird endlich am 30. 12. 1898 das erste Reiseziel, Baalbek, erreicht. Hier sollte Robert Koldewey im Auftrage des Kaisers eine Voruntersuchung der Ruinen für die

spätere Ausgrabung derselben unternehmen. Der große Tempel (Jupiter-Tempel) hat 19
Säulen in der Länge und 10 in der Breite. Jetzt stehen nur noch 6 Stück von 19 m Höhe, dar-
über ein mächtiges Hauptgesims (s. Bildmitte), auf mächtigen Fundamentmauern. Vom
kleinen Tempel (»Bacchus«-Tempel) stehen noch die Zella und etwa 20 Säulen von 1,80 m
Durchmesser und 5,20 m Umfang (Nr. 13. 14). Die Architektur mutet uns barock an, innen
mächtige Nischen, immer zwei übereinander mit Ornamentik, immer aus den mächtigsten
Blöcken konstruiert. Eine Säule ist beim Erdbeben gekippt und lehnt an der Zellawand. Das
Ganze ist von Saladins Nachfolger im 13. Jh. zur starken, uneinnehmbaren Festung ausgebaut, mit allen fortifikatorischen Verschmitztheiten. Es sind an sich wieder architektonische
Meisterstücke der islamischen Baukunst, herrliche Kreuzgewölbe und Stalaktitennischen,
Falltüren, Schießscharten und Brücken (Nr. 16. 17). Leider haben diese späteren Arbeiten
den Abbruch mancher schönen Antiken-Teile erfordert; der Grundgedanke ist jedoch leicht
zu erkennen.
Für den Maler ist die Ruine eine wahre Fundgrube. Ihr glaubt nicht, wie golden die mächtigen Kalksteinsäulen gegen den blauen Himmel glänzen, dahinter die blendenden Höhen des
Libanon und Antilibanon, die hier ihre höchsten Gipfel haben.
Jetzt schmilzt im Tale der Schnee, und die fruchtbare Beka-Ebene färbt sich wieder rot,
intensiv rotbraun und stellenweise grün. Abends wird's besonders herrlich, eine unge-
wohnte Farbenpracht entzückt das Auge, der Antilibanon erglüht in rosarotem Schein der
untergehenden Sonne, das Tal hüllt sich in blauen und violetten Dämmer, und der Himmel
verändert sich von Minute zu Minute (Nr. 12); dann steigt der blankgeputzte Mond hinter
dem Schneegebirge herauf und beleuchtet die nächtliche Landschaft so hell, daß man lesen
und schreiben kann in seinem Schein. Wir sehen von unserem Zimmer aus die ganze Flanke
der gespenstischen Ruine mit dem weißen Sannin (3200 m hoch) dahinter. Die Luft ist hier
herrlich, denn wir sind 1200 m über Meereshöhe.«
»Meine Arbeit ist sehr interessant, man dringt vollständig in die Absichten der großartigen
Planung ein, und ich skizziere und aquarelliere aus Leibeskräften, zumal die Landschaft ganz
herrlich ist. Von den Zinnen der arabischen Festungsmauer, die in den alten Tempelbezirk
eingebaut ist, hat man einen herrlichen Fernblick über die weite rötliche Ebene der Beka
und auf den ganzen mächtigen weißbeschneiten Libanon, der da glänzt im Sonnenschein
(Nr. 11. 14). Und abends, wenn die Sonne hinter die Schneegipfel sinkt, dreht man sich um
und sieht das Alpenglühen des Antilibanon (Nr. 12), an dessen Fuß die Ruinen liegen.«

12 2. 1. 1899 – Aquarell – 19,5 × 17,8
    Baalbek, Abendstimmung über dem Libanongebirge.
    Vgl. Zitat bei Nr. 11.

13 16. 1. 1899 – Aquarell und Bleistift – 35,3 × 25,3
    Baalbek, Am »Bacchus«-Tempel.
    Vgl. Zitat bei Nr. 11.

14 Jan. 1899 – Aquarell – 35,3 × 25,3
    Baalbek, »Bacchus«-Tempel.
    Vgl. Zitat bei Nr. 11.

15 Jan. 1899 – Bleistift – 34,0 × 24,3
Baalbek, Detail vom Tempel des »Jupiter Heliopolitanus«, am Vorhof.
Vgl. Zitat bei Nr. 11.

16 1. 1. 1899 – Bleistift, Buntstifte – 33,5 × 24,2
Baalbek-Nord, bei der arabischen Bastion.
Vgl. Zitat bei Nr. 11.

17 1. 1. 1899 – Bleistift – 18,5 × 27,3
Baalbek, im 1. Stock der arabischen Bastion.
Vgl. Zitat bei Nr. 11.

18 Febr. 1899 – Bleistift – 24,0 × 33,5
Aleppo, Tekke (Derwisch-Moschee). Vgl. Nr. 154: Takīya aš Šaiḫ Abū Bakr und
Nr. 228. Berlin, Staatsbibliothek, SPK, Nachlaß Andrae 15/6.

19 22. 1. 1899 – Bleistift – 27,7 × 18,6
Iskenderun, Markt.

20 22. 1. 1899 – Bleistift – 27,1 × 18,5
Iskenderun, Weg zum Amanus-Gebirge.
Beschreibung von W. Andrae, ungefähr 1950 (bisher unveröffentlicht): »Bei unserer Landung in dem kleinen Hafen empfing uns ein einheimischer Vizekonsul in einer sehr primiti-
ven Lokanta. Wir waren zu Viert und kamen von Beirut mit dem winzigen österreichischen
Lloydschiff ›Nettuno‹. Hier gab es keine europäische Kultur mehr. Eine kümmerliche
Bazarstraße durchzog den kleinen türkischen Ort. Aber hier mußten wir den mit drei Pferden bespannten sogenannten ›Landauer‹ besteigen, der auch das Gepäck mitnahm. So ging
die Reise über den Bailon-Paß des Amanus-Gebirges in drei Tagen nach Aleppo.«

21 1. 1. 1899 – Bleistift – 17,3 × 20,6
Baalbek, der Wirt Perikli Mimikaki (Hotel Palmyra).
Vgl. RK 106.

22 Febr. 1899 – Bleistift – 24,4 × 14,4
Aleppo, 'Ain at-Tell. Picknick mit Frau Koch. Von links nach rechts: drei Diplomaten
(wohl der deutsche Konsul Zollinger, der englische Barnham und der englische Vizekonsul
Falanga, vgl. LE 37), Frau Koch, R. Koldewey, zwei nicht mehr identifizierbare Personen.
Vgl. RK 114 ff.; LE 35. 229:
»Bei der Zusammenstellung der Karawane konnte ich Unerfahrener nicht viel helfen. Hilfe
kam uns von ganz anderer Seite, und ohne sie wären aus den 14 Tagen Aufenthalt sicher
3 Wochen geworden. Martha Koch, die Gattin des Kaufmanns Carl Koch, besorgte alles
Notwendige. Ihr schien ganz Aleppo dienstbar zu sein. Sie wußte, woher man die besten
und billigsten Maultiere und Packpferde, die zuverlässigsten Treiber, Diener, Köche, die
besten Zelte, Decken, Säcke, Nahrungsmittel, Laternen und Reitpferde bekam. Sie besaß
Würde und Autorität, Erfahrung im endlosen Aushandeln der Preise und Energie im
Ablehnen der Überforderungen, kurz im ›Bet Madame Koch‹ (Haus der Frau Koch), das in

Aleppo jedes Kind kannte, spielte sich das ganze Karawanendrama ab.« Vgl. auch
Nr. 160.

23 10. 2. 1899 – Bleistift – 18,6 × 27,5
Derhafer: Bienenkorbhäuser (zwischen Aleppo und Meskene). LE 37 f.:
»Am 9. Februar ging's nach Derhafa weiter über ebene Felderflächen. Felder sind seit wenigen Jahren, seit die sogenannte Straße ›sicher‹ ist, aus der vorhandenen Wüste wenigstens in
der Nähe der ›Straße‹ entstanden. Recht gedeihlich kann aber kein Wohlstand trotz des ganz
vorzüglichen Bodens werden, weil überall, wo etwas Rentables geschaffen wird, die Regierung Hand auflegt und wegnimmt oder hohe, fast unerschwingliche Steuern in Naturalien
zieht. Die Dörfer sehen hier aus wie Kolonien von Maulwurfshaufen, lauter Kuppeln aus
ungebrannten Ziegeln, oben einen Kranz als Schornstein, jedes Dorf für sich eine kleine
Festung.«

24 11. 2. 1899 – Bleistift – 18,5 × 27,3
Im Euphrat-Tal bei Meskene (Karawane), LE 38 f.:
»Am dritten Tage langten wir am Euphrat an, der dann durch 3 Wochen unser steter Begleiter und Wasserspender war. Es sieht ›närrisch‹ aus, würde man bei uns sagen, es ist überhaupt die ganze Gegend geologisch ganz merkwürdig – eine unverfälschte, ungestörte Darstellung geologischen Werdens und Vergehens. Eine mächtige Tertiärformation, darüber
gleichmäßiges Alluvium (Bretsche, Konglomerat), erstreckt sich über das ganze Zweistrom-
gebiet des Euphrat und Tigris. Das Tertiär ist unter dem Konglomerat zunächst Mergel,
dann Gips und ganz unten auch Kalkstein. Der Mergel steht bei Meskene bis zu 30–40 m.
Dieses ganze System ist alluvial nach Entstehung eines Stromrisses durchbrochen, bezie-
hentlich zerstört und zermalmt, und an den Rändern sieht man fast mathematische Schnitte
durch die ganze ungeheure Schichtung. Das Alluvialgebiet besteht nun zum großen Teil aus
dem bekannten fruchtbaren Euphratschlamm, der oft 3–5 m tief ist, das heißt also aus fet-
tem Lehmboden. Durch diesen windet sich jetzt in unabzählbaren Krümmungen der Euphrat, zahlreiche Inseln und Schlammschlieren bildend. Die Ufer sind fast immer senkrecht,
stets sind sie es an der konkaven Seite, wo eine ständige Zerstörung stattfindet. Wir hörten
in der Wüstenstille oft einen schußartigen Donner, wenn wieder eine solche Lehmwand ins
Wasser fiel. Die Fruchtbarkeit ist bei der heutigen Wirtschaft nur eine immanente Eigen-
schaft des Landes, denn bebaut wird es nur an verschwindend wenigen Stellen, weil für die
künstliche Hebung des Wassers bzw. die Kanalisierung nichts getan wird, außer wenn der
Profit der Regierung, d. h. den obersten Herren des Landes zufließt. Alles Land gehört mit
seinen Bewohnern dem Sultan, er kann machen damit, was er will. Es kann sich jeder ein
ödes Stück Land nehmen und bebauen, bringt's dann was ein, so muß er entweder den
Besitz durch eine bestimmte Reihe von Jahren oder den Kauf schriftlich nachweisen, was
natürlich nie möglich ist, sonst kann es ihm weggenommen werden. Unbeliebte Personen
werden mit Vorliebe so schikaniert. Jetzt wachsen da in der Hauptsache wilde Tamarisken-
gebüsche in großer Menge oder Dornen und manchmal etwas Gras. Felder haben wir bisher
sehr vereinzelt gesehen, das frische Grün darauf tat als seltener Genuß immer sehr wohl.«

25 11. 2. 1899 – Bleistift – 16,5 × 18,2
Qal'at Baalis (Barbalissus), byzantinisches Praetorium.
Sarre-Herzfeld I 123 ff. III Taf. 23.
Vgl. LE 40.

26 12. 2. 1899 – Tusche – 13,5 × 18,8
Qal'at Dja'bar, 5.–14. Jh.
Ein ca. zehn Jahre jüngeres Foto davon bei Bell, AtA, Abb. 50: den heutigen Zustand zeigt
A. Mahmoud, in: Land des Baal (1982) Abb. 77.

27 14. 2. 1899 – Bleistift – 9,0 × 18,2
Tell Menachir, zwischen Hammâm und Sabḫa. Wie uns Dr. Kay Kohlmeyer mitteilt, handelt es sich hier nicht, wie in der ersten Auflage angenommen, um einen Kranzhügel, sondern um einen erloschenen Vulkan. Zu Basalt in diesem Bereich vgl. auch Nr. 141 und 142
sowie den Text zu Nr. 222.

28 15. 2. 1899 – Aquarell – 16,4 × 24,5
Euphrat bei Dibne (at Tibne), vgl. Nr. 140–142.
Vgl. LE 41.

29 15. 2. 1899 – Bleistift – 9,3 × 18,5
Halebije (Zenobia), byzantinisches Stadttor. Ein ca. zehn Jahre jüngeres Foto von Halebije
bei Bell, AtA Abb. 46.
Vgl. auch Sarr-Herzfeld I 166 ff. II 365 ff. III Taf. 72–75. RK 125 f.:
»Halebije ist meines Wissens außer durch E. Herzfeld mit F. Sarre noch nicht weiter
erforscht worden. Es liegt in der Enge des Euphrattals, deren Hänge wohl 100 m ansteigen
und oben an der großen Basaltlavadecke von Strata-Vulkanen, also am Ledscha beginnen.
Von dem schwarzen Basalt erscheint überall so viel in der Landschaft, daß ein düsterer Eindruck entsteht, gegen den die hellen Bauten der merkwürdigen Abhangstadt nicht recht auf-
kommen. Sie sind aus silbrig-grauem durchscheinenden Gipsstein oder Alabaster, der,
schön gequadert und sorgfältig gefügt, von tüchtigen Baumeistern zu Toren, Stadtmauern
und Kirchen sowie in dem der Stadtmauer eingefügten Pallas verarbeitet war. Was man sah,
war in byzantinischer Zeit errichtet. Die Stadt hieß nach der bekannten palmyrenischen
Königin Zenobia. In der Höhe der Hochebene liegt eine kleine Akropolis, nach allen Seiten
steil abfallend, von der die beiden Stadtmauerarme divergierend zum Fluß hinabsteigen, den
eine Flußmauer mit Auslässen begleitet. Gegenüber liegt eine kleinere Stadt, jetzt Zelebije
genannt, deren Überreste wenig imposant sind und von uns damals nicht besucht werden
konnten.«

30 19. 2. 1899 – Tusche – 23,5 × 34,2
Qal'at ar-Rachba, seldschukische Ruine, 13. Jh., Sarre-Herzfeld II 382 ff. III 79.80; heutiger
Zustand: A. Mahmoud, in: Land des Baal (1982) Abb. 76 (Bleistiftausführung des Bildes in
Berlin, Staatsbibliothek, SPK, Nachlaß Andrae 15/9) RK 127; LE 42:
»Am nächsten Tag ritt ich mit Dr. Koldewey und zwei Soldaten zunächst zu der arabischen
Burgruine Rachaba, die von einem 40 m tiefen Graben umzogen auf vollständig unersteig-
barem Fels lag mit hohen Ziegel- und Steinmauern, einst die Burg einer großen Stadt, die
sich von da bis Mejadin erstreckte mit Gärten und Feldern – jetzt ist alles öde.«

31 20. 2. 1899 – Aquarell und Bleistift – 33,8 × 24,3
Der Felsen von Chan Kalessi (Dura Europos).
Vgl. Sarre-Herzfeld II 386 ff. III Taf. 81–83; RK 122. 125 f.:
»Koldewey führte die Karawane so, daß wir zwei größere Ruinenstätten berührten und
nicht nur das, sie auch sehen, zeichnen und schnell aufnehmen konnten: Halebije und Islahije
(Kan Kalessi), das alte Dura-Europos, von dem er in dem oben angeführten Briefe sprach.
Die letztgenannte Ruinenstadt ist später von einer französisch-amerikanischen Expedition
mehrere Jahre hindurch durchforscht und veröffentlicht worden. Für mich war es die erste
Aufnahmepraxis in Mesopotamien. Koldewey umschritt mit mir routierend das ganze Stadt-
gebiet, dessen Maerumzug schön erhalten an zwei tiefen Schluchten und zwischen ihnen
am ›Hals‹ der Festung mit einem gewaltigen Bogentor zu sehen war, während die Akropolis,
durch einen riesigen Felzsturz dezimiert, den Steilabfall zur Euphrataue hin bildete. Der
Blick von der Burg talauf und talab drückte sich unauslöschlich ein.«
LE 42:
»Der 20. Februar wurde benutzt zur Aufnahme der noch ganz unbekannten Stadtruine Kan
Kalessi (Blutschloß), die eine halbe Stunde rückwärts am Euphrat liegt. Sie ist ebenfalls in
Alabaster gemauert, aber fast ganz abgetragen. Interessant ist, daß man den Grundriß der
Häuser und Straßen auf dem glatten Erdboden genau erkennt.«

32 24. 2. 1899 – Aquarell – 35,0 × 25,0
Ana, Ortseingang. Rechts am Ufer der heute im Stausee von Haditha verschwundenen Insel
ein Schöpfrad.
LE 42:
»In Ana sah ich die ersten Dattelpalmen, und was für welche! Der Fluß bildet hier eine
gewundene, enge Oase mitten in den gelben kahlen Kalkfelsen und Hügeln, die sich rechts
und links 20–40 Tage weit erstrecken. Ana selbst ist 3 Stunden lang, immer in Palmen. Wir
lagern am Serail, mitten unter den mächtigen Wedeln der Dattelpalmen am rauschenden
Euphrat, in dem gegenüber fruchtbare Inseln liegen. Die Na'uren (Wasserschöpfräder pri-
mitivster Konstruktion) quietschten sanft, der Mond ging glanzvoll auf, tiefe, heimliche
Stille breitete sich über das herrliche Tal. Ich schrieb im Mondschein meine Erlebnisse auf,
so hell ist die Mondnacht hier.«

33 24. 2. 1899 – Farbstifte – 14,5 × 22,4
Ana, von der Euphratinsel gesehen.
Vgl. Nr. 32 und das ca. zehn Jahre jüngere Foto bei Bell, AtA Abb. 51.

34 24. 2. 1899 – Aquarell – 25,3 × 35,3
Der Euphrat unterhalb von Ana. Im Vordergrund ein Stock, der Schatten wirft, im Hinter-
grund Na'uren (Schöpfräder; vgl. z. B. solche auf dem ca. zehn Jahre jüngeren Foto bei Bell,
AtA Abb. 49 und Nr. 165.166).
Vgl. Nr. 32.

35 26. 2. 1899 – Bleistift – 33,9 × 24,6
Haditha im Euphrat. Am diesseitigen Ufer Na'uren (vgl. Nr. 32.34.165.166).
(Ausführung des Bildes in Tusche: Berlin, Staatsbibliothek, SPK, Nachlaß Andrae 15/14).

36 28. 2. 1899 – Aquarell und Bleistift – 24,4 × 34,0
    Hit, Grabbauten vor der Stadt (ähnliches Bild: Berlin, Staatsbibliothek, SPK, Nachlaß
    Andrae 15/17). Vgl. das ca. zehn Jahre jüngere Foto bei Bell, AtA Abb. 54. LE 43:
    »Auch in den folgenden Tagen belohnten uns herrliche Mondnächte am Euphrat für die
    Anstrengungen der Tagesritte, bis am 28. Februar Hit erreicht wurde (das alte Is des He-
    rodot). Sechs Stunden vorher sahen wir den Rauch der Asphaltquelle von Hit, die schon den
    Alten bekannt war. Es ist jetzt eine vertrocknete Quelle, die eine bituminöse Kalkschicht
    erzeugt hat, welche auf unrationellste Art in kleinstem Kleinbetrieb von den Eingeborenen
    ausgebeutet wird. Salziges Wasser und Schwefelwasserstoffgestank machen die Gegend
    Sodom und Gomorrha ähnlich, vor allem, wenn noch das Glührot der Abendsonne darüber
    leuchtet. Hit liegt auf einem alten Tell (Ruinenhügel) und ist ein gutes Beispiel für das Ent-
    stehen solcher Tells. Am Fluß gibt es hier auch schöne und viele Palmen.«

37 10. 3. 1899 – Tusche – 13,8 × 22,3
    Baghdad, »Drachentor« oder Talismantor (Bab el Tilism), seldschukisch. Vgl. Bell, AtA
    190 f. Abb. 114 f.; Sarre-Herzfeld III Taf. 10. 11. 49; T. Jawad al-Janab, Studies in Media-
    eval Architecture (1982) 46 Taf. 6.

38 März 1899 – Aquarell – 18,6 × 25,7
    Baghdad, Kathimein, Grabmoschee der Brüder Kathim.
    LE 44:
    »Baghdad! Was man zuerst sieht, sind die Goldkuppeln von Kathimein (Kathmen mit engli-
    schem th), welche 4 Stunden, ehe man hinkommt, im Sonnenschein am Horizont wie zwei
    goldene Sterne erstrahlen. Mit echtem Goldblech von der Dicke eines Fingernagels sind die
    Kuppeln abgedeckt, ein großes Heiligtum der Schiiten!«
    Die Grabschreine stehen jeweils in einem der Kuppelräume, zu denen je zwei der Minarette
    gehören.

39 15. 3. 1899 – Bleistift – 22,0 × 13,6
    Baghdad, Khan Mirjan (seldschukisch, 760 nH/1359). Sarre-Herzfeld II 187 ff. III Taf. 51;
    T. J. Al-Janab a. O. 140 ff.
    Taf. 134–140, Abb. 30–35.

40 7. 3. 1899 – Bleistift – 13,4 × 9,1
    Baghdad, Gasse (Briefbeilage: erster Gruß an die Eltern).

41 März 1899 – Bleistift – 22,4 × 13,6
    Baghdad, Hof im Haus Berk.
    Vgl. AK 131 f. und LE 38 sowie Abb. 17.

42 1900 – Tusche, Feder – 17,6 × 27,5
    Das Dorf Kuweirisch, von Babylon aus gesehen.

43 1901 – Aquarell – 23,4 × 16,4
    Babylon. Kuweirisch, Szene auf der Dorfstraße: Kinder beim Astragal-Spiel
    (vgl. R. M. Boehmer – N. Wrede, Baghdader Mitteilungen 16, 1985, 399 ff.)

Abb. 17 Baghdader Holzkeilchen-Kapitell, 19. 3. 1899

44 1900 – Aquarell – 14,0 × 24,7
Babylon. Dorfstraße in Kuweirisch nach Gewitterregen.

45 1901 – Aquarell – 35,0 × 25,0
Babylon. Kuweirisch, Euphratufer südlich vom Expeditionshaus.

46 1899 – Aquarell – 35,3 × 25,3
Babylon. Palmengarten vor Kuweirisch.
LE 59 f:
»Wir haben jetzt die wunderschönsten, zuckersüßesten reifen Datteln. Das ist etwas anderes als der klebrige, pappige Kram, den man in Europa unter dem Namen Datteln bekommt. Man kennt hier hundert verschiedene Arten, gelbe, graue, rote, schwarze, große, kleine: alle haben verschiedene Namen. Es beginnt auch die Zeit des Dattelraubes, überall sitzen tags und nachts Wächter, oftmals wird geknallt mit alten Donnerbüchsen, meist aber nur, um die Anwesenheit des Wächters zu dokumentieren. Ab und zu kommen auch Soldaten und führen einige Datteläuber hinweg, das fällt aber nicht weiter auf. Das Bild der Palmengärten ist jetzt prächtig. Die Datteln sind das reinste Goldgelb, umgeben von den mattgrünen, stilvoll geordneten Palmwedeln auf dem tiefblauen Himmel und mit dem weißlich-braunen Stamm.«
LE 77:
»Meine Erfahrung mit den störrischen Dattelpalmen muß ich noch anfügen. Diese Pflanze – es ist nämlich kein Baum, auch wenn sie 20 und mehr Meter hoch wird – führt den Maler zwingend wieder ins Zeichnerische. Sie aus der Farbe allein zu entwickeln, führt unweigerlich zu einem Wischiwaschi und gibt weder ihr Wesen noch ihre Erscheinung wieder. Will man also nicht »gegenstandslos« oder »abstrakt« darstellen, so muß man sich schon bequemen, sorglich und geduldig Wedel zu malen mit allen ihren feinen Blattrispen, also Pinselzeichnung.
Wenn man vier Jahre lang unter Palmen lebt, sie knospen, blühen, fruchten sieht und endlich von ihren süßen Früchten lebt, fühlt man sich als Maler verpflichtet, sie ehrlich und nicht karikiert oder verstümpert darzustellen. Man lernt, sie ehrfürchtig zu betrachten. Man weiß, welcher Pflege sie bedürfen und wie reich sie diese Pflege dem Menschen lohnen, man versteht, weshalb die Menschen des Altertums sie beinahe göttlich verehrten und in ihre Symbolwelt einbezogen wie kaum eine andere Pflanze.«

47 1899 – Aquarell – 25,5 × 17,9
Babylon, Kuweirisch, Koldeweys Reisezelt am Abend des Ankunftstages der Babylon-Expedition im Hofe des zukünftigen Expeditionshauses.
LE 38:
»Koffer, Sattelsack, Flinte und Pistole, Patronengürtel und Feldstuhl, alles fand seinen Platz. In der Mitte wurde sogar der Tisch aufgestellt, und wir speisten daran auf Stühlen sitzend, äußerst gemütlich und angenehm. Tisch und Stühle sind von Bambus und so leicht, daß das ganze Paket mit einer Hand zu heben ist.«

48 1899 – Aquarell – 25,7 × 17,7
Babylon. Kuweirisch. Haus der Babylon-Expedition von Westen über den Fluß gesehen.

49 1900 – Aquarell – 25,0 × 17,5
Babylon, Hof des Expeditionshauses im ersten Bauzustand, mit Funden.

50 1901 – Aquarell – 25,2 × 35,2
Babylon, Blick vom Dach des Expeditionshauses in einen Nachbarhof.

51 1901 – Aquarell – 9,3 × 12,1
Babylon, Expeditionshaus, Hofansicht nach dem Ausbau.
LE 54 f.:
»Kurz nach Beginn der Ausgrabung begannen wir auch schon mit dem Um- und Neubau
des von Habib el Alaui, dem Dorfscheich, gemieteten Hauses. Darüber schrieb ich damals
an den Großvater in Dresden: ›Der Hausbau hat einen fürchterlichen Spektakel in unseren
sonst so stillen Hof gebracht. Es sind jetzt etwa 20 Menschen dabei beschäftigt, von denen
kein einziger auch nur eine Minute still sein kann, ein fortwährendes Schreien, Rufen,
Schimpfen, Aufmuntern, auch wenn's nicht nötig ist – aber es geht wie in einem Ameisen-
haufen, alles rennt und schuftet mit einer eisernen Zähigkeit durch 10 Stunden ohne Ermat-
ten. Das ganze Erdgeschoß ist in 8 Tagen fertiggestellt worden. Kleine Jungen, die den Tag
2 Piaster = 35 Pf bekommen, bringen den Tin (Schlamm) zur Baustelle, den zwei unausge-
setzt den ganzen Tag bis an die Knie in ihm stehende Männer herstellen, indem sie den von
der nächsten Umgebung genommenen Erdboden mit Wasser vermischen. Das ist der Mörtel. An heiklen Stellen, z. B. bei einem Bogen, wird auch mal Gips genommen, und dann
wird ein Stein auf den anderen geklebt, und da der Gips schnell erhärtet, ist das Gewölbe in
einer halben Stunde fertig und wird betreten. Gerüste gibt es nicht, die Treppe geht außen
herauf und wird massiv gebaut, alles mit Ziegelbrocken, die Stufen aus je drei ganzen Nebu-
kadnezar-Ziegeln. Es ist ein ganz gelungener Betrieb, für mich äußerst interessant zu beobachten, wie man's hier handhabt.‹
Als Baumeister waltete bei diesem Bau Ustad Emin, d. h. Meister Emin, aus unserer Kreis-
stadt Hille, mit dem Zollstock messend, planend und die Baububen hauend. Er war ein wür-
diger Herr mit großem Turban und trug nur ein Musterbuch mit geheimen Bauschlüsseln in
der Tasche. Er ging auf alle Wünsche des Bauherrn ein. Den gewünschten Grundriß zeichnete er mit dem Zollstock auf den Erdboden, begann sofort, auf diese Zeichnung Schlamm
als Mörtel und Ziegel auflegen zu lassen und nach oben hin so weiter zu pappen, bis das
Gewünschte dastand. Er hat auch das Ziegelornament am Eingangsort entworfen und vor
unseren Augen ausgeführt, alles auf dem Erdboden, den er vorher mit der Hand glattstrich.
Die weichen gelben Ziegel modernen Brandes bearbeitete er mit einer Fuchsschwanz-Säge
und legte sie nach dem geheimen Musterbuch zu allerhand geometrischen Figuren oder
Sternen am Boden aus, hinterpappte sie mit Gipsmörtel und Schilfstengeln, so daß ein gro-
ßes »Ornament-Brett« entstand, das man als Ganzes an die Wand über dem Tore kleben
konnte. In Koldeweys Zimmer schuf er ein Kombinat von Dachtreppe, Nische, Fenster und
Ruhebank mit Euphrataussicht, wo Koldewey Siesta halten konnte und den landesüblichen
Tschibuk zu rauchen gedachte. Das neue »Schloß« gedieh prächtig und wurde mit blendend
weißem Gipsmörtel geputzt und hieß daher bei den Arabern Kasr-el-abiad, das weiße
Schloß. In ihm gab es auch keine Flöhe mehr, sie mochten die schneeweißen gipsenen
Wände nicht und verkrochen sich lieber in den alten erdigen Klamotten-Mauern. Aber auch
diese vergipste der wackere Ustad Emin und mauerte so die Verkrochenen lebendig ein.«

52 1902 – Aquarell – 25,2 × 35,3
    Babylon, Expeditionshaus, Hofansicht.

53 Sommer 1901 – Aquarell – 35,5 × 25,5
    Babylon. Expeditionshaus, Loggia im Obergeschoß; der Diener bringt Kaffee. Berlin,
    Staatsbibliothek, SPK, Nachlaß Andrae 15/18.
    Bisher unveröffentlichte Beschreibung von W. Andrae, etwa 1950:
    »Das Haus der Ausgrabungsexpedition hatte Robert Koldewey, ihr Leiter, gleich nach der
    Ankunft der Expedition in Babylon am Nordende des Dorfes Kuweiresch in dem Hofe des
    Dorfschulzen Habib el Alaüi nach einigermaßen europäischen Begriffen ausbauen lassen.
    Während des Baues bewohnten die vier Expeditionsmitglieder: Koldewey, Meissner, Meyer
    und Andrae das Mudif des Dorfschulzen, d. h. den Versammlungsraum für die Wintermo-
    nate (im Sommer versammelte man sich auf dem Hofe längs dessen Lehmmauern). Durch
    den Auf- und Ausbau gewann man ein Obergeschoß mit den Wohnräumen, dem Speise-
    raum, dem Bad und dem ›Museum‹. Im Hof war ein Stall und eine offene Halle für die Fund-
    kisten entstanden. Das Mudif erhielt der türkische Kommissar Bedri Bey als Wohnraum,
    von dem ein Aufbewahrungsraum für wertvolle, in Kisten verpackte Funde abgetrennt war.
    Die Küche befand sich unter den Wohnräumen im Erdgeschoß. Später wurde ein Vorhof
    im Palmenhain dazu genommen, in dem ein weiterer Stall und im Obergeschoß weitere
    Wohnräume entstanden, der sogenannte Kavalierflügel, den die jüngeren Expeditionsmit-
    glieder bewohnten. Das Bild zeigt die Veranda des alten Obergeschosses mit dem Diener
    Murad in der üblichen Bagdader Städtertracht. Er war ein chaldäischer Christ.«

54 1899 – Kolorierte Bleistiftzeichnung – 21,1 × 33,3
    Babylon. W. Andrae in seinem Arbeits- und Wohnzimmer im Expeditionshaus.
    LE 56 f.:
    »Auch in der nun einsetzenden Julihitze schrieb ich Briefe nach Hause: »Zwei heiße Julitage
    ohne Wind haben wir hinter uns, wenigstens sagte man uns, daß es heiß gewesen wäre, und
    da waren wir sehr froh, denn es war ganz lustig. Alle Welt schwitzte, selbst die ältesten
    Leute. Wenn's warm wird, verlieren sie die Energie, lassen alles schlapp hängen, trinken
    Wasser und denken an nichts anderes als an die Hitze. Wir machen uns dann immer was zu
    schaffen, langsam, weil jede körperliche Anstrengung große Mengen Schweiß kostet, aber
    bei der Länge des Tages wird immer etwas fertig, und wir haben auch viel zu tun. Glück-
    licherweise geht die Sonne hier erst nach 5 Uhr auf und schon um 7 Uhr unter, selbst am
    längsten Tage. Die Nächte waren noch schön. Als eines der Erholungsprodukte der heißen
    Tage schicke ich Euch ein naturgetreues Bild meines Salons, wo Ihr mich am Arbeitstisch,
    umgeben von den Funden des Tages, sitzen und schwitzen seht, leicht und luftig gekleidet,
    dahinter die »dekorierte« Wand. Die Teppiche sind noch nicht da, so ist die Eratonenfahne
    der einzige Schmuck, das deutsche Fähnchen und der runde Lederschnitt am Speer sind
    Geschenke der Frau Koch – Aleppo; darunter ist der Bücherschrank, die Bibliothek besteht
    fast nur aus Skizzenbüchern. Schöne braune Schranktüren aus indischem Holz, die braune
    Decke aus Palmstämmen, Tisch und Tischchen aus weißem Holz, Krugständer rechts – alles
    Arbeit unseres Tischlers aus Hille. Links ist der Wandschrank, auf dem das Hemd zum
    Trocknen hängt, es war durchgeschwitzt, oben steht der Windleuchter und Koffer, unten
    der geheimnisvolle Sack mit den von mir schon gezeichneten Funden. Die Kiste enthält
    ebenfalls solche. Rechts steht der bekannte graue Koffer, jetzt gleichzeitig Geldschrank der

Expedition, wo immer 2 bis 3000 M darin liegen, außerdem die eingenähten Wintersachen. Der Wandschrank darüber enthält die Toilettenartikel, unten alle Sorten Papier, Schrot und Schießbedarf; das Handtuch trocknet auch. Der schlangenartige Gegenstand, der ferner an der Wand hängt, ist Bindfaden, der viel gebraucht wird. Unten im Korb aus Palmblättern steht das Pensum des Tages, das zu bearbeiten ist. Dann seht Ihr eines von den Fenstern mit selbstkonstruiertem Vorhang, den Wasserkrug und etwas Gelbliches, die in nasse Tücher gewickelte Teekanne, dann den Wassereimer und die geliebte Flinte. Der Fußboden besteht aus monumentalen Fliesen; nun noch 40° Wärme, und die Sache ist vollständig.«

55 1900 – Aquarell – 18,0 × 25,8
Babylon. Abendstimmung auf dem Dach des Expeditionshauses. Der Diener bringt die Wasserpfeife.

56 1899 – Tusche – 19,0 × 9,5
Babylon, Expeditionshaus, Fenster im Arbeitszimmer von W. Andrae. Vgl. Nr. 61. Im Hintergrund die Dschird (vgl. Nr. 61. 62. 63).

57 Babylon, 1899 – Bleistift – 21,7 × 14,2
Babylon, Loggia im Obergeschoß des Expeditionshauses.

58 1927 – Tusche –
Babylon, Expeditionshaus, Innenhof.
Nach RK Abb. 18

59 1927 – Tusche –
Das Expeditionshaus in Babylon am Euphrat.
Nach RK Abb. 19

Abb. 18 Babylon, Expeditionshaus, Innenhof, 1927

Abb. 19 Babylon, Expeditionshaus am Euphrat, 1927

60 1901 – Aquarell –
Babylon, Euphrat: Blick auf den Hügel Babil im Norden der Ruine vom Expeditionshaus, und zwar wohl vom Fenster R. Koldeweys. Nach Gewitter. Vgl. Nr. 206.

61 1899 – Aquarell – 25,5 × 14,0
Palmengarten am Euphrat mit Schöpfwerk (vgl. Nr. 62 und 63), vom Fenster W. Andraes im Expeditionshaus (vgl. Nr. 56) in Babylon. Vgl. Foto bei R. Koldewey, Das wiedererstehende Babylon. 5. Aufl. (1990) Abb. 9.

62 April 1900 – Aquarell – 35,3 × 24,4
Babylon, Schöpfwerk an einem Nabuk-Baum = Christdorn: Ziziphus spina Christi, vgl. Michael Zohary, Pflanzen der Bibel (1983) 154 f. mit Abb.; D. Zohary – M. Hopf, Domestication of Plants in the Old World (1988) 178 f. (freundlicher Hinweis von U. al-Sadoon). Vgl. Nr. 61. 63.

63 1902 – Aquarell und Tusche – 28,8 × 45,2
Babylon, Euphrat, Säuberung des Zug-Zuflusses eines mit Tieren betriebenen Schöpfwerkes (Dschird): die Tiere ziehen die Eimer oder Wassersäcke hoch, die dann vom Menschen entleert werden. Vgl. zu solchen z. B. H. E. Wulff, The Traditional Crafts of Persia (1966) 256 ff. und R. Koldewey a. O. (Nr. 61) 30. Zu den Arbeiten vgl. ebenda Abb. 10.

64 1902 – Bleistift und Aquarell – 22,5 × 28,5
Babylon, mit Reusen fischende Jungen im Euphrat.

65 1901 – Aquarell und Tusche – 22,0 × 28,0
Babylon, Arabische Fischer im Euphrat vor dem Expeditionshaus in Babylon. Das Schlepp-
netz wird vom Boote ausgelegt. Einer treibt mit der langen Stange aufs Wasser schlagend
von unterhalb mit Geschrei die Fische stromauf ins Netz.
Berlin, Staatsbibliothek, SPK, Nachlaß Andrae 15/15.

66 1900 – Tusche – 13,5 × 22,0
Babylon, am Euphrat.
Berlin, Staatsbibliothek, SPK, Nachlaß Andrae 15/12.

67 1900 – Aquarell – 35,5 × 24,5
Palmen am Euphrat nach nächtlichem Gewitter in der Morgendämmerung kurz vor Son-
nenaufgang.

68 1901 – Aquarell – 35,5 × 21,5
Babylon. Abendstimmung über Palmengärten am Euphrat.
Berlin, Staatsbibliothek, SPK, Nachlaß Andrae 15/20.

69 Julimorgen 1901 – Aquarell – 35,5 × 25,5
Babylon. Im Palmengarten bei Kuweirisch.
Berlin, Staatsbibliothek, SPK, Nachlaß Andrae 15/23.

70 1902 – Aquarell – 35,0 × 25,2
Babylon. Euphrat beim Hügel Amran.

71 1901 – Aquarell – 24,9 × 17,6
Babylon. Abendstimmung am Euphrat.

72 1900 – Tusche – 14,2 × 27,5
Islamische Grabbauten auf Tell Amran ibn Ali.

73 1901 – Aquarell – 24,5 × 35,0
Auf der Straße Baghdad – Hille bei Babylon.

74 Januar 1900 – Tusche – 16,5 × 33,0
Babylon. Kasr von Nordosten.
Berlin, Staatsbibliothek, SPK, Nachlaß Andrae 15/11.

75 o. J. – Aquarell – 16,0 × 24,0
Schutthalde in der Grabung Babylon.
Berlin, Staatsbibliothek, SPK, Nachlaß Andrae 15/32.

76 1899 – Aquarell – 9,3 × 6,4
Habib el Alauwi, der einäugige Scheich von Kuweiresch (Beilage eines Briefes von W. A. an
seine Eltern); G. Buddensieg, MDOG 42, 1902, 53 ff.

77 1902 – Bleistift und Aquarell – 26,5 × 19,3
Der Knabe Dschum'a ibn Barakli.
LE 315:
»Dschum'a bedeutet Freitag. Er war ein lustiger, etwas lumpig bekleideter Knabe mit einem
übergroßen, fröhlichen Munde. Dieser Junge war überall beliebt, fand aber einen frühen
Tod. Bald nachdem ich ihn gezeichnet hatte, stand er nämlich zu nahe bei einem Europäer,
der ungeschickt mit seiner Flinte umging und den armen Knaben unversehens zu Tode
brachte. Man kann sich denken, daß der Vorfall unter Arabern nicht ohne großes Aufsehen
vorüberging. Wenn die Schuld nicht rasch beglichen wurde, war mit Blutrache zu rechnen,
die sich natürlich nicht um das versehentliche Verschulden des Europäers kümmern würde.
Robert Koldewey hatte sich als Leiter der Expedition bei dem türkischen Bezirksgericht in
Hille und bei dem Dorfschech von Kuweiresch um Beilegung, bei den Angehörigen um das
Blutgeld zu bemühen. Der schuldige Europäer mußte schnellstens aus Babylon verschwin-
den.«

78 1900 – Tusche – 16,6 × 16,0
Babylon. Junger Araber an einer Lore der Feldbahn.
LE 57:
»Vorgestern ist unsere Eisenbahn zum Schutt-Transport angekommen. Das hat also von
ihrer Ankunft in Baghdad bis hierher genau 2 Monate, von Deutschland bis hierher 7
Monate gedauert.«

79 1901 – Aquarell – 17,7 × 25,0
Tanz der Männer von Kuweiresch.
LE 68 ff.:
»Nun haben wir auch das 3tägige Fest der Mohammedaner überstanden, mit welchem der
Fastenmonat Ramadhan geschlossen wird. Dasselbe besteht aus allgemeinem großen Fres-
sen (Essen ist es schon nicht zu nennen), mit Gesang, Tanz, Schießen, Trommeln und jeg-
licher Art ohrenbetäubenden Lärms. Sie haben sich wochenlang darauf gefreut und uns
ebenso lange an das unumgängliche Bakschisch, das jeder zum Fest haben müßte, erinnert,
so daß wir schließlich nicht umhin konnten, es zu zahlen. Zum Feste selbst stolzierten alle in
neuen prächtigen Gewändern, viele in Seide und Silber, umher, die grellsten roten und gelben Stoffe sind bevorzugt, die Weiber lieben dunkelblau und schwarz vom Scheitel bis zur
Sohle, nur die jüngeren Damen gehen in den stechendsten violetten Farben. Jeder Mann, ja
jeder Junge von 8 Jahren hatte seine Flinte, mindestens ein Pistol, mit dem jeder umzugehen
weiß.
Die Tänze haben etwas Ungarisch-Urtümliches, es wird viel gestampft, und rote Tücher
werden geschwenkt; im ganzen geht es aber sehr langsam, nicht wild. Die Musik macht
einer mit der Doppelflöte, die Backen dienen als Windsack dabei, und einer mit der Neger-
trommel. Das Hauptvergnügen scheint die lange Dauer eines Tanzes zu sein, an dem sich
übrigens nur Männer beteiligen.
Wir haben zum Fest auch unsere Staatsvisite in Hille beim Kaimakan gemacht und sind auf
Hin- und Rückweg dem bunten Zuge der Pilger begegnet, die ihre Sure (Gebet) auf Tell
Amran zu verrichten gingen. Von Babylon bis Hille unaufhörlich Menschen, Reiter auf
Eseln und Rossen, Weiber, Kinder, Greise und ausgewachsene Männer, alle im Sonntags-
staat. Von dessen Buntheit macht Ihr Euch schwer eine rechte Vorstellung, sie wirkt so

mächtig auf den hellgrau schimmernden Kanaldämmen und dem wüsten Erdreich, den ebenso mattweißlich grünen Palmen als Hintergrund. Hier sieht die gräßlichste Farbe glänzend aus. Die Mode bringt immer Neues, oder besser gesagt, ein neuer Transport aus Manchester oder sonstwo aus Europa; jetzt waren schwefelgelbe Kopftücher an der Mode, grasgrüne oder schweinfurter-grüne Hemden, feuerrote Röcke, apfelsinengelbe Sammetjacken und ähnliche Zusammenstellungen. Alles strahlt, und nichts beleidigt das Auge, wenn man es auch oft in der Nähe überhaupt nicht ansehen kann. Auch unsere christlich chaldäischen Diener Murad, Mansus, Rasuki und Abdallah hatten ihre besten Sachen an, himmelblaue Ärmeljäckchen mit Goldstreifen, goldgelbe oder zitronengelbe Hemden und goldgestickte Gürtel, dazu karminrote Saffianschuhe einheimischen Fabrikates, wie sie alle Wohlhabenden an Festen anziehen.«

80 1899 – Aquarell – 17,0 × 27 (= 1/9 natürlicher Größe)
Erstes Bild des Löwen von der Prozessionsstraße in Babylon.
Berlin, Staatsbibliothek, SPK, Nachlaß Andrae 15/79.
RK 90:
»Babylon wird [zur Grabung] angenommen, und zwar ausdrücklich wegen der von Koldewey gerühmten Ziegelreliefs. Koldewey hat oft hervorgehoben, daß [Richard] Schönes [Generaldirektor der Berliner Museen] Erkenntnis vom Wert der Schmelzfarbenkunst und sein energisches Eintreten für die Untersuchung Babylons die Entscheidung herbeigeführt haben. Seit die Museen die Ziegelreliefs in ihrer Vorderasiatischen Abteilung haben wiederaufstehen lassen, zeigte ein kleiner Wandkasten die drei unscheinbaren Bruchstücke von emaillierten Ziegeln, die Koldewey von der Vorexpedition aus Babylon mitgebracht und Schöne vorgelegt hat. Es ist ein unbestreitbares Verdienst Schönes, aus diesen wenigen handgreiflichen Proben den hohen eigenartigen Wert des so vollständig zerstörten babylonischen Schmelzfarbenwerks erkannt und darauf mutig eine Unternehmung von langer Dauer und hohen Kosten eingeleitet zu haben.«
LE 96:
»Endlich Ende Februar [1901] konnte ich nach Hause schreiben: »Dr. Koldewey gräbt nun seit einer Woche in Birs. Gegenwärtig habe ich also in Babylon viel zu schaffen, weil unsere Arbeit eine große Anzahl emaillierter Ziegel herausbefördert, deren Zusammenstellung mir obliegt und die wieder drei ganz einzigartige Objekte ergeben werden. – Davon später! Da ich das alles allein tun muß – es sind täglich zwei bis drei große Kisten voll Bruchstücke auszulesen, zu waschen und zu numerieren, dann zu gruppieren und in die Skizze einzutragen –, so nimmt es mir fast den ganzen Tag in Anspruch. Man kann das keinen anderen tun lassen. Aber trotz der Schmutzerei ist es eine feine Arbeit wegen des Resultates! Sie bringt jeden Tag etwas Neues und größere Vollständigkeit bei der Zusammensetzung.«
R. Koldewey, MDOG 3, 1899, 4 ff. 10 ff.; F. Delitzsch, MDOG 6, 19, 15 f.:
»Erst der von Koldewey und Andrae in unermüdlicher Ausdauer glücklich wiedergewonnene ›Löwe von Babylon‹, welcher den Vorzug hat, vom Kopf bis zum Schweif völlig und ausschließlich aus echten Stücken wiederhergestellt zu sein, und dessen Reproduktion nunmehr in den Händen aller Mitglieder der Deutschen Orient-Gesellschaft sein dürfte, lehrt unwidersprechlich, daß die Künstler Nebukadnezars, wenigstens was die Darstellung des Löwen betrifft, es zu hoher Meisterschaft gebracht hatten.«
LE 275 ff.:
»Wie berichtet, waren schon im Jahre 1926 der Vorderasiatischen Abteilung Sockelgeschoß

und 1. Obergeschoß des Südflügels im Neubau zugesprochen worden. Mitte 1928, als Otto Weber seiner Familie und dem Museum durch den frühen Tod entrissen worden und seine Nachfolge an mich übergegangen war, änderte sich gerade in dem Augenblick die Sachlage, in dem alles zu den Entscheidungen über die Raumdispositionen und den inneren Ausbau der großen Ausstellungsräume im Obergeschoß hindrängte. Insbesondere wurde es jetzt dringend nötig, die Zusammensetzung der babylonischen Tier-Ziegel-Reliefs zu beschleunigen, die bis dahin sehr schleppend und nicht nach meinem Wunsche, ja in falscher Art vor sich gegangen war (s. S. 198). Ich erhielt auch sofort beträchtliche Mittel und große Arbeitsräume zur Verfügung. ließ den tatkräftigen Bildhauer Willy Struck engagieren, der etwa 30 Gehilfen bekam und in zwei Jahren das gewaltige Werk, 72 Relieftiere, große Rosetten- und »Ornament«-Streifen, versatzbereit machte. Dazu gewann ich drei Berliner keramische Werkstätten, die jede nach ihrer Art Versuche anstellten, die sechs babylonischen Schmelzfarben möglichst getreu nachzuahmen, was derjenigen von Frau Helene Körting weitaus am besten gelang.
In den zwei Jahren von Sommer 1928 bis Sommer 1930 hatten wir 30 Löwen, 26 Stiere, 16 Drachen, zwei Thronsaalfront-Teile und die parthische Palastfassade fertiggestellt und im Südflügel aufgebaut. Prozessionsstraße und Ischtar-Tor konnten bei der Hundertjahr-Feier der Museen 1930 zusammen mit dem Pergamon-Altar eröffnet werden.«
LE 279: zu weiteren fertiggestellten farbigen Relieftieren:
»Einige Exemplare dieser Tiere konnte ich als Geschenk an das Antiken-Museum in Istanbul und an das Irak-Museum in Bagdad absenden. Andere bot ich mit besonderer Genehmigung des Ministeriums in- und ausländischen Museen an. Sie gingen nach Wien, Paris, Kopenhagen, Göteborg, Chicago und an andere Museen der USA, endlich nach Dresden und München.«

81 1927 – Aquarell – 35 × 24,5
Entwurfsskizze für die Rekonstruktion der Prozessionsstraße in Berlin, Vorderasiatisches Museum: Block zum Syrischen Saal.
Berlin, Staatsbibliothek, SPK, Nachlaß Andrae 15//82 LE 278:
»Bei uns freilich hatte ›die Kunst der Museumsarchitekten‹ verschuldet, daß unsere Straße nur 8 statt 16 Meter breit geworden war. Nur die Höhe der beiden Festungsmauern zu beiden Seiten, an denen die Löwen dahinliefen, stimmte. Man fühlte sich occidantalisch beengt, statt orientalisch erweitert. Bedrückend war dieses für denjenigen, der aus Babylon kam und die Enge der Museumsräume verwünschte.«

82 1927 – Aquarell – 35 × 24,5
Entwurfsskizze für die Rekonstruktion der Prozessionsstraße in Berlin, Vorderasiatisches Museum: Blick zum Ischtar-Tor
Berlin, Staatsbibliothek, SPK, Nachlaß Andrae 15/81. Vgl. LE 277.

83 1927 – Aquarell – 37,5 × 27,0
Entwurfsskizze für die Rekonstruktion der Thronsaal-Fassade in Berlin, Vorderasiatisches Museum. Links das Ischtar-Tor, rechts Fassade des Parther-Palastes.
Berlin, Staatsbibliothek, SPK, Nachlaß Andrae 15/80.

84 1927 – Aquarell – 24,5 × 35,0
Entwurfsskizze für die Rekonstruktion des Ischtar-Tores in Berlin, Vorderasiatisches
Museum
Berlin, Staatsbibliothek, SPK, Nachlaß Andrae 15/83.

85 etwa 1901 – Aquarell – 28,7 × 45,3
Babylon, Kasr, NW-Ecke.
Berlin, Staatsbibliothek, SPK, Nachlaß Andrae 15/27.

86 2. 6. 1902 abends – Aquarell – 25,2 × 35,2
Babylon. Ruinenhügel el Kasr von Osten.
Bisher unveröffentlichte Beschreibung von W. Andrae, in etwa aus dem Jahre 1950:
»Von Osten her ist der ganze Kasr-Hügel wie ein langgestrecktes Gebirge zu Beginn der
Grabungen wahrzunehmen gewesen, wenn man in gehöriger Entfernung die schönsten und
nur wenig bewässerten Flächen des alten Stadtgebietes durchschritten hatte. Palmengärten
schließen sich rechts, das ist nördlich, unmittelbar an dieses Gebirge an.«

87 1902 – Aquarell – 25,5 × 35,5
Babylon. Bis in das Grundwasser hineinreichende Ausgrabung in der Nordburg des Kasr
sowie der Löwe von Babylon. Vgl. das ca. sieben Jahre jüngere Foto bei Bell, AtA Abb. 104.
Berlin, Staatsbibliothek, SPK, Nachlaß Andrae 15/26.

88 Julimorgen 1902 – Aquarell – 17,0 × 35,0
Babylon. Ruinenhügel Amran ibn 'Ali von Norden gesehen.
Berlin, Staatsbibliothek, SPK, Nachlaß Andrae 15/24.

89 1902 – Aquarell – 24,5 × 34,9
Babylon. Ausgrabung im Ninmach-Tempel, nach Farbphotographie.

90 22. 6. 1902 morgens zwischen 5.30 und 7 Uhr – Aquarell – 20.0 × 35,5
Babylon. Ruinenhügel Babil von SO gesehen.
Vgl. LE Abb. 33.
Berlin, Staatsbibliothek, SPK, Nachlaß Andrae 15/25.

91 1901 – Aquarell – 25,2 × 35,3
Borsippa (Birs Nimrud), Ruine der Zikkurrat E-ur-imin-an-ki und davor der Tempel Ezida.
Auf den Mauern des letzteren die Zelte der Ausgräber. LE 90:
»Wegen der vielen Besuche machte ich mich am Sonntag aus dem Staube. Ich unternahm
eine kleine Sonntagspartie mit 7^1/2 Stunden Reiten und 3stündigem Kraxeln. Ich hatte nämlich diesmal offiziell durch den Konsul um Erlaubnis bitten lassen, die Ruinen von Borsippa,
das heutige Birs, besuchen zu dürfen. Das ist sogar über Konstantinopel gegangen und
bewilligt worden; freilich mit der Klausel, daß ich nur mit den Augen, nicht aber mit dem
Bleistift oder sonstigen gefährlich-künstlichen Instrumenten genießen dürfte. Ich bekam in
Hille, wo ich den neuen Kaimakam besuchte, einen Beamten mit, der über meine Wege zu
wachen hatte und das auch tat; außerdem zu den unsrigen noch einen bewaffneten Polizi-

sten, während ich als Gehilfen zwei unserer Araber auf Eseln mit hatte, die festlichen Waf-
fenschmuck trugen, jeder Doppelflinte, Doppelpistole, Dolch und Keule. Wir hätten es mit
hundert Feinden aufnehmen können, wenn welche dagewesen wären. Ich war zu Mittag in
Birs und bin dann in der Ruine herumgekrochen. Es ist der Tempel Ezida und der Stufen-
turm E-uriminanki, daneben der Wohnhügel Ibrahim ibn Chalil, nach einem kleinen Kuppelgrab so benannt. Der Tempel ist von Rassam vor etwa 20 Jahren ausgegraben
[1879/1880], war daher gut zu sehen, der Turm ist noch heute sehr beträchtlich, in der
Hauptsache pyramidal durch die nivellierenden Halden. Auf der Spitze steht noch ein großes Ziegelstück von ca. 15 m Höhe, dessen Spitze etwa 90 m über der Ebene liegt. Oben
hätte man eine wundervolle Aussicht, wenn da was zu sehen wäre. Es ist aber alles eben wie
ein Tisch, auf der Nordseite Sumpf, sieht aus wie ein großer See, manchmal einige Palmenhaine, sonst ist der Horizont gerade wie ein Lineal und der Himmel wie eine tadellose
Glocke. Gegen 8 Uhr abends war ich wieder in Babylon. –
Einen Monat später, Ende November, zog Koldewey nach Birs, um dort eine neue Grabung
zu beginnen ...«
Vgl. ferner LE 91 ff. 96 ff!

92 26. 3. 1901 – Aquarell – 18 × 25,5
Hof der Karawanserai Imam Dschasim.
Berlin, Staatsbibliothek, SPK, Nachlaß Andrae 15/16.
LE 81 f.: »Der Weg bis Imam Dschasim, halbwegs zwischen Hille und Diwaniye, welches
der Sitz des Mutessarifliks ist, dem der Kaimakam von Hille untersteht, führt glatt und
gerade, lange Zeit durch Palmengärten und Palmenhaine, Felder und überbrückte Kanäle,
bis die Gegend ziemlich wüst wird, je weiter man vom Euphrat abkommt, der hier einen
Bogen macht. Imam Dschasim ist eine kleine Moschee mit ein paar Häusern und einem Kaffeehaus, die meist als Absteigequartiere dienen. Die Kuppel liegt hoch und ist lange und
weithin sichtbar, der Aufenthalt und das Nachtquartier so angenehm und komfortabel wie
in allen orientalischen Dörfern, auf unergründlichem Mist, in einem Fitz von Eseln, Maultie-
ren und Pferden, fluchenden Soldaten und schreienden Arabern, dazu die obligaten Flöhe.
Ich hatte mich auf einer langen Sitzbank des Kaffeehauses häuslich eingerichtet, d. h. in vollem Anzug und ein Bündel Decken unter dem Kopf, war aber nicht imstande, einzuschlafen,
da die Flohangriffe trotz energischer Insektenpulverdefensive nicht abzuschlagen waren.
Der schönste Moment einer solchen Lage ist, wenn es anfängt zu grauen, d. h. wenn man
daraus fort kann. Die übrigen Schläfer haben es meist genau so eilig, fortzukommen.«

93 1902 – Aquarell und Kohle – 25,0 × 18,0
Kaffeehaus in Kifl.
Berlin, Staatsbibliothek, SPK, Nachlaß Andrae 15/29.
Kifl liegt an der Straße von Hille nach Nedschef (Abb. 5), im Städtchen wohnten zur Zeit
Andraes Juden, da hier das Grab des Propheten Hesekiel verehrt wird. »According to Gold-
ziher Dhu'l-Kifl is a second name of Ezekiel as is the case with four other prophets who have
two names, such as Ya'qub: Israe'il; Yunus: Dhu'l-Nus; 'Isa: al-Masih; Muhammad: Ahmad.
Other modern researchers also suggest that Dhu'l-Kifl is the Arabic and Islamic form of
Ezekiel.« (Tariq Jawad al-Janabi, Studies in Mediaeval Iraqi Architecture [1982] 97.) W.
Andrae beschreibt das Kaffeehaus 1950 wie folgt: »Das Kaffeehaus sieht so aus wie alle länd-
lichen Kaffeehäuser des Iraq, nämlich schwarz gerändert durch den offenen Kaffeeherd. Das

Dach besteht meist aus mehr oder minder zerfetzten Schilfmatten, die Holzbänke sind uralt und man sitzt kreuzbeinig auf ihnen. Tische gibt es nicht, der Wirt kredenzt das Kaffeetäßchen mit wenigen Tropfen des Gebräus jedem Gast nach Wunsch. Die Wasserpfeife ist dabei sehr beliebt.«

Vgl. auch LE 114 zum Kaffeehaus in Imam Dschasim (Nr. 92):

»Ich kehrte in meinem bekannten Kaffehaus ein, derselben schwarzen Höhle, die ich schon bei Gelegenheit meiner ersten Reise nach Nippur geschildert habe. Auf der eisernen Bettstelle habe ich im Schatten dieser Höhle geruht und Kaffee, Tee, Huhn, Ei, Brot und Gurke geschlemmt, während die Sonnenhitze draußen brannte und ihr Teil auch nach innen abgab. Übrigens äußert sie sich auch in der aufgelösten Verfassung der Leute, die um einen herumsitzen. Sie sehen in ihren herabhängenden und offenen Gewändern wie welke Blümchen aus, zu denen freilich die dunkelbraun bis violett-bläulich schimmernde und schweißglänzende Haut nicht ganz im Vergleich paßt. Was sonst nie geschieht und großen Horror verursacht, das kann man jetzt bisweilen doch sehen, nämlich das Abnehmen der Kopfbedeckung. Freilich ist es kein veredelnder Anblick, denn meistens sieht man sonderbare Spitzköpfe, während der umwickelte Kopf immer etwas Großes, Imponierendes hat. Draußen sengt die Sonne auf die Buckel der stampfenden Esel und Pferde, und oben an den schwarzen rohen Palmbalken der Decke, unter der sich der Rauch des Kaffeeherdes sammelt, hocken die Spatzen und sperren die Schnäbel auf.«

94 26. 3. 1901 – Aquarell – 25,0 × 17,5
Kuppelgrab des Imam Dschasim.
Vgl. Nr. 92.
Bisher unveröffentlichte Beschreibung von W. Andrae, ungefähr 1950:
»Die Grabkuppel des Imam Dschasim steht einsam am Wege von Hille nach Samaua. Im Abendschein bildeten die Strahlen der untergehenden Sonne eine Art von Gloriole um das einfache Gebäude, das unter der Kuppel nichts weiter enthält als den Kenotaph des verstorbenen Priesters. Solcher Imame gibt es sehr viele im Lande. Man benennt die Örtlichkeit nach diesem Grabmal mit dem Namen des Verstorbenen.«

95 27. 3. 1901 – Aquarell – 17,0 × 25,0
Diwanije, Landeplatz am Euphrat.
Berlin, Staatsbibliothek, SPK, Nachlaß Andrae 15/22.
Vgl. Nr. 96.

96 27. 3. 1901 – Aquarell – 17,6 × 25,0
Diwanije, Schiffsbrücke, Chan und Serail.
Vgl. Nr. 95 und 97. 98
LE 82 f.
»Der zweite Tag brachte mich nach Diwaniye. Der Weg ist Wüste, obwohl auch noch mitunter einige Felder passiert werden; je näher an Diwaniye, desto öder. Das Land liegt nur einige Zentimeter hoch und kann bequem bewässert werden, es bleibt aber brach liegen. Der erste Meftul (Festung) wurde gesichtet am Ufer …
Diwaniye erreichten wir gegen Mittag, ein paar Häuser rechts, das Gros links des Euphrat, eine von den wundervollen (mistbelegten) Pontonbrücken, die man ihrer allseitig krummen Beschaffenheit wegen gar nicht ansehen kann, ohne schwindlig zu werden, verbindet beide

Ufer, d. h. die Dschezire (Insel zwischen Euphrat und Tigris) mit der anderen Welt. Ich stieg im neuen Chan an der Brücke ab, wo ich ein leidliches Zimmer im oberen Stockwerk erhielt mit schönem Blick auf Brücke und Euphrat. Die Malerei war nicht einfach (vgl. Nr. 95), weil man fortgesetzt gestört wird durch neugierige Türken oder Araber, oder der Schweiß trieft, die Fliegen krabbeln auf der Nase und in den Farben, oder der heiße Wind dörrt Papier und Pinsel. Kunst mit Hindernissen!«

97 27. 3. 1901 – Aquarell – 25,0 × 17,0
Euphrat oberhalb Diwanije, Meftul (Festung) und Srefen.
Vgl. Nr. 96.
Berlin, Staatsbibliothek, SPK, Nachlaß Andrae 15/21.
LE 84:
»Es ist öfter nötig, daß den zahlungsunwilligen Scheichen ihr Meftul (Festung) eingeschossen wird, damit der Sultan zu seinem Gelde kommt. Dieses Letztere ist wohl auch das einzige Bindeglied der Untertanen zu ihrem Herrscher. Meftuls nennen die Araber ihre festen Burgen. Sie wohnen ja da unten allesamt nur in Srefen, d. h. Hütten aus Schilf oder Schilfmatten (vgl. auch Nr. 105. 106). Kommt ein feindlicher Angriff des Nachbarstammes oder der Regierung, so geht die waffenfähige Mannschaft, also alles Männervolk, in den Meftul, der meistens weiter nichts ist, als ein innen hohler runder oder eckiger Turm aus Lehm mit einer ungeheuren Anzahl von Schießscharten nach allen Richtungen hin. Zugänglich ist er durch ein kleines Loch am Boden, eine schmale Treppe führt zur Schießgalerie und der Zinne. Die ganze Gegend ist gespickt mit solchen kriegerischen Bauten.«

98 29. 3. 1901 – Aquarell – 18,0 × 25,5
Siedlung am Nahr Djeliha im Marschgebiet bei Afedsch, zwei Meftulbauten (vgl. Nr. 97) und LE 84 ff.

99 1. 4. 1901 – Aquarell – 17,7 × 25,0
Nedschef, Ansicht der Stadt von der von Kufa kommenden Straße.
LE 87 ff:
»Von Kufa nach Nedschef geht es etwa 1¹/₂ Stunden lang über reinen, wüsten Kies, wo jetzt etlicher verdorrter Frühlingspflanzenwuchs sichtbar war. Nedschef liegt von geturmter Festungsmauer umgeben und besteht aus einem Gewirr von Gäßchen um das gold- und fayencestrotzende Heiligtum herum …«

100 2. 4. 1901 – Aquarell – 17,3 × 24,5
Nedschef, Blick vom Stadttor auf Pilgerweg und Grabbauten.
Berlin, Nachlaß Ernst Heinrich.
Vgl. Nr. 99.

101 2. 4. 1901 – Aquarell – 25,0 × 17,5
Nedschef, Bazareingang und Moschee des Ali.
Vgl. Nr. 99.

102 4. 4. 1901 – Aquarell – 25,5 × 35,5
Kerbela, Moschee des Hussein.

Berlin, Staatsbibliothek, SPK, Nachlaß Andrae 15/19.
Vgl. LE 89.

103 4. 4. 1901 – Aquarell – 25,0 × 17,5
Kerbela, Moschee des Hussein.
Vgl. LE 89.

104 4. 4. 1901 – Aquarell – 25,0 × 17,7
Moschee des Abbas in Kerbela.
Vgl. LE 89.

105 1903 – Bleistift – 31,0 × 22,3
Empfang im Mudif, im Schilfmattenhaus eines Scheichs bei Fara.
Vgl. LE 121 f.

106 1903 – Farbige Kreiden – 27,5 × 22,0
Empfang im Mudif, im Schilfmattenhaus eines Scheichs bei Fara.
Berlin, Staatsbibliothek, SPK, Nachlaß Andrae 15/68.
Vgl. LE 121 f.
Beschreibung von W. Andrae, bisher unveröffentlicht (ungefähr 1950): »Im südlichen
Mesopotamien wird das Baumaterial aus den riesigen Schilfdschungeln des Überflutungsge-
bietes gewonnen. Das über 4 m lange Schilf wird gebündelt und in zwei Reihen in die Erde
gepflanzt, oben zu Bögen zusammengeschnürt. Durch Längsbündel erreicht man die Stabili-
tät und durch mehrere Lagen von Flechtmatten aus Schilf eine recht solide Dachdeckung,
die Schutz gegen Hitze und Regen bietet. Die Schechs haben hallenartige große Häuser dieser Art zu Versammlungsräumen ausgebaut, in denen man in der Nähe des einen der beiden
Eingänge sehr würdig mit Kaffee bewirtet wird. Die Gäste sitzen einander an beiden Seiten
der Halle gegenüber. Ein Somali-Neger aus der Sklavenzeit bedient sie mit Kaffee.«

107 1903 – Aquarell – 35,2 × 25,2
Anlegestelle in Kut el Amara am Tigris.
Vgl. LE 128.

108 1903 – Bleistift und Farbstift – 17,0 × 26,0
Die Stupa von Sandschi, Indien.
Vgl. LE 134 f.

109 1903 – Aquarell – 25,0 × 35,0
Tadsch Mahal bei Agra, Indien.

110 1903 – Aquarell – 25,0 × 35,0
Das Tor Purana Killa zu Indraput, Indien.

111 1903 – Aquarell – 30,0 × 22,0
Delhi. Blick aus einem Moscheetor.
Berlin, Plansammlung der Technischen Universität, 7730.

112 1903 – Aquarell – 25,2 × 35,0
     Aden, vom Schiff aus gesehen. (Unser Bild gibt einen Ausschnitt wieder, das im Vorder-
     grund befindliche Meer ist weggelassen.)
     LE 137.

113 1908 – farbige Kreiden auf getöntem Papier – 44,7 × 30,2
     Tigrisdurchbruch südlich von Assur. Enge Fatha. Bei den dunklen Flecken im Vorder-
     grund handelt es sich um austretendes Bitumen.

114 1909 – farbige Kreiden auf getöntem Papier – 31,0 × 25,3
     Assur, Nordfront mit dem fischreichen Wadi Umm es Schebabit der »Mutter des Karpfens«,
     von Ost nach West, vgl. LE 168.

115 1909 – Mischtechnik, Aquarell, farbige Kreiden u. Feder – 30,5 × 25,7
     Assur, Nordfront im Abendlicht, von West nach Ost.

116 etwa 1908 – Tusche, Pinsel – 9,2 × 13,3
     Blick über die Assur-Ebene und den Tigris nördlich von Assur.

117 etwa 1906 – farbige Kreiden auf getöntem Papier – 25,1 × 31,0
     Blick von Assur nach Süden. Dämmerung über der Tigris-Aue.

118 Dezember 1910 – Blei- und Farbstifte – 15,7 × 22,8
     Tigris-Ufer bei Assur.

119 etwa 1904 – Aquarell – 24,6 × 35,6
     Abziehendes Gewitter über der Assur-Ebene östlich von Assur.

120 1904 – Aquarell – farbige Kreiden auf getöntem Papier – 29,3 × 21,6
     Assur: Abziehendes Gewitter über dem Tigris südlich von Assur.
     Vgl. LE 170.

121 1904 – Farbige Kreiden auf getöntem Papier – 29,7 × 22,7
     Assur, Blick nach Süden, Abendstimmung über dem Tigris.

122 1904 – Aquarell auf getöntem Papier – 22,0 × 26,0
     Ziqqurrat von Assur im Abendlicht.

123 1908 – Aquarell – 17,0 × 25,0
     Assur. Wächterhütte in der Grabung im Anu-Adad-Tempel (vgl. Nr. 129), pralle Mittags-
     sonne (Bildbeschriftung »am Abend« nachträglich und falsch).
     Berlin, Staatsbibliothek, SPK, Nachlaß Andrae 15/31.

124 1906 – farbige Kreiden – 21,6 × 29,5
     Assur. Hütten der Schergatis und zwei Schuttkegel am Rande der Grabung.

125 1906 – farbige Kreiden – 25,5 × 31,0
Arbeiter aus Schergat bei der Vorbereitung zum Durchschwimmen des Tigris.
LE 170: Im Frühjahr trat der Tigris »… sechs und mehr Meter hoch über seine Ufer und
wälzte dicke Lehmfluten, die er sich oben mit der Schneeschmelze von eben jenen Kurden-
bergen abgeleckt hatte. Dann grollte er vernehmbar mit seinem rollenden Kieselgeschiebe
und schob sein Bett hin und her, als sei ihm alles nicht recht. Bei uns in Assur war er dann
3 km breit und machte das Übersetzen unserer Arbeiter vom jenseitigen Ufer fast zur
Unmöglichkeit. Aber die Mutigen unter ihnen ließen sich nicht durch Hochwasser und auch
nicht vom Eisgang abschrecken, der in kalten Jahren doch auch vorkam. Uns kam die Gän-
sehaut an, wenn die braven Schwimmer mit dem aufgeblasenen Ziegenbalg, der ihnen als
Schwimmblase diente, und ihren um den Kopf gewickelten Kleidern den eiskalten Gewäs-
sern splitternackt entstiegen und frisch und fröhlich an ihre Arbeitsplätze gingen.«

126 1937 – Tusche –
Die Nordfront von Assur, nach
W. Andrae, Das wiedererstandene Assur, Abb. 2.
Original verschollen

127 1937 – Tusche –
Die Assur-Aue von Norden, nach
W. Andrae, Das wiedererstandene Assur, Abb. 1.
Original verschollen

128 1937 – Tusche – 32,5 × 41
Blick über Assur nach Norden, veröffentlicht in:
W. Andrae, Das wiedererstandene Assur, Abb. 24.
Berlin, Staatsbibliothek, SPK, Nachlaß Andrae 15/85.

129 1908 – Tusche – 16,5 × 24,5
Assur. Anu-Adad-Tempel. Wiederherstellungsversuch.
Hier hat Andrae noch die Zikkurrat mit spiralförmig sich emporwindendem Aufgang
rekonstruiert, eine Ergänzung, von der er später Abstand nahm. Vgl. z. B. Nr. 126. 127. 130.
131 und seine Ausführungen zur Frage des Aufgangs im wiedererstandenen Assur S. 92 f.
Deutsches Archäologisches Institut, Abt. Baghdad.

130 1923 – Kohle – 31,0 × 44,5
Assur. Blick vom Festhaus auf die Stadt. Wiederherstellungsversuch.

131 1923 – Kohle und Kreide – 30,0 × 49,5
Assur. Blick von der Ziqqurrat über Tempel- und Palastbezirk der Stadt zum Festhaus.
Wiederherstellungsversuch. – Vgl. auch den gleichzeitigen Rekonstruktionsvorschlag für
Scham'al Abb. 20.

132 1907 – Aquarell – 31,5 × 44,9
Bühnenbild-Entwurf I zu »Sardanapal«:
Hof eines assyrischen Tempels mit Blick auf das Götterbild.

LE 180 f.:

»Dann mußte ich die Proben und die Aufführung der französischen Pantomime »Sardanapal«, die Kaiser Wilhelm II. angeordnet hatte, in Berlin mitmachen. Man mag über den
künstlerischen Wert dieser Darbietung denken, wie man will – auch damals waren die Mei-
nungen geteilt –, für die Orientalisten und für uns Ausgräber hatte die Idee des Kaisers, das
Stück nach neuesten Kenntnissen im echt assyrischen Stil auszustatten, sicherlich Reiz und
verdiente unsere Aufmerksamkeit. Man hatte mich schon zu Anfang des Jahres in Assur auf-
gefordert, drei Bühnenbilder für die Aufführung zu entwerfen, damit auch die Architektur
zeitgerecht erscheinen möge. In Berlin hielt man sich ängstlich an diese drei Entwürfe, und
ich fiel fast auf den Rücken, als meine kleinen bunten Bildchen in voller Bühnengröße in der
Staatsoper erschienen. Inzwischen hatte auch Friedrich Delitzsch dafür sorgen müssen, daß
der ganze assyrische Hofstaat von Ninive, Herren wie Damen, echt assyrisch frisiert und
kostümiert auf dieser Bühne erscheinen konnten und daß Möbel und Prunkgefäße stilecht
waren. Kaiser Wilhelm war bei den Proben persönlich anwesend. Es schien so leicht, nach
den zahllosen assyrischen Bildern, welche die großen Relieffreihen von Kalach, Ninive und
Chorsabad darboten, die Bühnenkostüme des Königs, des Hofstaates, der Soldaten und Diener nachzuschneidern. Man fand aber doch allerlei Probleme, die aus den assyrischen Darstellungen nicht ohne weiteres gelöst werden konnten, und stieß dabei auf Unterschiede
unseres heutigen Sehens gegenüber der alten assyrischen Darstellungsweise. Daraus hätten
die Ärchäologen viel lernen können.«

Vgl. ferner ebenda 181 f. und zum Aufgang der Zikkurrat im Hintergrund hier Nr. 129.

133 1907 – Aquarell – 29,0 × 45,3
Bühnenbild-Entwurf II zu »Sardanapal«.
Assyrischer Palastraum, Schatzkammer.
Vgl. Nr. 132.

134 1912 – Aquarell und Bleistift – 30,4 × 22,9
Assur. Der Garten beim Expeditionshaus.
LE 157:
»In unserer trockenen Mondlandschaft galt das Gärtchen vor dem Hause am Abhang zum
Tigris als Erholungsstätte, insbesondere, als es gelungen war, eine echte Weinlaube heranzu-
züchten. Ein altassyrischer Brunnen spendete Bewässerung, und Sultan, der Gärtner und
Vater unendlich vieler Kinder, bemühte sich um Malven, Mandeln, Kürbisse und andere
Gemüse.«

135 5. 4. 1908 – farbige Kreiden – 22,7 × 31,5
Tell Afer.

136 5. 4. 1908 – farbige Kreiden – 30,7 × 21,8
Bei Tell Afer, Blick zum Sindjar-Gebirge.

137 6. 4. 1908 – farbige Kreiden auf getöntem Papier – 18,5 × 31,7
’Ain Ghazal (zwischen Tell Afer und Sindjar, vgl. z. B. W. Andrae, MDOG 20, 1903, 11).

138 8. 4. 1908 – farbige Kreiden auf getöntem Papier – 26,0 × 32,1
Am Tell Schemsani am Chabur.

Ergänztes Stadtbild von Sendschirli – Schamʾal.

Abb. 20 Schamʾal, »ergänztes Stadtbild« von Osten, 1923

139 9. 4. 1908 – farbige Kreiden auf getöntem Papier – 26,2 × 31,8
Suar am Chabur.
Vgl. Sarre-Herzfeld I 177 ff.

140 11. 4. 1908 – Aquarell und Kreide – 31,5 × 23,0
Euphrat-Talrand im Frühlung, bei Tibne. – Vgl. auch Text zu Nr. 222 LE 194.

141 11. 4. 1908 – farbige Kreiden auf getöntem Papier – 26,2 × 32,0
Basaltformationen nahe Tibne. – Vgl. auch Text zu Nr. 222 LE 194 f.

142 11. 4. 1908 – farbige Kreiden auf getöntem Papier – 25,8 × 31,3
Der Euphrat bei Tibne (vgl. Nr. 28). Vorn in der Mitte: Ein Friedhof.

143 1908 – Mischtechnik Aquarell, farbige Kreiden und Bleistift – 30,9 × 21,0
Samos, Hafen von Vathi.
Berlin, Plansammlung der Technischen Universität, Nr. 7732.

144 21. 6. 1917 – farbige Kreiden – 20,6 × 25,9
Istanbul. Am Goldenen Horn.

145 1915 – farbige Kreiden – 25,9 × 21,1
Istanbul. Am Goldenen Horn.
Berlin, Staatsbibliothek, SPK, Nachlaß Andrae 15/60

146 24. 12. 1915 – farbige Kreiden und Bleistift – 14,5 × 22,5
Istanbul. Blick auf Pera.
Berlin, Plansammlung der Technischen Universität, Nr. 18349.

147 1918 – farbige Kreiden auf getöntem Papier – 30,6 × 22,7
Istanbul. Boulevard in Pera: Heute Tepebaşı caddesi in Beyoğlu. Im Vordergrund ganz links
das Hotel Bristol (K. Bittel).

148 19. 4. 1917 – farbige Kreiden auf getöntem Papier – 21,1 × 26,0
Istanbul. Café-Garten in Pera.

149 Juni 1917 – farbige Kreiden auf getöntem Papier – 20,0 × 25,8
Istanbul. Pera, Petits Champs (Café chantant).

150 Skizze von 1912, ausgeführt 1922 – farbige Kreiden – 18,6 × 29,4
Istanbul, Blick vom Bosporus auf die Stadt.

151 1916 – farbige Kreiden auf getöntem Papier – 12,3 × 15,2
Afyon-Karahissar in Anatolien, Burg und Stadt.

152 1918 – farbige Kreiden auf getönten Papier – 20,9 × 26,0
Paßstraße über das Taurus-Gebirge.

153 1917 – farbige Kreiden auf getöntem Papier – 16,5 × 25,5
Am Golf von Iskenderun/Adana.

154 1918 – farbige Kreiden – 16,1 × 10,5
Derwisch-Kloster (Tekke) bei Aleppo: Takīya aš Šaiḫ Abū Bakr, vgl. H. Gaube – E. Wirth,
Aleppo, Beiheft 58 zum Tübinger Atlas des Vorderen Orients, Reihe B (1984) 160. 408. –
Die genaue Identifizierung dieses Bildes sowie der Bilder 156, 158 und 169 verdanken wir
der Freundlichkeit von H. Gaube.
Vgl. Nr. 18. 228.
Beschreibung von W. Andrae, bisher unveröffentlicht (ungefähr 1950):
»Vor den Toren von Aleppo auf einer kleinen Anhöhe liegt der Kuppelbau einer kleinen
Moschee mit den Wohnungen der Derwische (Mönche) und umschließt mit seinem Hof eine
riesige Pinie, deren schwärzliche Krone gegen das helle Gemäuer absticht. In der Abenddämmerung erschien der rotbraune Ackerboden wie violett getönt, während die weißge-
kalkten Häuserwände, wie in ein magisches Licht getaucht, den letzten Tagesschein wider-
zuspiegeln scheinen. Eine Augenblicks-Impression!«

155 1917 – farbige Kreiden auf dunklem Papier – 30,5 × 22,4
Moschee. Raum Aleppo (?).
Der genaue Standort der Moschee ließ sich nicht ermitteln. Eine mit Bleistift ausgeführte
Beschriftung auf der Rückseite des dunklen Papiers ist völlig verwischt. Meine in Syrien tätigen Kollegen A. Becker, H. Kühne, M. Meinecke, E. Strommenger und T. Ulbert konnten
die Moschee nicht identifizieren, ebenso nicht K. Bittel. Das läßt erwägen, ob das Gebäude
heute überhaupt noch vorhanden ist. David Oates schließt – wie auch Boehmer – nordiraki-
schen Standort aus und faßt seine Beobachtungen an dem Bild wie folgt zusammen:
»The structure in the background suggests that the mosque (?tomb) is on the building opposite the entrance and beyond the dome – the river flows on its western side, and seems to be
flowing approximate from *south* to *north*. The gallery of the minaret looks to me West Syrian
or possibly South Turkish – compare, although it is on a very much larger scale and octagonal in plan, the gallery of the south-western minaret (AD 1488) of the Great Mosque in
Damascus. The dome also looks to me rather western in style than Mesopotamian.« (Brief
vom 28. November 1988).
Andrae war 1917 in Aleppo. Unser Bauwerk scheint in Lage und Bauweise verwandt der auf
den Bildern Nr. 18 und 154 gezeigten Tekke bei Aleppo. Von daher dürfte die Ortsangabe
»Raum Aleppo« in etwa das Richtige treffen.
Tübingen, Altorientalisches Seminar (zuvor im Besitz von A. Falkenstein).

156 1917 – farbige Kreiden – 29,5 × 22,5
Moschee am Stadtrand von Aleppo: Madrasa al-Firdaus, vgl. H. Gaube – E. Wirth a. O.
(Nr. 154) 87. 98. 150. 411.
Berlin, Staatsbibliothek, SPK, Nachlaß Andrae 15/78.

157 1918 – farbige Kreiden – 30,5 × 23,0
Aleppo. Blick in einen Hof (mit Hund).
Berlin, Staatsbibliothek, SPK, Nachlaß Andrae 15/76.

158 1917 – farbige Kreiden – 22,4 × 30,3
Abendliches Aleppo. Blick auf die Zitadelle, Begräbnisplatz vor der Stadt: Friedhof des
Stadtteils el Ǧubaila (H. Gaube).
Berlin, Staatsbibliothek, SPK, Nachlaß Andrae 15/75.

159 1918 – farbige Kreiden auf grauem Karton – 10.0 × 16,1
Abenddämmerung mit Vollmond über einem kleinen Dorf mit »Bienenkorb«-Häusern und
einem Tell, nahe Aleppo. Farbskizze während des Vorbeifahrens mit dem Zug.
Am Quwaiq-Bach.
Berlin, Staatsbibliothek, SPK, Nachlaß Andrae 15/69.

160 1918 – Kohle und farbige Kreiden auf getöntem Papier – 60 × 43
Blick auf die »Promenade« am Quwaiq-Bach bei Aleppo.
Berlin, Plansammlung der Technischen Universität, Nr. 18347.
Beschreibung von W. Andrae, ungefähr 1950 (bisher unveröffentlicht):
»Am Stadtrand von Aleppo in der Nähe des Hauses von Karl Koch, das die Aleppiner bêt
Madame Koch nannten, floß ein schmaler Bach in einem flachen Tälchen dahin, der wenige
Kilometer entfernt in einer kräftigen Quelle entsprang und den fruchtbaren Talboden
bewässerte. Jenseits erhob sich flacher, unbewachsener Felsboden, der zu rotbrauner Erde
verwitterte und kahle, helleuchtende Kalkflächen aufleuchten ließ. So muß man sich die
ganze Umgebung von Aleppo vorstellen, dann versteht man, daß das Kuweiktälchen mit
seinem dünnen Gewässer ein beliebter Promenadenweg der Aleppiner geworden ist. Man
sah sie an Feiertagen festlich gekleidet, die Damen in papageienbunten Seidengewändern,
die Herren im roten Fez, unter den lieben, schattigen Pistazien und anderen Bäumen durch
die frischgrünen Gemüse- und Getreidefelder lustwandeln. Vom Balkon des Hauses Koch
aus gesehen war dies eine ganz lustige Szenerie. Wahrscheinlich ist nicht viel davon mehr
erhalten, weil in der Nähe der ziemlich große Bahnhof von Aleppo angelegt worden ist, zu
dem die Hauptstraße durch das Kuweiktal hinführt.« Vgl. auch Katalog zu Nr. 22.

161 1918 – farbige Kreiden auf getöntem Papier – 10,4 × 16,5
Blick auf Aleppo.

162 1917 – farbige Kreiden – 30,0 × 22
Aleppo. Friedhof.
Vgl. auch Nr. 158, Vordergrund rechts.
Berlin, Staatsbibliothek, SPK, Nachlaß Andrae 15/77.

163 7. 2. 1916 – farbige Kreiden – 14,0 × 21,5
Euphrat, oberhalb von Ana.

164 7. 2. 1916 – farbige Kreiden auf getöntem Papier – 21,0 × 27,7
Euphrat, oberhalb von Ana.

165 11. 2. 1916 – farbige Kreiden – 14,0 × 21,0
Schöpfräder (Na'uren) aus Pappelholz am Euphrat bei Suwije.
Berlin, Staatsbibliothek, SPK, Nachlaß Andrae 15/67.
Beschreibung von W. Andrae, ungefähr 1950 (bisher unveröffentlicht):
»In Syrien am Orontes und am mittleren Euphrat sind die ortsüblichen Wasser-Hebe-Werke
der arabischen Bauern aus allerlei krummen Stangen an einem hölzernen Nabenklotz sehr
geschickt befestigt und an der Peripherie des Wasserrades mit ebenso krummen Hölzern
verbunden. Am Radkranz befestigt man Tonflaschen, die zugleich als Schaufeln das Rad in
Bewegung setzen und, sich mit Wasser füllend, aufwärts bewegen. Dadurch ward das Euphratwasser vom Wasserspiegel bis auf beträchtliche Höhe, nämlich fast um den Durchmesser des gewaltigen Rades gehoben. Die Tonkrüge sind so angebracht, daß sie ihr Wasser
seitwärts ausschütten, wenn sie oben angelangt sind. Das Ausschütten erfolgt in den Bewäs-
serungskanal, der hier auf einer Art Brücke angelegt ist und mit Gefälle das Wasser nach den
zu bewässernden Feldern führt. Die Nabe läuft in einem Lager aus hartem Holz und wenn
das Rad sich dreht, ertönt ein schaurig brummendes, quietschendes Geräusch, das dem
Na'ura-Besitzer verkündet, daß sein Schöpfwerk im Gange ist. Jede Na'ura hat ihre eigene
Melodie.«

166 11. 2. 1916 – farbige Kreiden auf getöntem Papier – 40,3 × 53,3
Schöpfräder (Na'uren) aus Pappelholz am Euphrat in der Nacht bei Suwije.

167 1917 – farbige Kreiden – 30,2 × 23,2
Mossul. Hof des Deutschen Vize-Konsulates.
Zu Andraes Aufenthalt in Mossul vgl. LE 233 ff.

168 30. 12. 1917 – farbige Kreiden – 12,0 × 18,1
Schöpfrad (Na'ura) bei Hama. Syrien.

169 1918 – farbige Kreiden – 30,0 × 23,0
Damaskus. Hof der Derwisch-Moschee: Osmanische Tekke Suleimanije (H. Gaube) mit
Platanen und Ecke eines Wasserbeckens. Letzteres wurde vom Bergfluß Barada gespeist.
Berlin, Plansammlung der Technischen Universität, Nr. 7731.

170 1917 – farbige Kreiden – 23,5 × 30,7
Türkischer Troß im Yarmuk-Tal an einer Wasserstelle.

171 Frühling 1918 – farbige Kreiden – 10,5 × 17,0
Blühende Orchideen im Yarmuk-Tal.

172 23. 1. 1918 – Mit Farbstift kolorierte Tuschzeichnung – 22,1 × 14,0
Nazareth. Blick von der Höhe auf die Stadt.
Vgl. LE 242 f.
»Von der Ebene Jesreel steigt man steil hinaus in die Hügel von Galiläa. Hier oben versteckt
liegt in einem Talkessel Nazareth, wie ein Theater ansteigend halbringförmig an den Berg
gelehnt (Nr. 174), Gärten ringsum, die mit Hecken von Feigenkaktus eingefaßt sind
(Nr. 173), darin Ölbäume, Obstbäume und Zypressen (Nr. 179. 180. 183. 185). Die Franzis-

kanermönche haben auf einer Hügelkuppe den schönsten, friedlichsten Garten (Nr. 178. 183–185). Es ist im Februar 1918, der erste Frühling. Einsame Wege führen mich durch die blühende, duftende Felslandschaft jenseits der Gärten. Drinnen im Gewühl des Ortes ist mir wieder alles stumm. Draußen in der Einsamkeit sprechen Orchideen, Zyklamen und blühende Aprikosenbäume, die zwischen blanken Kalkfelsen auf dem rotbraunen Boden gedeihen (Nr. 180). Ernsthaft stehen die dunklen Zypressen in dieser Pracht, und ganz frisch geballte reinliche Wolken schweben groß und nahe vom Meer herüber.«

173 1918 – farbige Kreiden – 40,5 × 29,0
Nazareth. Weg in die Stadt zwischen Hecken von Feigenkakteen.
Vgl. Zitat Nr. 172.

174 1918 – farbige Kreiden – 27,8 × 40,0
Nazareth, Stadtansicht.

175 1918 – farbige Kreiden – 18,5 × 12,2
Moschee in Tiberias, aus Basalt errichtet.

176 1917 – farbige Kreiden auf getöntem Papier – 40,1 × 28,3
Nazareth. Minarett der Moschee.

177 19. 1. 1918 – Farbstifte und Tusche – 13,3 × 9,9
Nazareth. Gasse in die Stadt hinunter.

178 15. 1. 1918 – Farbstifte und Tusche – 13,4 × 9,9
Nazareth. Blick von der Stadt zum Franziskanerkloster.
Vgl. Zitat Nr. 172.

179 Frühjahr 1918 – farbige Kreiden – 26,0 × 21,0
Nazareth. Esel im Obstgarten.
Vgl. Zitat Nr. 172.

180 Frühjahr 1918 – farbige Kreiden – 23,5 × 30,2
Nazareth. Weg auf eine Anhöhe mit blühenden Mandelbäumen.
Vgl. Zitat Nr. 172.

181 Januar 1918 – farbige Kreiden auf getöntem Papier – 30,3 × 23,7
Nazareth. Pforte des Franziskanerklosters.
Vgl. Zitat Nr. 172.

182 1918 – farbige Kreiden auf getöntem Papier – 28,0 × 21,0
Nazareth. Auf dem Wege zur Marienkapelle.
Vgl. LE 245:
»Die Legende erzählt, daß die Nazarener Ihn vom Berge hinabstürzen wollten, weil sie Ihm zürnten wegen der Wahrheiten, die Er ihnen sagte. Aber Er schwebte unbeschädigt hinab, und Maria war ohnmächtig hingesunken mitten auf dem Wege zum Berg des Absturzes,

wohin sie Ihm in Todesangst gefolgt war. Eine Kapelle steht an dieser Stätte am Ende der
Gärten. Und hier begann es schön und lebendig zu werden für mich.«

183 1918 – farbige Kreiden – 38,8 × 28,0
Nazareth. Im Garten des Franziskanerklosters.
Vgl. Zitat Nr. 172.
Das Franziskanerkloster auf einer Höhe über der Stadt Nazareth war 1917/18 nur von zwei
Mönchen, beide deutscher Herkunft – der eine stammte aus Biberach in Oberschwaben –
bewohnt und bewirtschaftet. Zum Kloster gehörte ein großer Garten. Die Skizze zeigt Zy-
pressen und Mandelbäume und die beiden Mönche.

184 1918 – farbige Kreiden – 28,8 × 40,9
Nazareth, Dämmerung.
Vgl. Zitat Nr. 172.
Berlin, Plansammlung der Technischen Universität, Nr. 7728.

185 Frühling 1918 – farbige Kreiden auf getöntem Papier – 40,0 × 28,5
Nazareth. Am Franziskanerkloster.
Vgl. Zitat Nr. 172.

186 1918 – farbige Kreiden auf getöntem Papier – 15,7 × 10,0
Ein aleppiner Kaufmann.

187 1918 – Kohle – 17,5 × 13,1
Aleppo. Portrait des türkischen Soldaten Omer.

188 1918 – farbige Kreiden auf getöntem Papier – 16,0 × 10,0
Aleppo. Zwei alte Männer.

189 1918 – farbige Kreiden – 11,2 × 8,0
Ein aleppiner Händler. Vgl. auch Nr. 232.

190 1916/17 – Bleistift – 9,9 × 15,0
Baghdad. Der Chef-Ingenieur des Baues der Baghdad- und Hedschas-Bahn, Meißner
Pascha.

191 1918 – farbige Kreiden – 10,6 × 16,4
Aleppo. Arabischer Kaufmann, ausgezeichnet mit dem Königlich Preußischen Verdienstkreuz für Kriegshilfe.

192 1918 – Kohle und Kreide – 13,8 × 17,9
Aleppo. Flötender Derwisch.
Beschreibung von W. Andrae, bisher unveröffentlicht (ungefähr 1950):
»Der Bettler lockt seine Schenkgeber mit einem mißtönenden Blasinstrument herbei und
machte einen wohlgenährten Eindruck. Offenbar genoß er in der Gilde der Bettler ein
besonderes Ansehen. Bettler und Diebe hatten in Aleppo einen Scheich als ihr Oberhaupt.

Bei Diebstählen konnte man über den Scheich der Diebe das gestohlene Eigentum zurückerhalten. Dafür war ein entsprechender Entgelt zu entrichten.«

193 12. 8. 1906 – farbige Kreiden auf getöntem Papier – 29,0 × 22,0
Assur. Abdallah im Festgewande.
Berlin, Staatsbibliothek, SPK, Nachlaß Andrae 15/34.
Beschreibung von W. Andrae, bisher unveröffentlicht (ungefähr 1950):
»Abdallah war behelfsweise im Expeditionshause beschäftigt und hatte sich dabei einmal
ausgezeichnet durch geschicktes Benehmen, das es zu belohnen galt. Die Belohnung bestand
aus einem Festgewand, das er bei dem großen Korban-Bairam, dem großen Opferfeste mit
Stolz anlegte, um bei seinen Stammesgenossen die gehörige Bewunderung einzuheimsen.
Zu dem Kostüm gehörte auch ein Festhemd mit Ärmeln, die auf der Erde schleifen muß-
ten.«

194 1916 – farbige Kreiden auf getöntem Papier – 13,8 × 9,0
Baghdad. Portrait eines Kriegskameraden.

195 19. 6. 1916 – farbige Kreiden – 23,8 × 16,9
Baghdad. Portrait des Oberstabsarztes Dr. Ludwig Külz. – Vgl. auch Abb. 21.
LE 231 f.
»Ein Stab deutscher Majore, Rittmeister und Kavallerieleutnants war 1916 schon in Kasr-i
Schirin und versuchte, einen Flankenangriff gegen Persien zu organisieren. Die Gegend ist
archäologisch höchst interessant, war aber gründlich verseucht. Die Leichenkarawanen der
Schiiten aus ganz Persien, von denen ich in Babylon erzählte, wurden hier bei Seuchengefahr
angestaut, wenn die Türken Quarantäne machten und die Grenze sperrten. So sammelten
sich hier Cholera, Typhus, Pest, Malaria, Fleckfieber und ähnliche interessante Seuchen. Die
deutschen Tropenärzte, die sie bekämpfen sollten, wurden alle ohne Ausnahme von einer
der Seuchen ergriffen und lagen auf den Tod darnieder. Ich traf Ludwig Külz, mit dem ich
in Grimma an einem Tisch gesessen hatte, als cholerakranken Oberstabsarzt wieder. In
Kamerun war er Gouvernementsarzt gewesen. Jetzt hielt er seinen Zustand für höchst küm-
merlich, kam aber noch davon.«
Ferner: W. Litten, Persische Flitterwochen (1925) 303. 335.

196 1919 – Kohle und Kreiden auf getöntem Papier – 26,0 × 18,2
Istanbul. Bektaschi-Derwisch im Kloster Tschamlidscha.
Beschreibung von W. Andrae, bisher unveröffentlicht (ungefähr 1950):
»Auf einem Berge nicht weit vom anatolischen Ufer des Bosporus hauste dieser alte, gemüt-
liche Derwisch und lebte als Kaffeewirt, beschaulich über Krieg und Dummheit der Menschen philosophierend. Er genoß die weite Aussicht über die fruchtbare Ebene zu Füßen des
Berges fern vom Leben der Großstadt. Seine helle, gesteppte Filzmütze, sein eisgrauer Bart
und sein hellbrauner Derwischmantel gaben ihm das würdevolle priesterliche Ansehen, und
man hörte gerne seine sehr deutliche türkische Aussprache der knappen Sentenzen, die er
zum Besten gab.«

197 1918/19 – farbige Kreiden – 25,6 × 17,8
Istanbul. Captain Moses, der britische Kapitän der »Patmos«. (Zweites, nahezu identisches

Abb. 21 Dr. med. Külz, Baghdad, 15. 5. 1916

Bild: Berlin, Staatsbibliothek, SPK, Nachlaß Andrae 15/54: Captain Moses mit geschlosse-
nen Augen).
Vgl. Nr. 198.

198 1918/19 – farbige Kreiden auf getöntem Papier – 34,8 × 27,2
Der Dampfer »Patmos« auf dem Bosporus vor Istanbul, im Hintergrund Haidar Pascha.
W. Andrae schreibt zur »Patmos« in LE 247 ff.:
»Im Oktober 1918 langten die Reste der deutschen Orient-Armee in Haidar-Pascha vor
Istanbul an. Wir waren noch 10 000 Mann, die alliierte Kriegsflotte lag im Marmara-Meer,
und so waren wir in einer Mausefalle. Der Krieg ging zu Ende, als Kriegsgefangene wollte
uns keiner haben – was sollte man mit uns machen? Wir wurden also in kleine deutsche Han-
delsschiffe eingesperrt, die auf dem Marmara-Meer gegenüber Istanbul vor Anker lagen. Ich
kam mit 960 Mann auf einen 3000 t großen Kohlendampfer der Levante-Linie, der den
bezeichnenden Namen »Patmos« trug. In die großen Laderäume des Schiffes waren proviso-
rische Kojen eingebaut, jede für vier Pritschen, zwei und zwei übereinander auf engstem
Raum. Hölzerne Treppen führten in die Tiefe des schwimmenden Hohlraumes aus Eisen-
platten, die Maschinerie war alt und ungenügend. Auf Deck gab es einen Raum von etwa
8 m² zum »Spazierengehen«. In unserer Koje waren zwei Überlange, ein Mittelgroßer und
ein rundlicher Kleiner. Dieser mußte fast stets im »Bett« bleiben, sonst hätten die anderen
sich nicht bewegen können. Wir litten am meisten unter der Nachrichtenlosigkeit aus der
Heimat, denn die Sieger hatten unsere Post gesperrt. Die Angehörigen in der Heimat sollten
nicht wissen, wer von uns noch am Leben war. Solche Erfahrungen haben unsere Menschheit nicht abgehalten, dieselben Grausamkeiten zu wiederholen und noch hundertmal ärgere
heraufzubeschwören.
Als wir drei und mehr Monate im Marmara-Meer gelegen hatten, wurde die Stimmung
bedrohlich. Findige Köpfe veranstalteten allerlei Wettbewerbe unter der Besatzung. Da es
für den physischen Leib keine Bewegungsmöglichkeit gab, mußten diese Turniere auf intel-
lektuellem Gebiet abgehalten werden, mit Dichten, Rechnen und anderen Aufgaben. Aus
der rauhen Zusammenpferchung auf engem Raum wurde eine Art Pädagogium. Unter den
Offizieren gab es Archäologen und Ausgräber, ein paar Redegewandte, nicht gerade Kory-
phäen. Aber jeder gab sein Bestes dazu, und diesen Bemühungen war es wohl zu verdanken,
daß unsere »Patmos« nach einem halben Jahr gänzlich unbolschewisiert in Hamburg
anlangte. Jedoch haben die Monate der Zusammenpressung wohl nicht hingereicht, eine
nachhaltige Seelenwandlung zu erzeugen, die nach den Erfahrungen dieses Krieges überall
hätte eintreten müssen, wenn eine Wiederholung dieser Barbarei verhindert werden sollte.
Wann beginnen wir nun nach dem zweiten Krieg uns zu besinnen?
Mich interessierten die Physiognomien meiner Gefährten, und ich versuchte, aus ihnen Portraits ohne Anspruch auf Ähnlichkeit zu gestalten. Die meisten davon sind verschenkt worden. Der ausgeprägteste Typus blieb der englische Captain Moses, der dem Schiff als britische »Besatzung« mitgegeben wurde, mutterseelenallein und ohne Waffe, als wir im März
zum Abtransport nach Deutschland die Anker lichteten (Nr. 197). Man konnte wirklich den
simplen britischen, von sich überzeugten Mut des einzelnen den 960 »Feinden« gegenüber
bewundern. Immerhin galten wir als entwaffnet, aber es waren noch einige Schießgewehre
an Bord versteckt geblieben, mit denen wir später in der Nordsee die treibenden Minen
abschossen. Aber Moses gehörte einfach zu unserer Schicksalsgemeinschaft. Wir waren aus

»Feinden« wieder zu Menschen geworden, wie es sich nach Schluß des Krieges doch gehörte.

Captain Moses verließ uns in der Nordsee, nachdem uns die Landung in Rotterdam verweigert worden war und wir unseren Weg durch die Minenfelder bis Hamburg fortsetzen mußten. Ehemalige Kameraden, die auf viel schnelleren Schiffen über Genua die Heimat früher erreichten, hatten unseren wartenden Angehörigen gemütvoll erzählt, die »Patmos« könne nie nach Hause kommen, ein so schlechtes Schiff ohne Rettungsboote mit so vielen Menschen, durch die gefährlichen Minenfelder um ganz Europa herum!

Aber Ende März 1919 kam die Patmos in Quarantäne nach Cuxhaven und nach drei Tagen in den totenstillen Hafen von Hamburg.«

KATALOG DER TEXTABBILDUNGEN

1 1902 – Bleistift – 23,0 × 15
Babylon. Selbstportrait.
LE Abb. 5.

2 Mesopotamien und Syrien/Palästina nach einer Karte des Jahres 1918.
Zeichnung: Corinna Maschin. Die Schreibung der Namen entspricht weitgehend der von W. Andrae verwendeten.

3 15. 2. 1899 – Bleistift –
Halebije.
LE (1. Aufl.) Abb. 10.

4 22. 2. 1899 – Bleistift – 24,4 × 33,4
Lager östlich Kischla Kajin.

5 nach 1917 – Tusche –
Umgebung von Babylon, nach einer Karte des Jahres 1917.
LE Abb. 14.

6 1902 – Tusche – 13,5 × 14,6
Karte der Umgebung von Fara und Abu Hatab.
Vgl. auch die 2. Fassung aus dem Jahre 1903 in E. Heinrich, Fara (1931) neben p. 2.

7 1903/1904 Bleistift – 22,8 × 15,3
Dresden. Selbstportrait.

8 nach 1916 – Tusche –
Umgebung von Assur, nach einer Karte des Jahres 1916.
LE Abb. 34.

9 Etwa 1908 – kolorierte Tuschezeichnung – 12,5 × 20,0
Assur. »Die Ausgräber von Assur in neuen Anzügen.«
Von links nach rechts: Paul Maresch, Walter Andrae, Julius Jordan, Conrad Preußer und der
sich über die Herren wundernde Ismain ibn Dschasim.

10 20. 1./7. 2. 1916 – Farbstifte – 14,2 × 22,8
Auf dem Euphrat von Meskene nach Baghdad: In der Kajüte des Kastenbootes (Safineh)
(vgl. Nr. 24. 26).
LE 227 f. und W. Andrae (etwa 1950, bisher unveröffentlicht):
»1916 erhielt ich den Auftrag, von Aleppo nach Bagdad den Euphrat hinunter zu fahren, um
die Möglichkeit von Schifftransporten zu erkunden. Man hatte zu diesem Zwecke bei Kar-
kemisch eine Marinestation installiert, die den vergeblichen Versuch machte, einen Flußver-
kehr flußabwärts zu organisieren. Leutnant v. Zitzewitz, Leutnant v. Gosern und ein türkischer Hauptmann waren für diese Erforschung, die gar nichts erbringen konnte, beigegeben.
Wir bekamen ein Paar jener schwimmenden Holzkisten, die nebeneinander gebunden wurden und eine leichte Hütte darüber gebaut erhielten, die ganz hübsch wohnlich war mit drei
Betten und einem Tisch, während außerhalb der Hütte vorn und hinten je zwei Ruderer ihre
Plätze erhielten. Das Gefährt folgte der Strömung des Flusses, die Ruderer hatten die einzige
Aufgabe, es einigermaßen im Gang zu halten und durch die verschiedenen Strömungen zu
lancieren. Sie waren also nicht verpflichtet, etwa eine schnellere Gangart herbeizuführen. Die
Fahrt dauerte infolgedessen einen Monat, statt der sonst üblichen 18 Reittage. Bei Wind war
das Fahren unmöglich, man lag still am Ufer.«

11 1918 – Tusche – Original: 1:25 000
Karte von Aleppo und seiner näheren Umgebung. Unter Anleitung von W. Andrae aufgenommen von Oberleutnant Erdmann.

12 März 1919 – Kohle und Kreide – 34,8 × 26,3
Der Schiffszimmermann der »Patmos«, vgl. Nr. 197. 198.

13 1909
Gertrude Bell vor ihrem Zelt in Babylon.
S. Hill, Gertrude Bell (1976) Abb. 1.

14 1926 – Feder – Maße unbekannt
Ali Dschamus, »der Wasserbüffel«: der einäugige Wasserträger der Babylon-Grabung.
MDOG 65, April 1927, 13 Abb. 5.

15 1926 – Tusche – 9,5 × 7,7
Tischler beim Vernageln einer Transportkiste.
MDOG 65, April 1927, 15 Abb. 8.

16 1952 – Aquarell, Kohle und Kreide – 40,0 × 30,0
Walter Andrae, Portrait von Irmin Grashey-Straub, der jahrelangen Pressezeichnerin der
LEIPZIGER ILLUSTRIERTEN. J. Renger in: Berlin und die Antike (vgl. Anm. 24), 185 Abb. 21.
Berlin, Staatsbibliothek, SPK, Nachlaß Andrae 15/38.

17 19. 3. 1899 – Bleistift – 21,6 × 13,3
Baghdader Holzkeilchen-Kapitell.
Vgl. Nr. 41. 52. 53. 57.

18 1927 – Tinte – 7,8 × 16
Babylon, Expeditionshaus, Innenhof.
Vorzeichnung zu Nr. 58.

19 1927 – Tinte – 8,8 × 14,8
Das Expeditionshaus in Babylon am Euphrat.
Vorzeichnung zu Nr. 59.

20 1923 – Kohle und Kreide – 19,5 × 33,6
Scham'al-Zinçirli, »ergänztes Stadtbild«.

21 15. 5. 1916 – farbige Kreiden auf getöntem Papier – 23,5 × 16,5
Baghdad. Dr. med. Külz (mit dem Eisernen Kreuz 2. Klasse und dem Königlich Preußischen
Verdienstkreuz für Kriegshilfe), vgl. auch Nr. 195.
Berlin, Staatsbibliothek, SPK, Nachlaß Andrae 15/44.

NACHTRAG ZUR 2. AUFLAGE

EINLEITUNG

Die erste Auflage dieses Buches ist vergriffen. Eine Babylon-Ausstellung der Berliner Museen, SPK, steht bevor. Sie soll in mehreren deutschen Städten gezeigt werden. Auch Bilder Walter Andraes gehören zu den Exponaten.

So hat sich die Abteilung Baghdad des Deutschen Archäologischen Instituts in Zusammenarbeit mit Herrn Ernst Walter Andrae und dem Verlag Gebr. Mann entschlossen, eine zweite Auflage herauszubringen, was sonst nicht ihrer Gepflogenheit entspricht. Aber den Besuchern der Ausstellungen soll es ermöglicht werden, sich von der Schönheit der Bilder Walter Andraes auch daheim einfangen zu lassen. Sie zeigen zudem vieles, was seit dem Bau der Baghdad-Bahn (vgl. W. Andrae bei Katalog-Nr. 233) im Laufe der Zeit dem sog. modernen Orient mit seinem Auf und Ab der Wirtschaftskraft und seinen leider nur kurzen Augenblicken von Geschlossenheit und danach folgendem, Waffengewalt nicht scheuenden Auseinanderbrechen zum Opfer fiel und fällt. So sind diese Bilder auch Zeugen einer noch vor kurzem bestehenden Welt, deren Tradition bis in die Tage jener Kulturen zurückreicht, um deren Erforschung sich Andrae sein Leben lang bemüht hat.

Die neue Auflage ist um 24 Tafeln und vier Textabbildungen, insgesamt 42 Bilder, erweitert worden. Der größte Teil davon stammt aus dem Besitz der Familie Andrae, darüber hinaus kommen einige aus der Staatsbibliothek Berlin, SPK und dem Vorderasiatischen Museum, Staatliche Museen, Berlin, SPK, dazu. Hier ist für freundliche Druckgenehmigung wiederum Dr. Brandis und Frau Dr. Stolzenberg zu danken, sowie erstmalig Frau Direktor Dr. L. Jacob-Rost; Bilder aus dem von ihr geleiteten Vorderasiatischen Museum standen uns vor der Vereinigung Deutschlands nicht zur Verfügung.

Aus Kostengründen ist die Anordnung der ersten Auflage beibehalten worden. Die neu hinzugekommenen Bilder sind als Nachtrag auf den Tafeln 129–152, ihre Beschreibungen auf Seite 93 ff. vorgelegt.

In seinem achtzigsten Lebensjahr standen dem nunmehr fast völlig erblindeten Walter Andrae (vgl. p. 2), die Bilder seines Lebens immer noch so deutlich vor seinem geistigen Auge wie eh und je. Er diktierte eine unveröffentlichte Schrift: Das Schöne – Das Gute – Das Wahre (im folgenden abgekürzt: SGW). Um Andrae besser zu erfassen, soll dem Leser ein Einblick in die Gedankenwelt seiner letzten Jahre gegeben werden. So sind dem ersten Teil dieses Manuskriptes die folgenden und die bei Nr. 210 und 224 gedruckten Abschnitte entnommen, aus einem unveröffentlichten Teil seiner Lebenserinnerungen (LE) die Charakterisierung des Erbauers der Hedschas-Bahn, Meißner-Pascha (bei Nr. 233).

Berlin, 8. August 1991   R. M. B.

WALTER ANDRAE

BILDBESCHREIBUNGEN

Zu Nr. 46. SGW, 12. 4. 1954

Phoenix dactilifera: Auch zwischen Palmen glutet unverhofft Schönheit für Augen, die am mitleidlosen Brennen weißer Mittagsstrahlen schon fast verzweifelten und alles Schöne fortgebrannt und ausgedörrt vermuteten. Nun neigt sie sich, die Glühende, zum Abendrande, und alle Farbentöne bis zum Purpur folgen ihr am Himmel wie Trabanten. Ein zartes Rosa legt sich hinter Palmenkronen, die sich am Tage noch wie Bündel blanker Schwerter so kriegerisch gebärdeten und jetzt wie weiche bunte Federwedel so harmlos in die Lüfte ragen. Und unter ihnen fangen Datteltrauben reifend schon wie pures Gold zu glühen an, ja auch die stumpfen erdengrauen Stufenstämme spielen ein in diese Farbakkorde. Am Boden steht das zartgefiederte Gelaub von Süßholz und Mimosen und scheint mit ganz verhaltenem Grün unhörbar fast mit einzustimmen. Am Euphrat, ganz im Abendschatten schon, sind braun und bläulich schimmernde Gestalten mit Spaten an der Arbeit, dem Schöpfwerk den Kanal neu zuzuführen. Das warme, gelbe Euphratwasser rundet dies friedvolle Farbgemälde schön nach unten ab.

zu Nr. 79. SGW, 30. 4. 1954:

Kurban bairam: Am Opferfest der Moslem strahlt die Mittagssonne grell im farblos-erdengrauen Hof der Dörfler-Hütten. Männer füllen ihn in Festgewändern, unter ihren braunen Mänteln leuchtet's gelb und rot und schneeig weiß, und neue blaue oder rote Tücher werden vom Agâl aufs Haupt gepreßt. Sie ordnen sich zum Tanz und bilden eine Schlange, die auf roten Schnabelschuhen geht. Am Haupt der Schlange führt Murâd, der erste Diener im »Palast« der Europäer, die in Babel graben. Er trägt den roten Fez und schwenkt das rote Schnupftuch. Sein Jäckchen leuchtet himmelblau, kanariengelb das lange seid'ne Hemd, der goldgeflocht'ne Gürtel baumelt an der Seite. Pausenlos ertönt die Doppelflöte; Achteltöneklang aus Röhrenknochen der Gazelle, vor jedem Tänzer knicksend dargebracht vom Künstler. Schüchtern staunt die Hausfrau ob der Pracht, den schwarzen Mantel übers Haupt gezogen. Sie zieht ihn sittsam vor die Nase bei jedem Männerblick und vor die Silberscheiben der Nasenflügel. Staunend steht der Europäer, denn im Westen pflegt der Tanz wohl andere Schönheit.

Die Sonne sank, mit ihr der heiße Tag, und in die Dämmerung tönt von ferne leises *brekekex*, dem sich piano und sonor *koax koax* gesellt. Es schwillt crescendo bald zum sanften Chor. Und ihr vermeint, es sei ein Wiegenlied. Doch, weit gefehlt! Wer jetzt den Frosch und seinen Nachbar sähe, der könnt' verstehen, warum der eine immer lauter singen muß als jener, der ihn übertönt. Das will der unsichtbare Dirigent. Und so ge-

schieht's: Das Wiegenlied, es ward zum Männerchor und dieser zum Gebrüll, bis plötzlich Pause – Neubeginn – und Schwellen wie Meeresbrandung auf- und abwogt und
euch um die Ohren schlägt. Jedoch Finale gibt es nicht. Der Mond geht auf, die lange
Nacht verrinnt, doch nicht verrinnt das Wogen des Gesangs, bis sich die Morgensonne
zeigt. Wem es zuviel, der reise ab!

Zu Nr. 101–103. SGW, 13. 4. 1954

Goldmoschee: Dem Heiligen, der einst vor tausend Jahren den Menschen sonnengleich
des Denkens Licht entzündet und den Herzen Farben gab, erbaute Erfurcht über seinem Grabe die mit purem Gold bedeckte Kuppel und das gold- und farbgeschmückte
Tor und den geweihten, vielgewölbten Hof, damit sein unvergängliches Wirken auch
heute wie die Sonne golden strahle und heute noch den Menschen zarte Farben in die
stumpfen Herzen gebe.

Nun ist so manche bunte Fliese von gierigen Händen aus der Wand genommen,
irgendwohin verschleppt und ihrem Zweck entfremdet. Jedoch der Rest blieb schön,
und wenn's noch Herzen gäbe, die sich öffnen könnten, sie würden auch der Herzens-
predigt dieses Heiligen noch offen stehen.

Denn dieses ist nicht Schönheit um des Schönen willen! Es geht um Gutes und um
Wahres gleichermaßen. Vergeblich würde sonst die gold'ne Kuppel, der gold'ne Son-
nenstern, weit über leere Felder alle Tagesstunden noch dem Wanderer leuchten. Der
Stern ist mehr als ird'scher Richtungsweiser!

Zu Nr. 109. SGW, 19. 3. 1954:

Tadsch Mahall: Eines edlen Menschenpaares unbegrenzte Liebe setzt ihr Denkmal hier
in unerhörter, großer, fleckenloser Reinheit, weißen Marmor edelster Gestaltung in
gebändigter Natur. Wo steht ein Grabmal gleicher Größe und doch nicht groß genug
für seinen Inhalt an gegebener und empfangener Menschenliebe? Der Mond beglänzt
die Kuppel und die schlanken Türme, und vor dem Sternenhimmel steht es wie ein
Schneegebirge und spiegelt sich in wohlgepflegten Marmorbecken, um die sich Rosen-
ranken und Palmwedel wiegen. In dunklen Hecken schlägt die Nachtigall ihr süßes
Lied. Wie seidener feiner Schleier weht es um die stillen Gänge. Wie Weihrauchwolken
weht es um die Marmorkuppel, als umarme noch die tote Kaiserin die Totengaben des
Gemahls, der trauernd diesen Wunderbau geschaffen, damit die flüchtige Liebe die
Erde nie verlasse. Mit Edelsteinen ließ er Hals und Wangen zieren, wie einst der Gattin,
so dem Totenmal.

Hier geht das Leben weiter! Wie edel spricht hier Wissen: Nicht endet Leben mit
dem Tode!

Zu Nr. 80–87. SGW, 7. 5. 1954:

Verborgene Schönheit: Die Königsburg zu Babel war ein Schuttgebirge, sonst nichts. Den Forscher graut's, man sah nur Erde und Klamotten. Nur manchmal leuchtete es himmelblau und weiß und gelb und schwarz, geschmolz'ne Farbe, unvergänglich, als käm' sie eben erst vom Ofen großer Künstler.

Da schimmert Hoffnung! Und der Kampf begann. Es wird gegraben und gesucht, Schatzgräberei, die nicht um Gold und Statuen sich müht, nein, um Klamotten nur, auf denen Farben prangen. Man findet Tausende, doch was bedeuten sie?

Schön sind die Farben! Doch die Gestalten, sind sie ebenbürtig schön? Man müht sich drei Dezennien, sucht zu verbinden, was in kleinste Brocken zwei Jahrtausende zerschlagen, was einst die Burg zur Weltberühmtheit machte und einigen Geschlechtern Lehr- und Seelenantrieb war: Die langen Reihen schöner Tier- und Pflanzenbilder, Kraftgebilde, die vom Himmel strahlen und auf Erden wirken, die den Menschen helfen, die sie recht betrachten und nach oben streben.

Nun, enthüllte Schönheit, kannst Du heute auch den Menschen helfen?

Zu Nr. 98. SGW, 6. 5. 1954:

Der Frösche Schönheit: Der Frösche Schönheit sei Gesang? Kommt an den Euphratsumpf von Afedsch, der neben der Ruine Nippur's, der Tempelstadt des Gottes Ellil, liegt, und kehrt beim Scheich des Afedsch-Stammes zur Nacht in seine gastliche, aus Schilf geflocht'ne Hütte ein. Sie liegt nicht weit vom Schilfsumpf, und man reist in Gondeln her.

KATALOG DER TAFELN 129–152 (NR. 199–237)

199 24. 1. 1899 – Bleistift – 10,0 × 18,0
    Amq-Ebene (Kirk-Chan, Hamamath etc.). Kurdisches Bauernhaus aus Schilf.

200 12. 2. 1899 – Bleistift – 13,3 × 18,0
    Zwischen Abu Chrere und Hamamath. Ruine einer Moschee. Minarett, Details.

201 Anfang 1899 – Öl – 41,6 × 30,8
    Damaskus. Am Abend.

202 19. 2. 1899 – Bleistift – 33,8 × 24,6
    Qal'at ar-Rachba. Vgl. Nr. 30.

203   25. 1. 1899 – Bleistift – 9,0 × 12,5
»Der Panzerkreuzer« auf der Straße von Alexandrette/Iskenderun nach Aleppo: Der Expe-
ditionsteilnehmer (und Berliner Teppichhändler) H. F. Ludwig Meyer betreibt Vogeljagd
von der Kutsche aus. Zu H. F. Ludwig Meyer, der Koldewey bereits nach Surghul und El
Hibba begleitete, vgl. RK 36.93. An anderer unpublizierter Stelle berichtet Andrae, daß
Meyer auch in Babylon auf Vögel schoß, diese aber von Koldewey, wenn er es bemerkte,
durch laute Rufe oder Händeklatschen kurz vorher vertrieben wurden.

204   16. 3. 1899 – Bleistift – 16,5 × 22,0
Ktesiphon. Taq i-Kisra v. SW. Links im Hintergrund Salman Pak.

205   1899 – Feder und Farbstift – 28 × 20,7
Babylon. Erster Plan nach Abschreiten der Ruine.
Aus einem Brief an die Eltern.

206   1899 – Aquarell – 8,3 × 17,8
Babylon. Expeditionshaus: Blick von Koldeweys Fenster nach Norden zum Hügel Babil,
nach Gewitter. Vgl. Nr. 60.

207   1900 – Feder – 27,7 × 17,8
Babylon. Arbeiter in der Grabung. Der feine Strich, der die späteren Rekonstruktionszeich-
nungen Andraes auszeichnet, ist im Ansatz bereits erkennbar, aber noch nicht erreicht.

208   1902 – Aquarell – 25,3 × 35,3
Babylon. Homera von N. Im Hintergrund links der Ruinenhügel der inneren Stadtmauer.

209   1902 – Bleistift – 14,1 × 15,6
Babylon. Das »Nilpferd«, W. Andraes Schimmel in Babylon. Vgl. auch Nr. 222 und Abb. 25
(mit Text).

210   1923 – Farbkreiden – 30,4 × 46,3
Babylon. Rekonstruktion.
Blick über die archäologisch bekannte Euphratbrücke zum Turm und Marduk-Heiligtum
Esangila. Eine zweite Brücke ist in den Texten überliefert, ihre einstige Lage konnte im
Gelände noch nicht identifiziert werden (vgl. E. Unger, Babylon, in: Reallexikon der Assy-
riologie 1 [1932] 349 §§ 75.76).
Andrae, der später für den Turm von Babylon die Stufenform annahm, hat ihn hier und auf
Abb. 211 noch blockhaft dargestellt und erwies mit diesem Rekonstruktionsvorschlag den
Vorstellungen seines Lehrers Koldewey eine Referenz. (Zu den verschiedenen Wiederher-
stellungsversuchen ist heute H. Schmid zu vergleichen, der selbst einen Vorschlag bringt:
H. Schmid, in: Das wieder erstehende Babylon, 5. Aufl., neu herausgegeben von B. Hrouda
(1990) 303 ff.)
Koldewey, seit 1917 in Berlin, starb ebenda. Andrae hat ihn bis zu seiner letzten Stunde
begleitet. Am 6. 4. 1954 diktiert er aus der Erinnerung (SGW):
»MORIBUNDUS.
Baumeister ohne Baugrund, ohne Tor und Weg und Wahrheit, lag der unheilbar Erkrankte,

Babylon
2. Pfingsttag 1899.

Abb. 22 Babylon. Der Euphrat am Expeditionshaus, mit Segelschiffen und Kellek, Pfingsten 1899

Abb. 23 Babylon. Expeditionshaus. Wohn- und Schlafraum, erster Zustand. Pfingsten 1899

und im wirren Auge glomm ein letztes Fünklein seines Lebenswillens. Ich aber sollte helfen, den Weg ihm zu erschließen und die rechte Pforte noch zu finden. Und ich sprach – nein, nein, – *Es* sprach aus mir:

›Wir Architekten kennen Kreis und Mitte und unser Ich ist unseres Lebenskreises Mitte. Was jenseits dieses Horizontes liegt, wir holen es mit scharfer Konstruktion als Bild in unseren Lebenskreis herein.

Nun sei es das unendlich Ferne, sei es Gott, den wir in unsern Kreis beziehen wollen – und siehe da, die Konstruktion beweist es haargenau: *Sein* Bild ist *unsere Mitte,* unser Ich. Wir spiegeln es unendlich oft, von allen Seiten herein in unser Ich. Es wird zur inneren Sonne, leuchtet uns im Herzen!‹

Der Kranke lächelt und von blauen Lippen kam ein leises: ›Ja, so ist es.‹ Weit öffnet sich sein Augenpaar, in tiefer, überirdischer Schönheit quoll dunkler die Erleuchtung.

Gefunden war der Weg, die Wahrheit und das Leben. Es fand ein Sterbender den Weg zum Vater durch des Sohnes Hilfe. Und uns auf Erden blieb erhalten seiner Augen Leuchten.«

Mir (R.M.B.) war es vergönnt, 1988 mit der wohl letzten Lebenden, die Koldewey noch persönlich kannte, über ihn zu sprechen: Frau Else Wasmuth geb. Püttmann (13. 10. 1901 – 26. 10. 1990), Inhaberin des in archäologischen Kreisen sehr wohl bekannten Verlages Wasmuth in Tübingen.

Frau Wasmuth verlebte einen Teil ihrer Kindheit im Baghdad der späten osmanischen Zeit. Ihr Vater, Ernst Püttmann, war dort als Export-/Importkaufmann und belgischer Honorarkonsul tätig. Koldewey wurde nach der zu seinen Ungunsten ausgegangenen Kontroverse mit dem Berliner Assyriologen F. Delitzsch über die doppelte Befestigungsmauer am Ischtar-Tor mürrisch und zurückhaltend (RK 170.205-208). Erschien aber das kleine Mädchen, das aus Baghdad mit der Kutsche angefahren kam, in Babylon, hellte sich sein Gesicht auf, er nahm sich Zeit und zeigte dem Kind alles in der liebenswürdigsten Weise. Was Frau Wasmuth bis in ihr hohes Alter ganz besonders stark erinnerlich war, war die strahlende Leuchtkraft seiner Augen. Mit dem Hinweis auf diese schloß auch Andrae sein oben zitiertes Memorial auf diesen ungewöhnlichen Menschen.

Berlin, Vorderasiatisches Museum, SPK.

211 1923 – Farbkreiden – 30,2 × 46,3
Babylon. Rekonstruktion. Prozessionsstraße bei Nacht. Links vorn das Marduk-Heiligtum Esangila, dann der Turm Etemmanki, das »Haus des Himmels und der Erde«, in der Koldeweyschen Rekonstruktion. Am Horizont noch die Mauerkronen des Palastbezirks Nebukadnezars II. erkennbar. Links über Esangila der Sirius, direkt über dem Heiligtum der Orion.
Berlin, Vorderasiatisches Museum, SPK.

212 1899 – Bleistift – 34,2 × 18,7
Babylon. Expeditionshaus. Fenster im Arbeitszimmer von W. Andrae. Vgl. Nr. 56.

213 1903 – Öl – 45 × 65
Basra. Auf dem Schatt el Arab. Unfertig.

214 o. J., ca. 1908 – Aquarell – 34,2 × 24,7
Assur. Blick über Tigris nach Gewitter mit Ansatz eines Regenbogens. Vgl. Nr. 120. 121.

215 o. J., ca. 1907/08 – Feder, Bleistift, Buntstift – 13,3 × 18,0
Assur. Ein Königspaar der Assyrer hält mit den Ausgräbern »Jour fix« im Hof des Grabungshauses. Das Gazellenböcklein »Gottlieb« stößt die Königin, wie bei allen fremden Gästen, von hinten.
Vgl. LE 159 f.:
»Das Gazellenböckchen Gottlieb wurde Mitbewohner des Hofes im zarten Alter von wenigen Tagen. Der Jäger hatte ihn aus der Steppe mitgebracht. Er mußte mit der Milchflasche großgezogen werden, was überraschend gut gelang, obwohl anfangs nur ein winziges Etwas mit klapprigen Beinchen dalag. Um so etwas Erdfarbenes in der erdfarbenen Steppe zu finden, mußte man die scharfen Augen des Jägers Mohammed haben, des einzigen seines Berufes in der ganzen Gegend. Gottlieb jedoch wuchs und gedieh, bekam stattliche spitzige Hörnchen und wurde der Liebling aller Hofbewohner, nicht aber der Fremden, die mit dem erdfarbenen schmuddeligen Araber-Mantel bekleidet den Hof zu betreten wagten. Denen lauerte er förmlich auf, wenn sie sich arglos unterhielten. Mit ein paar echten Gazellensätzen sprang er über den ganzen Hof, um seinem ahnungslosen Opfer die Hörnchen in den Hintern zu stoßen. Der Betroffene fiel langgestreckt auf den Rücken, und Gottlieb kehrte befriedigt in sein sakrosanktes Versteck zurück. Das passierte natürlich nicht oft, es wurde überall bekannt, und jeder Araber, der in den Hof kam, spähte zuerst nach Gottlieb und ging dann in voller Rückendeckung an den Wänden entlang, woran wir fast ebensoviel Spaß hatten wie an dem übermütigen Gazellensprung.«

216 Weihnachten 1907 – Feder – 7,5 × 26,0
Assur. »Die fröhlichen Assyrer«.

217 1912 – Bleistift – 6,8 × 10,5
Aleppo. Hotel Baron. Der Wirt und sein Bruder.

218 Dezember 1912 – Bleistift – 9,5 × 11,8
Passagier an Bord der Heluan.

219 1909 – Öl – 44,8 × 64,8
Assur, Blick vom Assurtempel zum Grabungshaus nach Süden. Berlin. Vorderasiatisches Museum, SPK.

220 1908 – Farbige Kreide auf getöntem Papier – 13,7 × 23,0
Assur. Wasserbüffel im Auwald des Tigris.

221 1905 – Öl – 31,7 × 41,3
Assur im Schnee.

222 1908 – Öl – 60,5 × 80,0
Euphrat südlich Meskene (vgl. Nr. 24).
Tränken der Pferde (zum Reisen im Planwagen vgl. auch Abb. 24 und 25). Im Vordergrund ein Blütenteppich aus Margeriten, Mohn, Rittersporn, wie er sich im Orient nur kurze Zeit im Frühling entfaltet.
Vgl. LE 189:

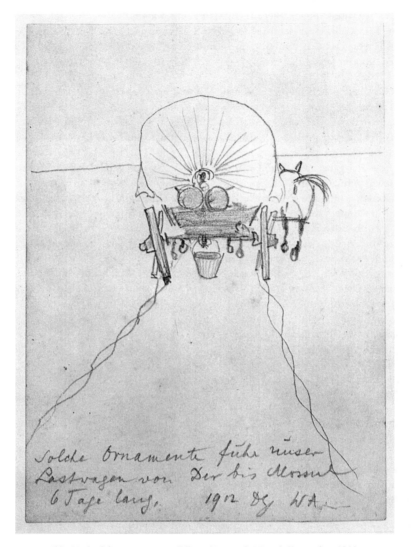

Abb. 24 Auf dem Wege von Dēr ez-Zor nach Mosul. Dezember 1912

»Wir ritten [von Assur] 15 Stunden durch grünes Gras und allerlei duftende Blumen. Immer sehen sie geschenkt aus, hingestreut von einer gütigen Göttin, verteilt auf den wüsten Boden, der überall durchschimmert und nicht verfilzt ist, wie eine deutsche Wiese.« – p. 191 f.: »Zum dreieckigen Zeltschlitz [bei Uwênât] sehe ich wie über einen grünen Teppich hinaus, der auf einem großen Tisch liegt. Sein Rand ist der Horizont… Viele Kamillen hat die Blumengöttin auf den grünen Tisch gesteckt…

Bald riecht es süß, bald kräftig; grün ist es überall, oft noch bunt, nirgends wüst, nur Bäume

Abb. 25 Auf dem Weg 'Ain Ghazal – Tell 'Afer – 31. 12. 1912

fehlen, das ist das einzig Fremdartige.« – p. 194 f.: »Die folgenden Tage haben ein jeder seinen eigenen Reiz, wenn auch immer die gleiche Ebene und der gleiche kahle Bergzug zur Rechten die Landschaft bildet. Aber das eine Mal sind feuerrote gewaltige Tulpen über diese Flächen verteilt (vgl. Nr. 140. 141), das andere Mal riesenhafte Kräuter mit Blättern wohlgedüngter Rhabarberstauden (vgl. Nr. 141), die zwischen sich für anderes keinen Raum zu lassen scheinen und jede Konkurrenz im Keime ersticken. Sie dehnen sich aus bis zum Horizont, und wie auf der See sieht man hie und da wie eine fürwitzige Welle ein besonders großes Blatt aus diesem Krautmeer herausgehoben. Dann wieder ist das welliger werdende Land mit kleinen und dann immer größer werdenden schwarzen Blöcken bedeckt, deren Geheimnis sich endlich an einem flachen Tälchen enthüllt, auf das nichts deutet, bis man unmittelbar vor ihm steht: Wir gehen über einen Basaltlavastrom, der in kaum meterdicker Schicht über die braven abgelagerten Schichten des Diluvium hinweggeflossen ist, als man noch nicht daran dachte, eine Eisenbahn über sie hinwegzulegen. Hier an dem armseligen Bächlein, das sich vom Gebirge zur Rechten in Steppen hinabwindet, um dort irgendwo zu versickern oder in einer unfruchtbaren Salzpfanne zu verenden, zeigt sich die Basaltdecke in ihrem Querschnitt, und von den Talrändern sind würfelförmige Blöcke zur Bachsohle abgerollt und bedecken diese in unordentlicher Weise (vgl. Nr. 141. 142). Hier und da bilden sich kleine Höhlen unter dem harten wasserdichten Stein.« Zum Basalt vgl. auch Nr. 29.
Hier ist ferner auch W. Andraes Erinnerung an den Frühling in Assur, SGW vom 12. 4. 1954, zu erwähnen:

»Zwei Sternenwunder:

Die Hände unterm Kopf gefaltet lieg' ich auf unseres Hauses flachem Dach. Und leise rauscht da unten der Tigris vorbei. Jedoch da oben dreht majestätisch sich die große Himmeluhr um den Polarstern, unhörbar, doch millionenfach beglitzert, wie eine große, dunkelblaue Wiese voll von Blütensternen, nur wenige mit Namen, ein ungenanntes, ungezähltes Heer von Blumen, die mich sanft mit Schlaf beträufeln.

Am Morgen reite ich hinab zur Tigrisaue. Sonst liegt sie kahl und dürr und erdengrau. Heut hat sie über Nacht sich wunderbar gekleidet in einen unermeßlich weiten Teppich aufgeblühter Margeriten, so dicht bei dicht geschmiegt die unschuldsvollen weißen Köpfchen mit den goldenen Perlen, daß kaum das Grün noch zwischen ihnen Raum hat. Ja, ja, du wunderst dich wie ich, mein Schimmelchen (vgl. Abb. 25 mit Text), daß jetzt auch unter uns ein Sternenhimmel ist, den wir bei unseren Ritten nächtens sonst nur über uns gewahrten. Das Rößlein schnaubt befriedigt. Wir trinken beide dieses Glück des Schönen. Und so kreisen wir, der Sonne gleich, durch uns're Sternenwiese auf der Erde, freudetrunken.«

223　1918 – Farbige Kreiden – 16,9 × 10,4
　　　Aleppo. Türkisches Bad.
　　　Berlin, Staatsbibliothek, SPK, Nachlaß Andrae 9.

224　1917 – Farbige Kreide – 15,4 × 9,9
　　　Aleppo. Kefr Salame. Wasserträgerinnen
　　　Berlin, Staatsbibliothek, SPK. Nachlaß Andrae 9.

225　1917 – Farbige Kreide auf getöntem Papier – 10,2 × 16,8
　　　Aleppo. »Die bunten Damen«.

226　1916 – Farbige Kreiden – 13,0 × 20,7
　　　Während der Schiffsreise von Aleppo nach Baghdad auf dem Euphrat. Ruinen einer Schöpfradanlage (Na'ura) am Euphrat.
　　　Vgl. p. 26, Abb. 10 Nr. 165. 168.

227　Frühjahr 1918 – Farbige Kreiden auf getöntem Papier – 10,1 × 16,7
　　　Derwisch-Kloster (Tekke) südlich Aleppo: Mašad al-Husain.
　　　E. Herzfeld: Inscriptions et monuments d'Alep (Kairo, 1955) 236–248, Taf. 94–101.
　　　Die Identifizierung des Bildes und die Literaturangabe verdanken wir H. Gaube.

228　1918 – Farbige Kreiden auf getöntem Papier – 10,1 × 16,5
　　　Derwisch-Kloster (Tekke) bei Aleppo: Takīya aš Šaih Abu Bakr.
　　　Vgl. Nr. 18. 154.

229　21. 12. 1918 – Farbige Kreiden – 11,6 × 18,0
　　　Bei Hama.

230　1918 – Farbige Kreiden – 10,5 × 17,9
　　　Damaskus, Altstadt.
　　　Berlin, Staatsbibliothek, SPK, Nachlaß Andrae Nr. 9.

231 15. 7. 1918 – Farbige Kreiden – 15,7 × 11,4

Meißner-Pascha, vgl. Nr. 190

LE, unveröffentlichter Teil:

»Mit echten ›Pionieren‹ in Berührung gekommen zu sein, darf man gewiß zu den bemerkenswerten Erlebnissen zählen. Für mich gehört Meißner Pascha zu diesen Pionieren. Er nahm einige Tage bei uns in Assur mit einer kleinen Vorexpedition für die Erkundung der Route der Baghdadbahn Quartier. In einem eisenbahnlosen Lande wie Mesopotamien darf man eine solche Tätigkeit wohl mit besonderem Rechte Pioniertätigkeit nennen. Stelle ich mir mein eigenes Vaterland eisenbahnlos vor, so muß ich mich schon in die Jugend meiner Großväter versetzen. Der eine derselben gehörte ja selbst zu den sächsischen ›Pionieren‹, allerdings bescheidensten Maßstabes. Die erste Bahn von Dresden nach Leipzig existierte bereits. Der Großvater hatte die Bauleitung eines Teiles der sächsisch-böhmischen Bahn durch das Elbtal.

Auch Meißner Pascha kam aus Sachsen, seine Sprache verriet es. Das Vaterland ist ihm, wie vielen seiner Landsleute, zu eng geworden, und seinen Ruf im Orient hatte er damals schon als Erbauer der Mekkabahn von Damaskus nach Medina begründet. Die Türken haben ihn mit allen Ehren für diese Leistung ausgezeichnet: Seinem Titel und einer hohen vererblichen Dotation. Er konnte sich daher berechtigt fühlen, die besten, längsten und schwersten Zigaretten der türkischen Tabakregie zu rauchen und sich dabei eine jährliche Nikotinvergiftung anzurauchen, die ihn manchmal wochenlang außer Kurs setzte. Dann war das Rauchen verboten und seine Laune fürchterlich. Die übrigen elf Monate des Jahres galt er als der vergnüglichste Anekdoten- und Schnurrenerzähler und der unerhört ideenreiche Ingenieur, der er war.

In Assur lernten wir ihn in seinen Arbeitspausen an unserem Tische kennen. Als Europäer macht man sich nur selten klar, von was für einem dichten Netz von Stahlschienen unsere Erde übersponnen ist. Hier aber sollte ein einziger Strang über 1000 km und mehr auf die wellige Erde gelegt werden, ohne daß man einem Grundbesitzer auf die Zehen zu treten genötigt war. Der Ingenieur erfaßte die Erde dort gewissermaßen mit ausgebreiteten Armen und tastete ihr die günstigsten Falten und Fältchen ihres Antlitzes ab. Und da rollen dann später die Lokomotiven darüber.

Bei seinen Bahnbauten hat Meißner Pascha die Türken und die anderen Landesbewohner gut kennengelernt und wußte ausgezeichnet mit ihnen umzugehen. Im kleinen hatten wir die gleichen Erfahrungen wie er gemacht. Zukunftsbilder durchzogen damals unsere Phantasie. Wir sahen das öde Land sich verändern und mit Wohlstand überziehen, weil wir meinten, dieser stählerne Strang, wenn er erst einmal bis hierher gekrochen kam, sei ausschließlich ein Segenbringer. In Wirklichkeit brachte er, noch nicht einmal ans Ziel gelangt, den Krieg. Einer der Kriegsgründe war die Erbauung der Bagdadbahn durch die Deutschen gewesen.

Heute scheint die Eisenbahnkultur überholt zu sein. Man kann zwar im Pullman-car durchaus komfortabel von Istanbul nach Bagdad und Basra fahren, aber der Schwerpunkt des Verkehrs liegt auf den asphaltierten Autostraßen. Diese gewann der junge Irak-Staat nach dem zweiten Kriege durch seinen Erdölreichtum.

Und nun werden meine obigen Erinnerungen vom Urzustand des Landes allmählich ausgelöscht und verblassen gegenüber seiner sehr diskutablen Europäisierung und Amerikanisierung. Wann werden jenem Lande die Pioniere des *geistigen* Fortschritts erstehen? Wann wird

bei uns Europäern eine genügend große Gefolgschaft den Pionieren unseres *geistigen* Fortschritts erstanden sein?«
Berlin, Staatsbibliothek, SPK, Nachlaß Andrae Nr. 9.

232 1918 – Farbige Kreiden – 16,1 × 9,4
Aleppo. Singender (?) Händler. Vgl. Nr. 189 derselbe Mann.

233 1918 – Farbige Kreiden auf getöntem Papier – 16,4 × 10,4
Damaskus. In den Gärten vor der Stadt beim Barada-Bach.

234 Frühling 1918 – Feder, Bleistift, farbige Kreide auf getöntem Papier – 13,4 × 17,8
Blumen aus der Gegend von Nazareth: Asphodelus- und Orchideenblüten, Alpenveilchen
etc.

235 20. 2. 1917 – Bleistift, farbige Kreiden – 12,7 × 7,5
Baghdad. Zelte im spätabendlichen Palmenhain.

236 19. 2. 1918 – Farbige Kreiden –18,2 × 11,8
Nazareth. Feldweg im Tal: Zypressen und Feigenkakteen
(vgl. Nr. 173).

237 26. 9. 1927 – Farbige Kreiden auf getöntem Papier – 10,2 × 16,8
Istanbul. Beikos am Bosporus. Während einer Reise nach Boğazköy kam Andrae 1927 ein
weiteres Mal durch Istanbul und griff, nur noch sehr selten in dieser Zeit, wieder zum Farbstift. Vgl. auch die Bilder früherer Besuche Nr. 144–150. 198.

KATALOG DER TEXTABBILDUNGEN

22 Pfingsten 1899 – Feder – 6,5 × 11,5
Babylon. Der Euphrat am Expeditionshaus, mit Segelschiffen und Kellek.

23 Pfingsten 1899 – Feder – 7,8 × 10.7
Babylon. Expeditionshaus. Wohn- und Schlafraum, erster Zustand.

24 Dez. 1912 – Bleistift – Original verschollen
Auf dem Wege von Dêr-ez-Zor nach Mossul. Planwagen mit hinten angehängtem Eimer,
seine Fahrspur deutet an, wie wackelig die Räder waren.
Andraes Beschriftung: »Solche Ornamente führt unser Lastwagen von Der bis Mossul,
6 Tage lang.« Zum Reisen im Planwagen vgl. auch Nr. 222 und Abb. 25.
LE 1. Aufl. Abb. 21.

25 31. 12. 1912 – Bleistift – Original verschollen

Andraes Beschriftung: »Soll man schmieren? Oder gehts noch? Auf dem Weg 'Ain Ghazal-Tell 'Afer. Mein Happel [der Schimmel rechts im Bild]«. Zum Reisen im Planwagen vgl. auch Nr. 222 und Abb. 24. Zu den Pferden in Assur äußert sich Andrae LE 158:

»Wir hatten Reitpferde, mit denen man sich freundschaftlich verband. Sie dankten uns die Freundschaft, wenn wir sie in der wege- und zäunelosen Gegend tummelten, die ihre eigentliche Heimat war. Und ihr Temperament antwortete entzückt auf die kleinen Winke, die sie erhielten.«

Vgl. auch Nr. 209.

Le 1 Aufl. Abb. 22.

TAFELN

PLATES

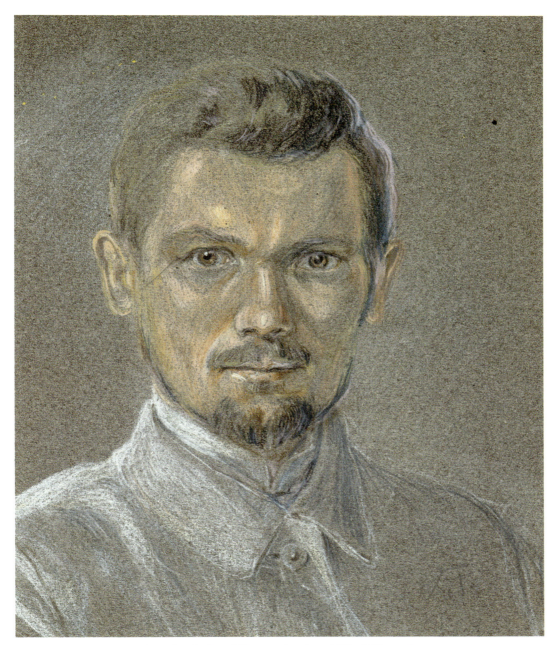

1. Walter Andrae, Selbstportrait – Assur 1908 – Self-portrait

2. Walter Andrae, Portrait von J. Walter-Kurau – 1915 – Portrait by J. Walter-Kurau

3. Walter Andrae, Portrait von O. Jäger – 1948 – Portrait by O. Jäger

4. Im Hafen von Alexandria – 18. 12. 1898 – In the harbour at Alexandria

5. Im Hafen von Port Said – 21. 12. 1898 – In the harbour at Port Said

6. Der »Nettuno« vor Jaffa – 22. 12. 1898 – The »Nettuno« at Jaffa

7. Jaffa. Vom Schiff aus gesehen – 22. 12. 1898 – View from the vessel

R. Koldewey   B. Moritz

2 Juden auf dem Saturno
vor Jaffa 22. 12. 1898.

8. Robert Koldewey und Bruno Moritz auf dem »Nettuno« – 22. 12. 1898 – Robert Koldewey and
Bruno Moritz aboard the »Nettuno«

9. Blick auf Beirut – 23. 12. 1898 – View of Beirut

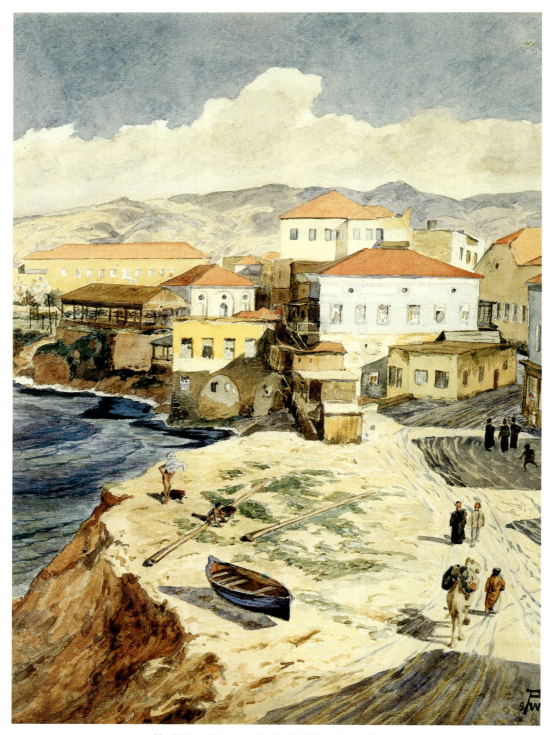

10. Blick auf Beirut – 23./26. 12. 1898 – View of Beirut

11. Ansicht von Nordosten – 28. 12. 1898 – View from the northeast

12. Abendstimmung über dem Libanon – 2. 1. 1899 –
Dusk over Lebanon

Baalbek

13. Baalbek. Am »Bacchus«-Tempel – 16. 1. 1899 – At the temple of Bacchus

14. Baalbek. »Bacchus«-Tempel – Jan. 1899 – Temple of Bacchus

15. Baalbek. Im Vorhof des »Jupiter Heliopolitanus-Tempel« – Jan. 1899 – In the forecourt of the temple of Jupiter Heliopolitanus

16. Baalbek. Bei der arabischen Bastion – 1. 1. 1899 – At the Arab bastion

17. Baalbek. Arabische Bastion. 1. Stock – 1. 1. 1899 – Arab bastion, first floor

18. Aleppo. Derwisch-Moschee Scheich Abu Bakr – Anfang/Beginning Febr. 1899 – Dervish mosque Sheikh Bakr

20. Aufweg zum Amanus-Gebirge. Path leading up the Amanus mountains

Iskenderun – 22. 1. 1899

19. Markt. Market

21. Baalbek. Der Wirt Perikli Mimikaki – 1. 1. 1899 –
The innkeeper Perikli Mimikaki

22. Aleppo. ʿAin at Tell: Drei Diplomaten. Frau Koch. R. Koldewey –
Anfang/Beginning of 1899 – ʿAin at Tell: Three diplomats, Mrs. Koch,
R. Koldewey

23. Derhafa – 10. 2. 1899

24. Euphrat bei Meskene – 11. 2. 1899 – The Euphrates at Meskene

Kalat Baalis (Barbalissus)

25. Qal 'at Baalis – 11. 2. 1899

KALAT DSCHABR B. ABU CHRERE. 12. 2. 1899. (EUPHRAT.)

26. Qal 'at Djabar – 12. 2. 1899

27. Tell Menachir – 14. 2. 1899

28. Euphrat bei Tibne – 15. 2. 1899 – The Euphrates at Tibne

29. Halebije. Byzantinisches Stadttor – 15. 2. 1899 – Byzantine city gate

30. Qal 'at ar-Rachba – 19. 2. 1899

31. Der Euphrat bei Dura Europos – 20. 2. 1899 – The Euphrates at Dura Europos

32. Ana. Ortseingang – 24. 2. 1899 – Entrance to the village

33. Ana. Von der Euphrat-Insel aus – 24. 2. 1899 – View from the Euphrates island

34. Euphrat unterhalb von Ana – 24. 2. 1899 – The Euphrates below Ana

35. Haditha – 26. 2. 1899

36. Hit – 28. 2. 1899

37. Baghdad. Bab el Tilism – 10. 3. 1899

38. Baghdad. Kathemein. Moschee – März 1899 – Mosque at Kadhimain

40. Gasse – 7. 3. 1899 – Alley

39. Khan Mirjan – 15. 3. 1899

Baghdad

41. Baghdad. Haus Berk. Innenhof – März 1899 – Berk house, inner court

42. Babylon, Kuweirisch. Von Osten – 1900 – From the east

43. Babylon, Kuweirisch. Dorfstraße – 1901 – Village street

44. Babylon, Kuweirisch. Dorfstraße nach Gewitter – 1900 – Village street after a thunderstorm

45. Babylon, Kuweirisch. Euphrat – 1901 – Euphrates

46. Babylon, Kuweirisch. Palmengarten – 1899 – Palm garden

47. Babylon, Kuweirisch. Koldeweys Reisezelt – 1899 – Koldewey's travelling tent

48. Babylon, Kuweirisch. Expeditionshaus vom Euphrat – 1899 – Expedition house seen from the Euphrates

49. Babylon. Expeditionshaus. Hof mit Funden – 1900 – Expedition house, courtyard with finds

50. Babylon, Kuweirisch. Expeditionshaus. Blick nach Süden — 1901 — Expedition house, view to the south

51. 1901

52. 1902

Babylon. Expeditionshaus. Hof – Expedition house, courtyard

53. Babylon. Expeditionshaus. Loggia im Obergeschoß – Sommer 1901 – Expedition house. Loggia on upper floor

54. W. Andrae in seinem Zimmer – 1899 – W. Andrae in his room

55. Auf dem Dach, Abendstimmung mit Mond – 1900 – On the roof, moonrise at dusk

Babylon. Expeditionshaus – Expedition house

56. Blick aus W. Andraes Fenster – 1899 – View from W. Andrae's window

57. Loggia im Obergeschoß – 1899 – Loggia on upper floor

58. Innenhof – 1927 – Inner court

59. Ansicht mit Euphrat – 1927 – View towards the Euphrates

Babylon, Kuweirisch. Expeditionshaus – Expedition house

60. Blick aus R. Koldeweys Fenster, nach Gewitter – 1901 – View from R. Koldewey's window, after a thunderstorm

61. Blick aus W. Andraes Fenster – 1899 – View from W. Andrae's window

Babylon. Kuweirisch. Expeditionshaus – Expedition house

62. Babylon. Schöpfwerk unter Christdorn – April 1900 – Water drawing device under a Spina Christi tree

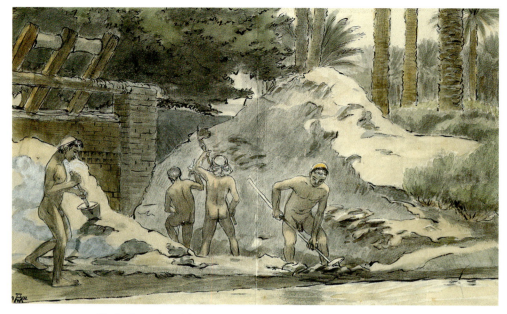

63. Säubern eines Schöpfwerkes – Cleaning of a water drawing device

64. Fischende Knaben – Boys fishing

Babylon. Euphrat – 1902 – Euphrates

65. Fischer – 1901– Fishermen

66. Am Fluß – 1900 – By the river

Babylon. Euphrat – Euphrates

67. Babylon. Morgendämmerung am Euphrat – 1900 – Dawn over the Euphrates

68. Babylon. Abendstimmung am Euphrat – 1901 – Dusk on the Euphrates

69. Babylon. Palmengarten – Julimorgen/July morning 1901 – Palm garden

71. Abendstimmung – 1901 – Dusk

Babylon. Euphrat – Euphrates

70. Beim Hügel Amran – 1902 – Near Amran hill

72. Islamische Grabbauten auf dem Hügel Amran – 1900 – Islamic tombs on Amran hill

73. Auf der Straße Baghdad–Hille, bei Babylon – 1901 – On the Baghdad–Hilla road near Babylon

Babylon

74. Kasr von Nordosten – Jan. 1900 – Kasr seen from the northeast

75. Schutthalde der Grabung – o. J. – Spoil heap of the excavation

Babylon

78. Grabungsarbeiter – 1900 – Excavation workmen

77. Dschum' a ibn Barakli – 1902

Babylon

76. Habib el Alaui – 1902

79. Babylon, Kuweirisch. Tanz der Männer – 1901 – Men's dance

80. Babylon. Erstes Bild des Löwen der Prozessionsstraße – 1899 – First representation of the lion of the Processional Way

82. Blick zum Ischtar-Tor – 1927 – View toward the Ishtar Gate

81. Blick zum Syrischen Saal – 1927 – View toward the Syrian Hall

Entwürfe für die Prozessionsstraße in Berlin – Drafts for the Processional Way in Berlin

83. Entwurf für die Rekonstruktion der Thronsaal-Fassade in Berlin – 1927 – Draft for the reconstruction of the facade of the throne room in Berlin

84. Entwurf für die Rekonstruktion des Ischtar-Tores in Berlin – 1927 – Draft for the reconstruction of the Ishtar Gate in Berlin

85. Babylon, Kasr. Nordwest-Ecke – etwa 1901 – Northwest corner

86. Von Osten, abends – 2. 6. 1902 – From the east, evening

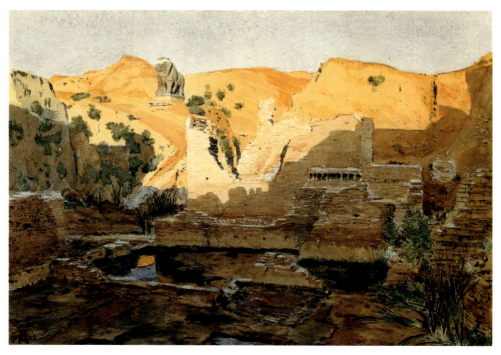

87. Grabung im Nordpalast sowie der »Löwe von Babylon« – 1902 – Excavation in the northern palace and the »Lion of Babylon«

Babylon. Kasr

88. Hügel Amran von Norden – Julimorgen 1902 – July morning – Amran hill from the north

89. Grabung im Ninmach-Tempel – 1901 – Excavation in the Temple of Ninmach

Babylon

90. Babylon. Hügel Babil von Südosten, frühmorgens – 22. 6. 1902 – Babil hill from the southeast, early morning

91. Borsippa – 1901

92. Imam Dschasim Karawanserai – 26. 3. 1901 – Caravanserai at Imam Jasim

94. Imam Dschasim. Kuppelgrab – 26. 3. 1901 – Domed tomb at Imam Jasim

93. Kfl. Kaffeestube – 1902 – Coffee house

95. Landeplatz am Euphrat – 27. 3. 1901 – Euphrates landing-place

96. Schiffsbrücke, Chan und Serail – 27. 3. 1901 – ›Pontoon bridge‹, Khan and Saray

Diwanije – Diwaniyeh

97. Euphrat oberhalb von Diwanije – 27. 3. 1901 – Euphrates above Diwaniyeh

98. Bei Afedsch – 29. 3. 1901 – Near Afedj

99. Ansicht von Osten – 1. 4. 1901 – View from the east

100. Blick vom Stadttor auf Pilgerweg und Gräber – 2. 4. 1901 – View from the city gate to the pilgrim's path and tombs

Nedschef – Najaf

101. Nedschef. Bazar und Moschee des Ali – 2. 4. 1901 – Bazaar and mosque of Ali

102. Kerbela. Moschee des Hussein – 4. 4. 1901 – Mosque of Hussein

104. Moschee des Abbas – Mosque of Abbas

Kerbela – 4. 4. 1901

103. Moschee des Hussein – Mosque of Hussein

105. 106. Bei Fara. Empfang im Mudif – 1903 – Reception in the Mudif

107. Kut el Amara. Landeplatz am Tigris – 1903 – Tigris landing-place

108. Indien. Stupa von Sandschi – 1903 – India. Stupa of Sanchi

109. Tadsch Mahal – Taj Mahal

110. Indraput

Indien – 1903 – India

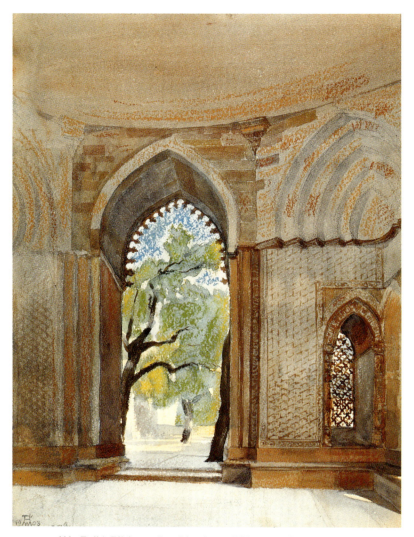

111. Delhi. Blick aus einer Moschee – 1903 – View from a mosque

112. Aden – 1903

113. Tigris. Enge Fatha, südlich von Assur – 1908 – Straits of Fatha, south of Assur

114. Assur. Nordfront von Osten – 1909 – North face from the east

115. Assur. Nordfront von Westen – 1909 – North face from the west

116. Blick nach Norden – etwa 1908 – View to the north

117. Blick nach Süden – etwa 1906 – View to the south

Assur

118. Tigris-Ufer – Dez. 1910 – Banks of the Tigris

119. Nach Osten abziehendes Gewitter – etwa 1909 – Thunderstorm retreating eastwards

Assur

120. Assur. Nach Süden abziehendes Gewitter – 1909 – Thunderstorm retreating southwards

121. Assur. Blick nach Süden. Abendstimmung – 1909 – View to the south, evening

122. Ziqqurrat, abends – 1909 – Ziqqurrat, evening

123. Wächterhütte, mittags – 1908 – Watchman's hut, midday

Assur

124. Arbeiterhäuser und Schutthalden am Tigris – Workmen's houses and spoil heaps on the Tigris

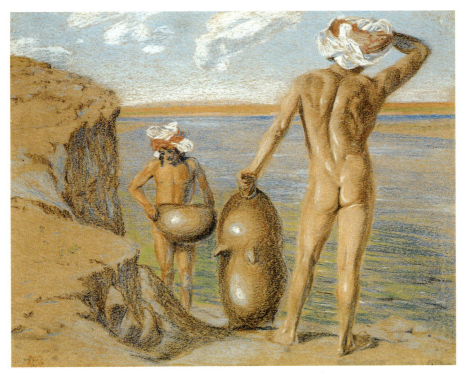

125. Schwimmer mit aufgeblasenen Ziegenbälgen – swimmers with inflated goat skins

Assur – 1906

126. Nordfront – Northern face

127. Aue nördlich von Assur – Water-meadow north of Assur

Assur. Rekonstruktionen – 1937 – Reconstructions

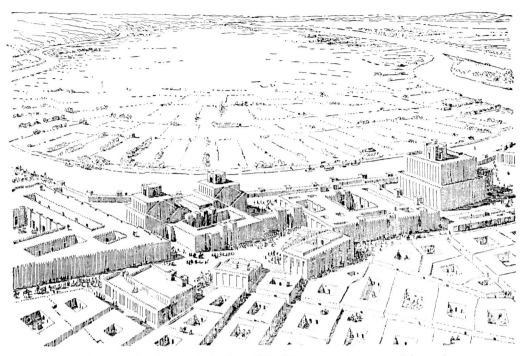

128. Blick über Assur nach Norden – 1937 – View accross Assur toward the north

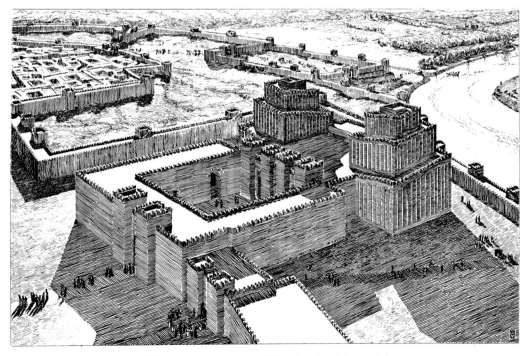

129. Anu-Adad-Tempel – 1908 – Temple of Anu-Adad

Assur. Rekonstruktionen – Reconstructions

130. Assur. Blick vom Festhaus zur Stadt. Rekonstruktion – 1923 – View from the festival hall toward the city, reconstruction

131. Assur. Blick zum Festhaus. Rekonstruktion – 1923 – View toward the festival hall, reconstruction

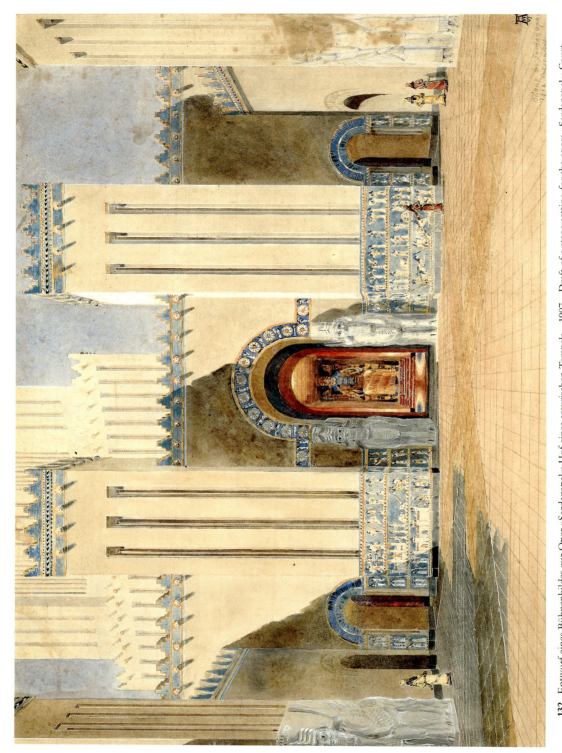

132. Entwurf eines Bühnenbildes zur Oper »Sardanapal«: Hof eines assyrischen Tempels – 1907 – Draft of a stage setting for the opera »Sardanapal«: Court of an Assyrian temple

133. Entwurf eines Bühnenbildes zur Oper »Sardanapal«: Schatzkammer – 1907 – Draft of a stage setting for the opera »Sardanapal«: Treasury

134. Assur. Expeditionshaus, Garten – 1912 – Expedition house, garden

135. Ansicht – View

136. Blick zum Sindschar-Gebirge – View toward the Sindjar mountains

Tell Afer – 5. 4. 1908

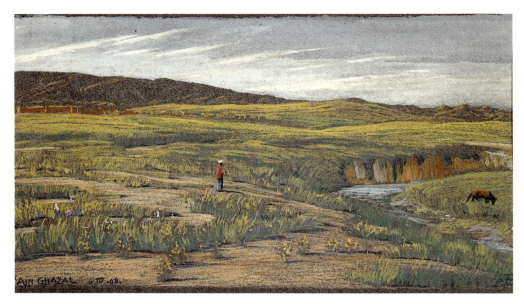

137. 'Ain Ghazal – 6. 4. 1908

138. Chabur bei Tell Schemsani – 8. 4. 1908 – Khabur near Tell Shemsani

139. Chabur bei Suar – 9. 4. 1908 – Khabur near Suar

140. Euphrattal bei Tibne – 11. 4. 1908 – Euphrates valley near Tibne

141. Basaltformationen bei Tibne – 11. 4. 1908 – Basalt formations near Tibne

142. Euphrat bei Tibne – 11. 4. 1908 – Euphrates near Tibne

143. Samos. Hafen von Vathi – 1908 – Vathi harbour

144. Istanbul. Am Goldenen Horn – 21. 6. 1917 – The Golden Horn

145. Istanbul. Am Goldenen Horn – 1915 – The Golden Horn

146. Istanbul. Blick auf Pera – 24. 12. 1915 – View toward Pera

147. Istanbul. Boulevard in Pera – 1918

148. Istanbul. Pera, Café-Garten – 19. 4. 1917 – Pera, café garden

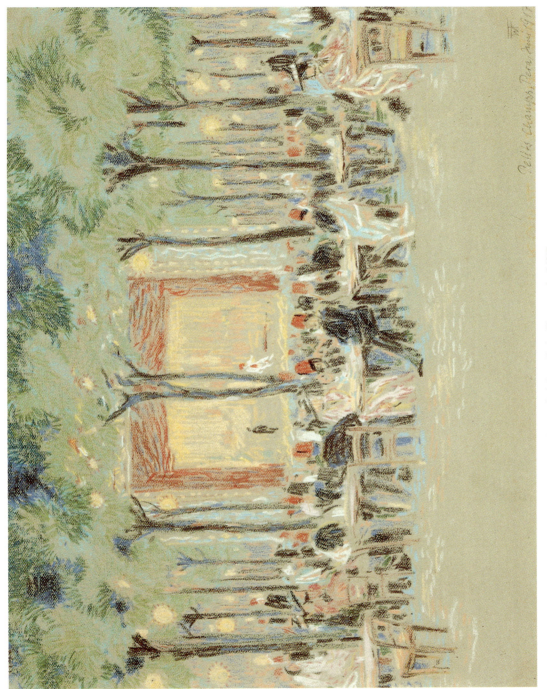

149. Istanbul. Pera. Petits Champs – Juni 1917

150. Istanbul. Vom Bosporus – 1912/1922 – View from the Bosporus

151. Afyon-Karahissar. Ansicht – 1916 – View

152. Im Taurus-Gebirge – 1918 – In the Taurus mountains

153. Am Golf von Iskenderun/Adana – 1917 – At the Gulf of Iskanderun/Adana

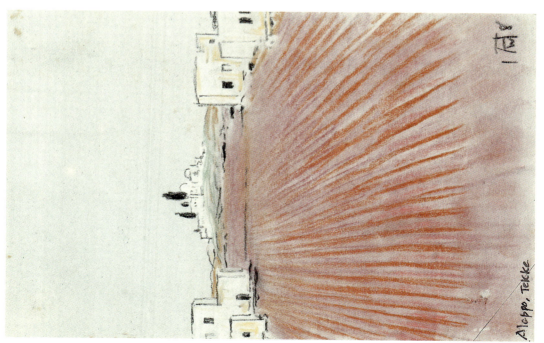

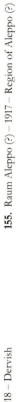

155. Raum Aleppo (?) – 1917 – Region of Aleppo (?)

154. Aleppo. Derwisch-Moschee Scheich Abu Bakr – 1918 – Dervish mosque Sheikh Abu Bakr

157. Hof eines Hauses – 1918 – Courtyard of a house

Aleppo

156. Madrasa al-Firdaus – 1917

158. Aleppo. Ansicht, abends – 1917 – Evening view

159. Dorf und Tell bei Aleppo – 1918 – Village and Tell near Aleppo

160. Aleppo. Am Quwaiq-Bach – 1918 – Quwaiq stream

161. Ansicht aus der Ferne – 1918 – View from a distance

162. Friedhof – 1917 – Cemetery

Aleppo

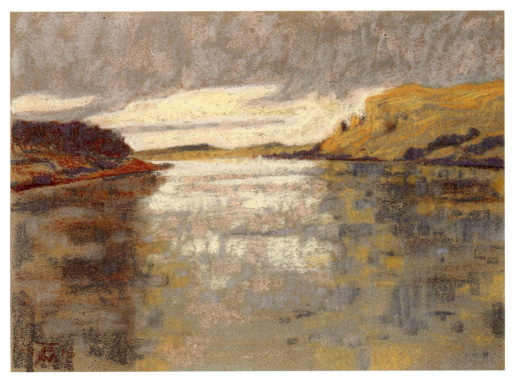

163. 164. Euphrat oberhalb Ana – 7. 2. 1916 – Euphrates above Ana

165. 166. Schöpfräder am Euphrat bei Suwije, tags und nachts – 11. 2. 1916 – Water wheels at the Euphrates near Suwije, by day and by night

167. Mossul. Hof des Deutschen Vize-Konsulates – 1917 – Courtyard of the German vice consulate

168. Schöpfrad bei Hama – 30. 12. 1917 – Water wheel near Hama

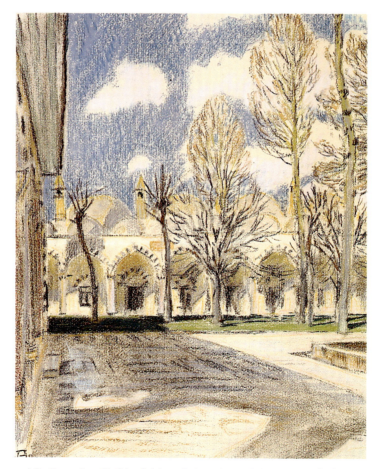

169. Damaskus. Hof der Suleimanije-Moschee – 1918 – Courtyard of the Sulaimaniyeh Mosque

170. Türkischer Troß – 1917 – Turkish camp followers

171. Blühende Orchideen, Frühling – 1918 – Orchids in bloom, spring

Yarmuktal – Yarmuk valley

172. Nazareth, von der Höhe aus – 23. 1. 1918 – Nazareth as seen from above

173. Weg zwischen Feigenkakteen in die Stadt –
Path to the town through prickly pears

174. In der Stadt – In the town

Nazareth – 1918

176. Nazareth. Minarett – 1917 – Minaret

175. Tiberias. Moschee – 1918 – Mosque

178. Blick zum Franziskanerkloster – 15. 1. 1918 – View toward the Franciscan monastery

Nazareth

177. Gasse in die Stadt – 19. 1. 1918 – Alley leading into town

180. Blühende Mandelbäume – Almond trees in blossom

Nazareth, Frühjahr – 1918 – Spring

179. Esel im Obstgarten – Donkey in an orchard

182. Auf dem Weg zur Marienkapelle – 1918 – On the road to the Chapel of the Virgin Mary

Nazareth

181. Pforte des Franziskanerklosters – Jan. 1918 – Gate of the Franciscan monastery

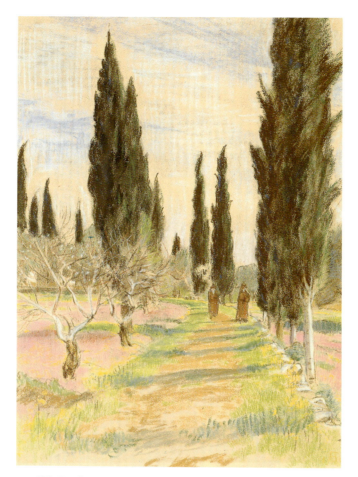

183. Im Garten des Franziskanerklosters – In the garden of the
Franciscan monastery

184. Dämmerung – Dusk

Nazareth – 1918

185. Am Franziskanerkloster – Frühling 1918 – At the Franciscan monastery

187. Omer, ein türkischer Soldat – Omer, a Turkish soldier

Portraits, Aleppo – 1918

186. Ein Kaufmann – A merchant

189. Ein Händler – A vendor

Portraits, Aleppo – 1918

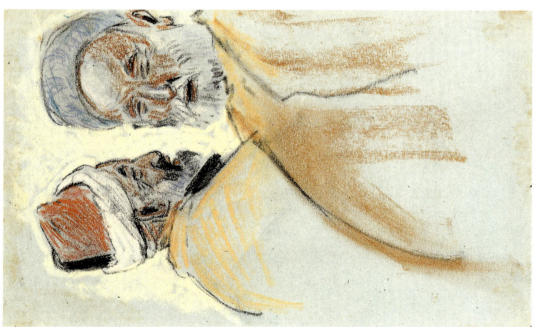

188. Zwei alte Männer – Two old men

190. Baghdad. Meißner Pascha – 1916/1917

191. Aleppo. Ein Kaufmann – 1918 – A merchant

Portraits

192. Aleppo. Flötender Derwisch – 1918 – Flute-playing dervish

193. Assur. Abdallah im Festgewand – 12. 8. 1906 – Abdallah in
festive dress

195. Dr. med. Ludwig Külz – 19. 6. 1916

Portraits, Baghdad – 1916

194. Kriegskamerad – Fellow soldier

197. Captain Moses von der »Patmos« – Captain Moses of the »Patmos«

Portraits – 1918/19

196. Bektaschi-Derwisch – Bektashi dervish

198. Die »Patmos« vor Haidar Pascha – 1918/19 – The »Patmos« at Haidar Pasha

199. Amq-Ebene. Kurdisches Bauernhaus – 1899 – Amq Plain. Kurdish farmhouse

200. Zwischen Abu Chrere und Hamamath. Minarett – 12. 2. 1899 – Between Abu Khrere and Hamamath. Minaret

201. Damaskus. Am Abend – Anfang/Beginning 1899 – Damascus. Evening

202. Qal'at ar-Rachba – 19. 2. 1899 – Qal'at ar-Rakhba

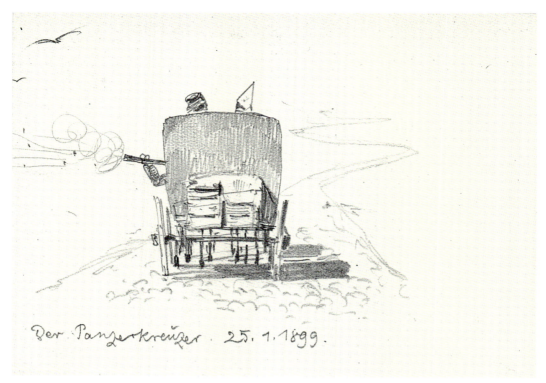

203. »Der Panzerkreuzer« unterwegs nach Aleppo – 25. 1. 1899 – »The Armoured cruiser« on the road to Aleppo

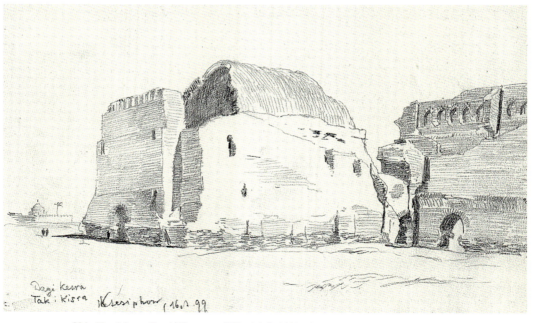

204. Ktesiphon. Taq i-Kisra von SW – 16. 3. 1899 – Taq i-Kisra from the south-west

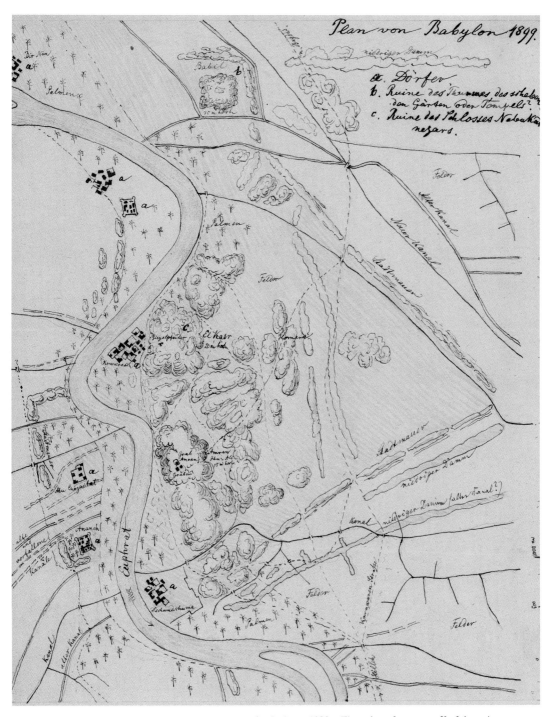

205. Babylon. Erster Plan nach Abschreiten der Ruine – 1899 – First plan after pace-off of the ruins

206. Euphrat und Hügel Babil nach Gewitter – 1899 – Euphrates and mound Babil after a thunderstorm

207. Arbeiter in der Grabung – 1900 – Workmen on the excavation

Babylon

208. Hügel Homera von N. – Mound Homera from the north

209. Das »Nilpferd«, W. Andraes Schimmel – The »Hippopotamus«, Andrae's grey horse

Babylon – 1902

210. Babylon. Rekonstruktion. Turm, Euphratbrücke und Marduk-Heiligtum – 1923 – Reconstruction. Tower, Euphrates bridge and Marduk sanctuary

211. Babylon. Rekonstruktion. Prozessionsstraße bei Nacht − 1923 − Reconstruction. Processional Way by night

212. Babylon. Blick aus W. Andraes Fenster – 1899 – View from W. Andrae's window

213. Basra. Auf dem Schatt al-Arab. Unfertig – 1903 – Along the Shatt al-Arab. Unfinished

215. Ein »assyrisches Königspaar« mit den Ausgräbern im Hof des Grabungshauses – A »royal Assyrian couple« with the excavators

Assur – o. J./undated ca. 1907/08

214. Blick über Tigris nach Gewitter – View over Tigris after a thunderstorm

216. Assur. »Die fröhlichen Assyrer« – Weihnachten/Christmas 1907 – »Assyrians« celebrating

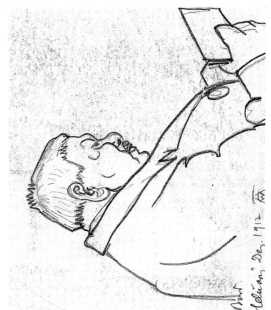

218. Passagier an Bord der Heluan – Dezember 1912 –
A passenger on board the Heluan

217. Aleppo. Hotel Baron. Der Wirt und sein Bruder – 1912 – The Baron hotel.
The landlord and his brother

219. Blick vom Assurtempel nach Süden – 1909 – View from the Assur temple looking south

220. Wasserbüffel im Auwald des Tigris – 1908 – Water-buffalo in a wooded meadow by the Tigris

Assur

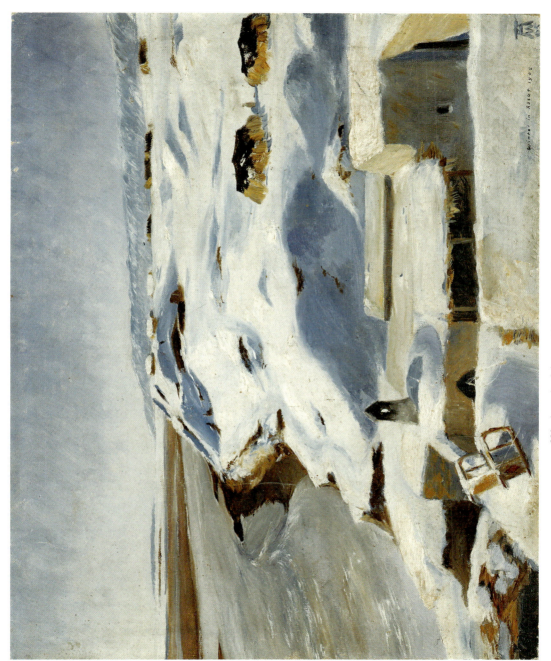

221. Assur im Schnee – 1905 – Assur in the snow

222. Euphrat südlich Meskene – 1908 – Euphrates south of Meskene

224. Keft Salame. Wasserträgerinnen – 1917 – Keft Salama.
Watercarrying women

Aleppo

223. Türkisches Bad – 1918 – Turkish bath

225. Aleppo. »Die bunten Damen« – 1917 – ›Gay ladies‹

226. Ruinen einer Schöpfradanlage (Na'ura) am Euphrat – 1916 – Ruins of a water-wheel (Na'ura) on the Euphrates

227. Tekke Mašad al-Husain, südl. Aleppo – Frühjahr/Spring 1918 – Tekke Mashad al-Husain, south of Aleppo

228. Tekke aš-Šaih Abu Bakr – 1918 – Takiya ash-Sheikh Abu Bakr

Derwischklöster – Derwish monasteries

229. Bei Hama – 21. 12. 1918 – Near Hama

230. Damaskus. Altstadt – 1918 – Damascus. Old city

232. Aleppo. Singender (?) Händler – 1918 – A merchant, possibly singing

231. Meißner-Pascha – 15. 7. 1918 – Meissner Pasha

233. Damaskus. In den Gärten am Barada-Bach – 1918 – Gardens by the Barada-stream

234. Blumen aus der Gegend von Nazareth – Frühling/Spring 1918 – Flowers from the Nazareth region

235. Baghdad. Zelte im spätabendlichen Palmenhain – 20. 2. 1917 – Tents in a palm-grove, late evening

236. Nazareth. Zypressen und Feigenkakteen – 19. 2. 1918 – Cypresses and prickly pears

237. Istanbul. Beikos am Bosporus – 26. 9. 1927 – Beikos on the Bosphorus

ERNST WALTER ANDRAE
RAINER MICHAEL BOEHMER

WALTER ANDRAE'S ORIENTAL SKETCHES

INTRODUCTION

It was on my first meeting with Walter Andrae's eldest son Ernst, who visited our Berlin Institute in the spring of 1988, that I learnt how many of Andrae's sketches and paintings were still in the family's possession. These pictures illustrate facets of Andrae's manifold achievement previously only known to scholars in the field of Oriental studies, and only then from a few examples. Pending the time they can all be made available to a wider audience, a representative collection of about two thirds of the total number is offered here.*

Thanks are due to Mr. E. W. Andrae for bringing together the family's collection, and not only giving permission for publication but also actively helping to make it possible. We are grateful also to Dr. Brandis and Dr. I. Stolzenberg, heads of the manuscript section of the National Library, (Staatsbibliothek) SPK, Berlin, and to Dipl.-Ing. D. Radicke, head of the plan collection of the Technical University, Berlin, who all gave permission to reproduce pictures in their collections. Further thanks are to the following: Mrs. Barbara Grunewald for her painstaking preparation of most of the

---

* Abbreviations:

Bell, AtA	Gertrude Lowthian Bell, Amurath to Amurath (1911)
Mem.	Walter Andrae, Lebenserinnerungen eines Ausgräbers (Memoirs of an Excavator) 1988, 2nd Edition.
Mem. 1st Ed.	Walter Andrae, Lebenserinnerungen eines Ausgräbers (Memoirs of an Excavator) 1961, 1st Edition.
MDOG	Mitteilungen der Deutschen Orientgesellschaft (Communications of the German Oriental Society)
RK	Walter Andrae, Babylon, Die versunkene Weltstadt und ihr Ausgräber Robert Koldewey (The Buried City of Babylon and its Excavator Robert Koldewey) 1952
Sarre-Herzfeld	Friedrich Sarre and Ernst Herzfeld, Archäologische Reise im Euphrat- und Tigris-Gebiet (Archaeological Travels along the Tigris and Euphrates) Vol. 1 1911, Vol. 2 1920, Vol. 3 1911.
SPK	Stiftung Preussischer Kulturbesitz (Prussian Cultural Foundation)
WVDOG	Wissenschaftliche Veröffentlichungen der Deutschen Orientgesellschaft (Research Publications of the German Oriental Society)

Ektrachromes used for the colour reproduction; Mr. B. Fischer of Offset-Repro-Technik (Berlin); Mr. D. Eckert and Dr. F. Redecker of Gebr. Mann Verlag (Berlin) for the carefully executed printing; and Mrs. Jane Moon for the English translation. I am especially grateful to Dr. Beate Salje for her patient professional editorial assistance with the layout and text.

I first encountered Walter Andrae in my first year as a student: an imposing, unbowed individual then in his late seventies. He used to attend evening lectures both in the Faculty of Architecture at the Technical University and at the German Archaeological Institute's heavily bomb-damaged main building in Maienstrasse in Berlin, which was finally demolished in the late fifties. He was able to follow slide-lectures, despite a serious handicap incurred in 1948 when he was 73. He damaged one eye chopping wood, and the other suffered subsequently from overstrain. And he could always add something worthwhile to the subsequent discussion and give a balanced opinion both on archaeological subjects or on general or specific matters, such as Lenzen's report during the winter of 1955/56 of the fighting between Arab factions from Larsa and Uruk.

A serious visual handicap! One can only guess what that must have meant to a man like Andrae – artist, painter, constant observer. But the strength of his personality withstood even this cruel stroke of fate, knowing as he did, from a lifetime of growing self-awareness, that suffering has its place in the process of maturity. As his external vision regressed, so his inner sight gained in strength. Of his many surviving sketches and paintings, those of the East make up the greatest number, along with ones of his home, from Bohemia, Austria, Italy and Portugal. Those published here make up a representative collection of the former. They have a certain historical significance, for much of what he saw no longer exists. Certain places have changed completely: Beirut and Iskenderun, for instance, which were small towns 90 years ago (Nos. 9, 10, 19, 20).

The pictures are mainly arranged chronologically. Thus this volume complements Andrae's own memoirs (henceforth Mem.) and the biography of his mentor Robert Koldewey, which Andrae published himself (W. Andrae, Babylon. Die versunkene Weltstadt und ihr Ausgräber Robert Koldewey ‹The Buried City of Babylon and its Excavator, Robert Koldewey› Berlin 1952). Both books are much invoked, and quoted, below. The chronological arrangement of the pictures also highlights Andrae's development as an artist.

It will be immediately obvious that Andrae was a genuine artist, not just an archaeologist. With an equal ability for drawing or watercolour (Mem., 77), he modestly considered himself a mere dilettante. There are many quickly-executed sketches (e.g. No. 39), used, when time allowed, to illustrate letters home (e.g. No. 40). He handled pencil, chalk, pen and brush with masterly facility. We have examples of landscape as well as animals and people, even portraits. Remarkable too is the strength of his imagination, which enabled him to produce such clear yet detailed pen-and-ink reconstructions. He breathed new life into the old city of Assur, recreating for the observer views or details of the otherwise unimpressive structural remains (cf. Nos. 126–131, and fig. 20).

While unemployed after the First World War Andrae devoted himself for a short while entirely to art, but then painted little subsequently. His professional publications are richly illustrated with splendidly drawn reconstructions of the kind already mentioned. These demonstrate the inner vision of the man to whom we owe not only the excavations at Assur (carried out under Spartan conditions) but also the Near Eastern section of the Berlin Museum and a whole generation of first-class scholars of architecture. Most prominent among the latter is his pupil and successor to the Chair of Architectural History at the Berlin Technical University, Ernst Heinrich. His appreciation of Andrae, reproduced below (p. 133ff.), is one of the best. It brings out in particular his role as a major exponent of the well known 'Koldewey School' of architectural research.

R.M.B.

WALTER ANDRAE
18. 2. 1875–28. 7. 1956

Life and Work

'He was the excavator of Assur. He set up the Near Eastern Section of the State Museums (Staatliche Museen Berlin).'

This is the most succinct epitaph to Andrae, his own words, written in 1956, the year of his death.

Childhood and Youth 1875–1893

Andrae began his life during the last quarter of the 19th century. He was born in Leipzig on the 18th February 1875, the son of a railway engineer. His father, who was for several years in charge of the building of a bypass railroad, was well known in bourgeois circles in Leipzig, and was popular as a virtuoso piano player, singer, and amateur actor. He ended his days as director of the State Railway of Saxony. So from this bourgeois background Andrae began his education in the humanities at the Chemnitz and Grimma Grammar School, and after a year of military service went on to study architecture at the Technical College in Dresden. His artistic talent dates from his earliest years, but received little encouragement while he was at school.

Student Years 1893–1898

The further development of his gift for drawing was much influenced by the artists Andrae met during his studies at the Technical College in Dresden. He mentions the draughtsmen and engravers Otto Greiner and Max Klinger,[1] exponents of the 'Jugend-stil' (Youth-Style) and admired and imitated them. His sister Elisabeth,[2] who later executed the great paintings of Assur, Uruk and Boğazköy for the permanent exhibition at the Near Eastern Museum, was studying at the Academy of Art in Dresden. This provided an entrée to the students and teachers there.

The teachers Andrae mentions are Cornelius Gurlitt (History of Architecture),[3] Karl Weißbach,[4] Ernst Giese[5] and Paul Wallot.[6] Gurlitt encouraged his pupils to sketch the Baroque buildings of Dresden and Vienna: the more serious side of studying architecture. Paul Wallot, the man entrusted with the construction of the 'Reichstag' (Parliament) in Berlin, showed his student how to handle great building mass, at any rate on the drawing board. Andrae admired Wallot. This was the background to his preparation for the state examination for Master Architect (Dipl. Ing.), which he passed with distinction after eight terms. He had been in practice for a few weeks in a government office when his student friend and future brother-in-law Paul Ehmig sent him a newspaper advertisement: 'Draughtsman wanted for expedition to the Near East'. At the time Andrae was engaged in designing an equipment depot for a forestry bureau, while just a few weeks before he had been commended in his exam for his plan of a County Hall conceived on a grander scale than Wallot's 'Reichstag'. He applied at once for a place on Koldewey's Babylon Expedition, and was chosen from sixteen candidates.

His father, concerned for his son's career, strongly advised him against giving up his 'safe' civil service appointment. Later on (in 1903 and 1908), when Andrae was on leave in Europe, his father tried to retrieve him from excavation in the East to work in an architects' practice in Germany.

On the 12th December 1898 Koldewey and Andrae set sail from Trieste on the 'Cleopatra', of Lloyd's Austrian line, and after a stopover in Alexandria (No. 4) reached Port Said (No. 5) on the 20th. There they changed to the 'ancient Syrian coaster 'Nettuno', another of Lloyd's', which conveyed them and Bruno Moritz of the Khedive's Library in Cairo via Jaffa (Nos. 6–8) and Haifa to Beirut (Nos. 9–10).

---

1 Otto Greiner, painter, lithographer, engraver, 16. 12. 1869 – 24. 9. 1916, see Allgemeines Lexikon der Bildenden Künstler von der Antike bis zur Gegenwart (General Lexikon of Fine Artists from Ancient Times to the Present). Founded by Ulrich Thieme and Felix Becker (henceforth abbreviated 'Thieme-Becker'). Vol. 14 (1921) 588 f. – Max Klinger, graphic artist, painter, sculptor, 18. 2. 1857–5. 7. 1920, see ibid. 20 (1927) 513 ff.

2 Elisabeth Andrae, landscape painter and lithographer, 3. 8. 1876 – May 1945, Thieme-Becker 1 (1907) 442; H. Vollmer, Künstlerlexikon des 20. Jahrhunderts (Lexikon of 20th Century Artists) 1953, 47; L. Jakob-Rost – E. Klengel – R.-B. Wartke – J. Marzahn, Das Vorderasiatische Museum (The Near Eastern Museum) 1987, 61 Fig. 56 (Same as E. Andrae before her picture of the 'King's Gate' at Boğazköy-Ḫattuša).

3 *Cornelius* Gustav Gurlitt, 1. 1. 1850–25. 3. 1938, art-historian, Professor and Doctor, see Otto Schubert, Neue deutsche Biographie (New German Biography) 7 (1966) 327 ff.

4 *Karl* Robert Weißbach, 8. 4. 1841–8. 7. 1905, architect, Professor, see Thieme-Becker 35 (1942) 22.

5 Ernst Giese, 16. 4. 1832–12. 10. 1903, architect, Professor, see Thieme-Becker 14 (1921) 5.

6 Paul Wallot, 26. 6. 1841–10. 8. 1912, architect, Professor and Doctor, Assistant Development Councillor and Assistant Privy Councillor, see Thieme-Becker 35 (1942) 103 f.

Fig. 1 Walter Andrae, Babylon. Self-portrait, 1902

Babylon 1899–1903

Andrae (Fig. 1) was quite unqualified to serve at the side of someone as experienced in architectural research as Robert Koldewey. The latter remarked on this in connection with the planning of Baalbek (Nos. 11–17, 21), which they undertook at the behest of Kaiser Wilhelm II. He wrote thus to his friend Otto Puchstein in early January 1899: 'I wish we were together again like at the temples in Sicily. Here I have an innocent lad who can't tell a post-hole from a fox-hole. Though he does paint and draw most enchantingly.'[7]

From Baalbek back to Beirut, from there by boat to Alexandretta (Nos. 19–20), modern Iskenderun, which they reached on 22nd January 1899, then on to Aleppo (Nos. 18, 22), to arrive three days later (see MDOG 1, 1898/1899, 10).

Martha Koch, wife of the German trader Karl Koch (compare catalogue entry for Nos. 22 and 160), gave them every conceivable assistance, as she was to again in 1915 and 1916, when she helped the 'completely helpless German General Staff to get to Baghdad'. 'The people of Aleppo wanted nothing to do with the mighty gentlemen, but they would do anything for Frau Koch' (Mem., 229). She also had the courage to speak up for the Armenians, even to the German High Command, to von Falkenhayn himself. But this is all looking ahead. Andrae has left us only a back view of this exceptional lady (No. 22). On the 8th February they started on the 26-day caravan trek to Baghdad (Nos. 23–41, figs. 2–4), and arrived on the 5th March. Andrae's apprenticeship had begun.

Koldewey's route down the Euphrates took in two previously unexplored ruins: Halebiyeh (ancient Zenobia – No. 29, Fig. 3), and Islahiyeh – Khan Kalessi (ancient Dura Europos, (Nr. 31).[8] Koldewey and Andrae surveyed the ruins systematically, making a provisional plan. This was the junior partner's first practical experience of planning in Mesopotamia. Andrae made an almost daily record of the then desert wastes of parts of the Euphrates valley in pencil and watercolour (Nos. 23–36), just as he had done the landscapes of the Mediterranean and Baalbek. In Babylon Koldewey introduced him to the kind of drawing required on an archaeological site: 'I learnt something special from Koldewey: how to make the surface of our prosaic-looking mound appear three-dimensional to the observer, as though the sun were shining from the south-east. The uninitiated often call this over-fussy, even artificial. To us it seemed essential, for this ground-surface represents the latest, the present day phase of the ruins of Babylon.

The important thing about Koldewey's way of representing landscapes and buildings is not his shading but the way everything was drawn from nature. Triangulation points were joined up indoors, but everything else was drawn from life. This is the only way to avoid the sources of error which inevitably occur when sketches executed outside are brought home to 'fill in'. We hated topographical maps and drawings of ruins which were shadeless and flat, however perfectly correct.

Once everything had been incorporated into our grid-system, excavation could begin at the right spot on this surface landscape. Then building remains began to appear. These too were represented as under a south – eastern light, throwing shadows the length of their height.

---

7 Mem. 34, after C. Schuchhardt, Ernste und heitere Briefe aus einem Archäologenleben (Serious and Not-so-serious Letters from a Life in Archaeology), 1925.

8 See Catalogue No. 31.

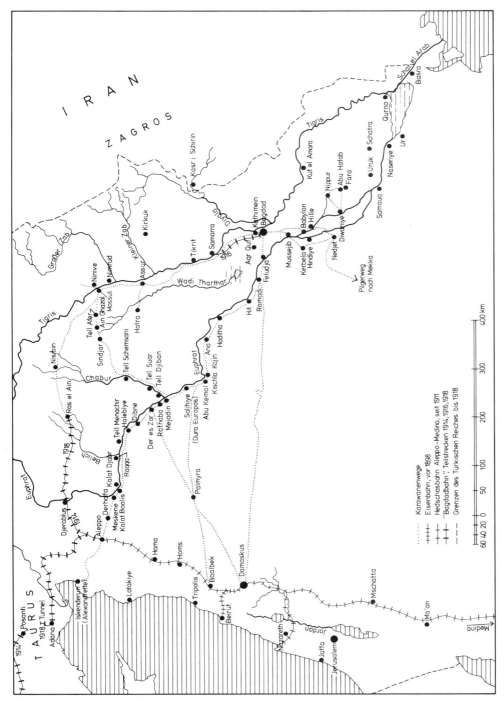

Fig. 2 Mesopotamia and Syria/Palestine according to a map of 1918

Fig. 3 Halebiyeh, 15. 2. 1899

Anyone looking at illustrations treated in this way can take in the whole situation at a glance. The method is adhered to on all German excavations in Iraq.'[9]

The excavation assembled in Babylon on 22. 3. 1899 (Nos. 42–90, Fig. 5). Here Andrae was to learn from Koldewey how to excavate. The result is not easily surpassed by anyone in breadth or depth, spatially or spiritually. Soon the twenty-four year old architect was aware that this initiation was a twist of fate away from architecture *per se* towards architectural research. It was to shape his whole life. In old age he looked back on the first couple of years at Babylon, and saw himself as an acolyte being initiated into the secrets of historical research. The 'Koldewey School' was born, and with it scientific excavation in Mesopotamia.

When work began in Babylon Koldewey gave his assistant a task which was to pervade the rest of his life – indeed to become his life's work.

Koldewey began his excavation on the Kasr mound (Nos. 85–87), where numerous fragments of glazed brick were to be found, still brightly coloured. They indicated the presence of some lost, shattered, major work of art .[10] It was relatively easy to see what many of these pieces were meant to be from the designs in relief that they bore. They represented dragons and bulls the same as the unglazed baked-brick reliefs unearthed

---

9 Mem. 78 f.
10 See Catalogue No. 80.

Fig. 4 East of Kishla Kaeen, 22. 2. 1899

on the foundations of the Ishtar Gate. But there were also bits of coloured brick, with and without relief, from the area of the Processional Way and the Palace Court. They did not match the bull and dragon figures, and it was Andrae's job to discover what they did mean. After a year of patiently piecing them together he met with success (compare the backgrounds of Nos. 2 and 80). The lions of the Processional Way with their rosette decorations, the lions of the Throne Room facade with their floral tendrils and palmette decoration were found. Twenty seven years later, after negotiations with the Iraqi authorities, Andrae managed to bring about 300,000 of these coloured brick fragments back to Berlin.[11]

Koldewey soon had complete confidence in his assistant. Otherwise he would never have trusted him, twenty years younger as he was, with the direction, in turn, of excavations at Babylon, Borsippa (Birs Nimrud – No. 91, Fig. 5), and Fara (compare Fig. 6). And in 1901 that was what he did.

These 'subsidiary excavations' began with Birs Nimrud. Koldewey and Andrae took it in turn to direct there and at Babylon.[12] Only a year later (1902), Andrae found himself installed alone at Fara, and had to exercise what he had learnt from Koldewey about leadership.[13] Fara was a long way from such rudiments of modern civilisation as could be found in the towns of Mesopotamia, such as police, administrative authority, post and telegraph. He lived among a population as yet quite untouched by such monuments to progress. There were conflicts occasioned by the greedy importunities of tribal and ancestral leaders, transmitted to the workforce, who were obliged to support them.[14] The Europeans had to keep in with the sheikhs at all costs. These conflicts at Fara and Assur are detailed by both Andrae and Koldewey – and their outcomes. The effect for the modern reader is quite comical: both authors took pains to describe hardship in an amusing fashion. At Fara and Assur they found themselves with people to whom a careless fatal shooting accident could lead to a blood feud, an insulting word or gesture to hot-blooded and unpredictable fighting. As he had in Fara, Andrae exerted gentle but firm, even-handed authority over such dissensions, bloodless or otherwise, which took place among his workforce. His was an authority not based on power. Later incidents at Assur, also not bloodless, proved this point. They took place under the very noses of the armed police, who as representatives of the Turkish State, were supposed to be protecting the archaeologists.

Neither Koldewey nor Andrae ever said what it was that enabled them to co-exist so peacefully with Arab peasants and bedouin over the course of decades. Their long,

---

11 See below p. 122 ff.

12 See RK 149 ff., Mem. 91 ff., 96 ff. and Catalogue No. 91; also R. Koldewey, Die Tempel von Babylon und Borsippa (The Temples of Babylon and Borsippa), WVDOG 15 (1911).

13 RK 195. Andrae later handed over the results and finds of the Fara excavation to Ernst Heinrich to work on, see E. Heinrich, Fara (1931).

14 R. Koldewey, MDOG 15, 1902, 8 ff. (for description of living conditions, 18 ff.); MDOG 16, 1902/3, 9 ff.; W. Andrae, ibid. 16 ff. 24 ff.; MDOG 17, 1903, 4 ff. (for description of living conditions, 18 ff.); A. Nöldecke, ibid. 35 ff., RK 153 ff., Mem. 112 ff., 123 ff.

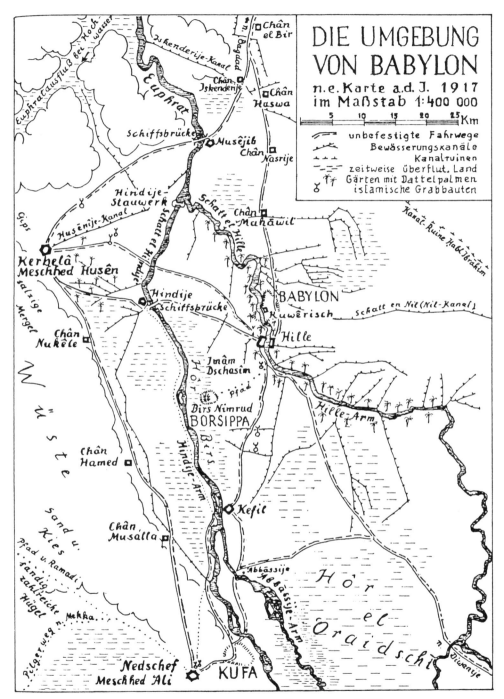

Fig. 5 Environs of Babylon, according to a map of 1917

almost unbroken presence in the country made them familiar with language and custom. Was that enough? Both tactfully observed the local customs, apart from religious observances. Trust and integrity were the real cause.

Both before and after the Second World War the German Expeditions to Warka had reason to appreciate the help of Ismain ibn Jasim (far right, Fig. 9).[15] In 1904 he accompanied Andrae as a young man from Babylon to Assur as his servant. In 1914, after the end of the excavation, he returned to his home town of Hilla. In 1915, when Andrae found himself back in Mesopotamia as an army officer, Ismain re-appeared at once. Until 1918 he followed Andrae like a shadow through all the dangers and vicissitudes of wartime, up the Tigris and Diyala, and in Syria and Palestine. He functioned not only as servant but as mentor, and kept Andrae from a lot of trouble. And he did so of his own free will, for as an Arab he was not obliged to serve in the Turkish army. A lifetime friendship developed.

Apart from dealing with the coloured brick-fragments Andrae's work at Assur encompassed much of the city plan and the Marduk Temple.[16]

At the same time he remained faithful to his 'hobby', his watercolours and drawings. The gift of precise representation is evident here as well, and means that the pictures are in a sense records too. Here in Babylon his study of colour and experimenting with it began. In his memoirs he documents for us his eventual transition from draughtsman to fully-fledged painter, as demonstrated in his later pictures. He modestly considered his Oriental sketches as the dabblings of a dilettante.[17]

---

15 See H. J. Lenzen, UVB 22 (1966) 8 f. – The Baghdad Department of the German Archaeological Institute has a bronze bust of Ismain ibn Jasim, done in 1955 by Peter Steyer. See Mem. 154 f., 264 ff. – 154 f.:
'Getting on with the servants at the Expedition House did not require great diplomatic skill. It only worked half as well as it did because most of these people were naturally good-natured, some quite exemplary. Thus in particular was my dear Ismain, who as a landowner and merchant still depends on me, though we have not been able to see each other for 20 years. The following anecdote will serve to demonstrate the relationship between us: One day he came to my door as usual, his hands folded across his chest, and said: ›Master, today a son has been born to you. What should he be called?‹ I gave him the name Ali, and from then on that was what he was called, and he gave his father Ismain 16 grandsons, of whom 10 are still living and are a great joy to their grandfather, especially the youngest. And all the grandchildren know all there is to know about the German excavations and about us. At Assur too Ismain was indispensable as arbitrator in Arab disputes, which sometimes raged right up our very door. We knew from him exactly which of the people out there we could trust, and which not. They were very variable.
There is also more to tell about Ali ibn Ismain. At the time that Ali needed a cradle, my genuine Dresden untanned leather case had got damp and acquired the form of a Japanese roof. It could not be closed any more, having got wet on the journey. Ismain had his eye on it. At his suggestion it was torn apart at the hinges, and Ali used the one half to swing in until he was big enough to walk. The other half found employment too, but not at Ismain's hands. Still today I am aware of a sin of omission: I forgot to ask after Ali's mother. That might however have been the correct thing to do in Arab terms: only man and son count!'
Ismain joined the Uruk-Expedition during the last ten years of his life, see Lenzen, op. cit. His son Ali took over his position as commissar to the excavation. He was awarded the Cross of the Order of Merit of the Federal Republic of Germany (Bundesverdienstkreuz am Bande) on 16. 12. 1981, his father's service also being taken into account. Ali ibn Ismain died in Hilla on 20. 2. 1985.
16 See R. Koldewey, Die Tempel von Babylon und Borsippa (The Temples at Babylon and Borsippa), WVDOG 15 (1911) 37 ff.
17 See below p. 104 (after Mem. 77).

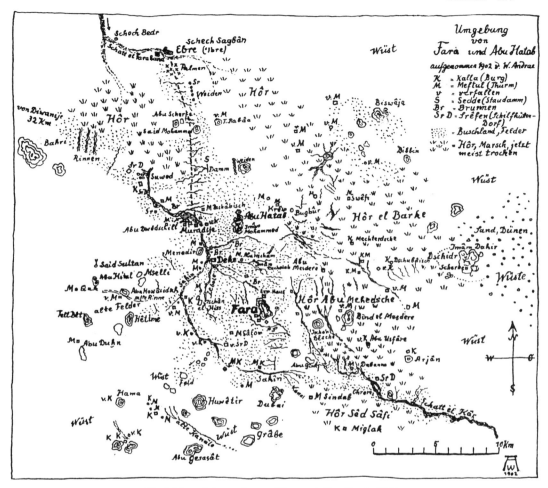

Fig. 6 Map of the environs of Fara and Abu Hatab, 1902

These remarks on his apprenticeship have a bearing on a question he asked himself in old age: What was our approach to religion while at Babylon? 'Although we were surrounded by religious practice I ceased to pay much attention to the religion I had practised myself in youth. It had vanished. What had taken its place? Was it really just a vacuum?'[18] 'Was that the only reason Koldewey advised me to read Schopenhauer, to fill the gap? I did so, not because I felt there was a gap to fill, but because I thought he must know better. It was something to study in peace, Schopenhauer and his world of Will and Imagination, a true bachelor's philosophy!

18 Mem. 75 ff.

These readings meant as little to me from the religious point of view as glances at Immanuel Kant's 'Dreams of a Spirit-seer Illustrated by Dreams of Metaphysics (Träume eines Geistersehers. Erläutert durch Träume der Metaphysik)', and his various critics, whose overlong sentences put me off more and more.'[19] 'By my second year in Babylon a more fundamental and less philosophical light dawned on me: colour, which Goethe called 'the experiences and sufferings of light', and form – the shapes that nature places before our eyes for us to wonder at. I felt almost as thought this revelation had been bestowed upon me as a complete substitute for religion.

There was something of a celebratory inspiration about the manifestations of Nature's colours on my page. On my free Sundays, after a hard six-day working week, I liked to get away from the ruins into the open country, to the palm groves or the river bank, to the green or golden fields. There I gradually acquired an affinity with the strange beauty of the apparently formless tells, in which the practised eye could see much that was hidden. With increasing confidence, I like to visit the groves of lanky palm trees, which I had not dared attempt to try and capture for a whole long year. Various setbacks had beset me in the meantime. First of all the standard four weeks of debilitating dysentery; the local Baghdad boils, for which there was then no cure but to put up with them for twelve months; and of course work on the wonderful coloured Babylonian lions, which held me in thrall day and night for all of a year. In the second year a new regime began: six days of planning on the mound, measuring and drawing and minute detailing of the brickwork of the excavated walls, and of course the daily round of excavation tasks, observing progress and results. The free Sundays, revelling in colour, were an effective tonic. More effective than reading. The remedy was fresh and healthy. I can recommend it to anyone gifted in the same unusual fashion as I. I remembered my studies with Erwin Oehme[20] in Dresden. Now I was faced with quite different problems of rendering colour from those at home. What unsettled me for a long while was the intense light, which could not even be mastered by the use of contrast. So it was no great feat to paint at dawn and sunset, without direct sunlight, however pretty the colours might be. No! We also want to treat the much, much longer scorching day with its brilliant sunshine! How could it be done? Most artists of the East fail this test. I believe I only succeeded rarely. A trained artist would have painted differently. My works are amateurish and have but a certain dilettante value. They do, however, bear witness to the joys and sorrows of an artist: that I can honestly maintain.'[21]

'Dear Reader, you would be wrong to suppose that painting meant more to me than research and draughtsmanship. I would liken it more to the wild herbage around the edge of our native cornfields, running by the side of the roads and paths which the har-

---

19 Unpublished, form a passage omitted in Mem.

20 Erwin Ernst E. Oehme, landscape and genre painter (among others pupil of Ludwig Richter), 18. 9. 1831–10. 10. 1907, see Thieme-Becker 25 (1931) 566.

21 Mem. 76 f.

vest wagon travels. This wild herbage includes all the good healing plants which attend to our health. I could also describe my painting as a 'by-product', though I find the term less sympathetic. It reminds me too much of the chemical industry, whose 'by-products' can have more that is of harmful nature than useful medicaments, and which are most often linked with the most depraved of poisonous and explosive substances. I have learnt to distrust them. If, dear reader, your opinion differs from mine, you may prefer this metaphor to that of the herbage. I do not.

Following what I consider to be a healthy instinct, I have not attempted in my water-colours to be slavishly true to nature in form or colour in the way of a colour photograph. The emotional content of the motifs and the sympathetic juxtaposition of the colours are the essential points, after a natural rendering of the perception of my senses. As I never became a true master, I remained faithful to my early ambition. If the pictures had transcended nature, had achieved 'mastery' in Goethe's sense of the word, despite being true to nature's laws, then they might have impressed the observer as being somehow larger than life. As it was, this one or that happened to please this person or that, each being judged on its merits. For my own part I found they took me back instantly to the time of their creation. They could not do the same for anyone else, even someone who had visited all the same places. This observation belongs to the realm of quest for self-awareness, and deserves to be included here.'[22]

These reminiscences from old age demonstrate how Andrae himself viewed his artistic creativity. Anyone who knows the country where Andrae did his drawing and painting is familiar with the special problem he describes. It creates particular difficulty for the artist, and can in fact be inferred from the pictures: the great intensity of the light. The unrelenting glare of the daylight, together with the dust in the atmosphere (absent only during rain) makes the countryside almost colourless. A single colour dominates: the earth colour of the desert, which engulfs the greens of the river-banks just as it does the human settlements. It conceals colour, which only emerges under particular conditions. The minute the light is subdued, morning, evening, by approaching or retreating thunder, by cloud, rain, or even by nocturnal phenomena, then colour re-appears, to the enchantment of the artist.

Andrae tried to capture these fleeting manifestations of colour, and it was not easy. The right conditions never lasted long, neither in the atmosphere nor on the ground. Near the northern tropic twilight is very short, lasting for less time it takes to execute a watercolour. The colours of retreating thunder-clouds vanish quickly. Even moisture after rain, which greatly enhances the hues of plants and earth, disappears fast with the sun's returning heat, and with it, the colours.

In a letter to his parents of 11. 6. 1899 Andrae mentions a further problem:

'Sometimes I do a little watercolour painting, but only in the evenings, when the hard, dry wind has let up. The colours dry up with extraordinary speed, so one must

---

22 From an unpublished early draft of Mem.

paint very quickly. Ink drawing is quite impossible, as the ink dries onto a fine pen as soon as it leaves the pot, and the pot itself stays moist only for a short time.'

Meanwhile the propensity for charicature which first manifested itself during his schooldays at Grimma had not been lost.[23] One need only glance at the Babylon Expedition's unpublished visitors' book, in which Andrae added a humorous margin-sketch to every entry from 1900 to 1902. Later on, in the State Museums at Berlin, particular circumstances prompted him to sarcastic or sartirical illustration, as for instance the long-standing feud among scholars over how and where the Pergamon Altar should be displayed. It should be said, though, that there are few examples of one-sided charicatures, just designed to make the observer laugh. More frequent are expressions of a life-long tendency to see the funny of human experience – including his own – and to capture it in a few humorous strokes, with or without accompanying verse. Grete Güterbock-Auer remarked upon this facility in respect of her children:

'While telling a story he could illustrate it as he went along, with quick, lively sketches, wonderfully humorous in expression and movement. He gave them a number of children's books made specially for them, not excessively childish, nor excessively whimsical, with glorious colours and drawings. He not infrequently used my eldest boy's own attempts at poetry as text to put pictures to. He also illustrated fairy-tales in a charming manner, and occasionally tried to get them published, without the success he deserved.'[24]

When Andrae had been a practising archaeologist for five years, Koldewey made over to him the excavations at Assur.

At Babylon (1899–1903) Andrae concentrated on watercolours. At Assur (1904–1914) he used this technique but rarely, and worked mainly in coloured crayon on tinted paper. At this stage he found that the use of a coloured background made it easier for him to represent the mood of nature.

Assur 1904–1914

In 1903 Andrae went on leave, obliged to do military service in Germany (Fig. 7). He chose to return via India (Nos. 108–111). His fairly comfortable six-week journey by rail and sometimes ox-cart, staying in hotels, official European rest-houses, and as guest of a Maharajah, took him in search of a goal which the architect in him had chosen. He wanted to pay homage to the Islamic architecture of the Mogul emperors at Delhi, Agra and Bijapur, to the Hindu temples at Tanjor, Trichinopli and Madura, to the Buddhist ones of Ceylon, to the oldest visible shrines: the Stupa of Sanchi, the Ice Pillar of Ashoka, the cave temples of Karli and Ellora.

---

23 See Mem. Fig. 3.

24 J. Renger, in: Deutsches Archäologisches Institut, Berlin und die Antike, Aufsätze, (German Archaeological Institute, Berlin and Antiquity, Essays). W. Arenhövel and C. Schreiber ed. (1979) 187.

In his memoirs Andrae examines the significance of this Indian experience, and felt nothing of the old spirituality.[25] He did not come into close contact with the Indian people. He found that his encounter with India was premature, and that he had gone through it like a sleepwalker. However, as a constructive element in his life, he considered it in retrospect to have had a fundamental effect.

In April 1904 Andrae rode from Damascus across the desert via Palmyra, across the Euphrates to the Jebel Sinjar and on to Mosul. There he embarked on a kelek (raft) to Qal'at Shargat, ancient Assur (Nos. 113–134, Fig. 8). Koldewey, who had already begun work there in 1903, had now returned to Babylon.

When Andrae took on the directorship of excavations at Assur, he felt much too young for the task (No. 1). However, supported by the confidence of Koldewey and his colleagues (Fig. 10), he made a complete success of it. He found it totally fulfilling, even after actual excavation finished in 1914. Over and over again he reviewed the work from different points of view and sought not only to make the most of what had been found, but to bring a present-day relevance to the results. In the process he had to put up with numerous tribulations and to overcome difficulties compared with which the sufferings which cause sighs among modern archaeologists are mere irritations. There was then no major town, no doctor, no grocer's store within easy reach. It took two days to get to Mosul, between five and seven to get to Baghdad. They lived like the local people of Shargat, on bread from their grain, on meat from their sheep, and fish from the Tigris. That is, as long as drought or locusts had not destroyed the crops (c. f. e. g. No. 134). In times of need Andrae had to send out caravans to obtain grain for the people of Shargat.

There was no real precedent for the excavations at Assur. The experience of Babylon was only of limited relevance. Here one encountered older levels than those at Babylon, where the ground-water prevented access to lower levels. New methods had to be found to penetrate deeper places, and Andrae was the first to conduct a careful stratigraphic excavation in Mesopotamia. This later allowed him to draw exemplary sophisticated conclusions such as the relationship between the archaic and the later Ishtar temples.[26] The French archaeologist André Parrot remarked in this connection that Andrae came to surpass his master, Koldewey.[27] Andrae would not have agreed. He considered

25 Mem. 130 ff.

26 W. Andrae, Die archaischen Ischtar-Tempel in Assur (The Archaic Ishtar Temples at Assur), WVDOG 39 (1922); idem, Die jüngeren Ischtar-Tempel in Assur (The Later Ishtar Temples at Assur), WVDOG 58 (1935).

27 A. Parrot, Archéologie mésopotamienne, Les Étapes (Mesopotamian Archaeology. Main developments.). (1946) 214:
'Nevertheless one can hardly overemphasize with what mastery W. Andrae directed his expedition. During an age when a technique was still being sought it was impossible to do better in any field, excavation or interpretation, and the excavator of Assur was an amazing precursor. This is not to detract from Koldewey, only to say that the pupil surpassed his master.'

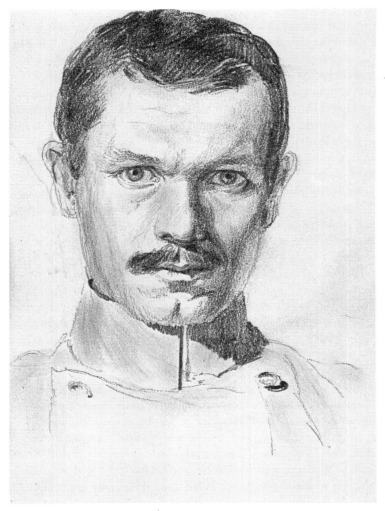

Fig. 7 Walter Andrae, Dresden. Self-portrait, 1903/04

it fortuitous that Assur provided the opportunity to develop excavation technique in Mesopotamia, making it possible to investigate in turn even older sites, such as Uruk.[28]

What did the work of eleven years achieve? Andrae's book 'Assur Rediscovered (Das wiedererstandene Assur)'[29] encompasses a chronological and historical perspective

---

28 Julius Jordan, W. Andrae's deputy then took over the directorship at Assur.

29 W. Andrae, Das wiedererstandene Assur (Assur Rediscovered), 9th Communiqué of the DOG (German Oriental Society), 1938; 2nd edition (edited and ammended by B. Hrouda), 1977.

of the city, the defences, the palaces, living quarters, graves, major and lesser finds, and also the climate and other physical conditions. The finds and results are described and evaluated in detail in the Research Publications of the German Oriental Society (WVDOG) about Assur.[30] The results of the nearby excavation of Kar Tukulti Ninurta were published by Andrae and his colleagues in the Communications series of the same institution,[31] and the investigations at Hatra, carried out on serveral very short visits are written up in two comprehensive volumes of WVDOG.[32]

Andrae twice left Assur in the ten years he was there, in 1908 and 1912. In 1908 he attained his doctorate at the Technical High School at Dresden.[33] He was invited to the première performance of the historical opera 'Sardanaplus' at the Royal Opera House in Berlin. In 1907 Wilhelm II had commissioned Andrae to provide a stage design for this play, which was harshly treated by the critics.[34] The play concerned the end of the Assy-

---

30 W. Andrae, Der Anu-Adad Tempel in Assur (The Anu-Adad Temple at Assur), WVDOG 10 (1909); idem, Die Festungswerke von Assur (The Fortifications at Assur), text and plates, WVDOG 23 (1913); idem, Die Stelenreihen in Assur (The Relief Orthostats at Assur), WVDOG 24 (1913); idem, Hethitische Inschriften auf Bleistreifen aus Assur (Hittite Inscriptions on Lead from Assur), WVDOG 46 (1924); idem, Kultrelief aus dem Brunnen des Assurtempels zu Assur (Cult Reliefs on the Fountain of the Assur Temple at Assur), WVDOG 53 (1931); W. Andrae and H. J. Lenzen, Die Partherstadt Assur (Assur the Parthian City), WVDOG 57 (1933); idem, Vorwort und Einleitung (Foreword and Introduction) to Conrad Preusser, Die Wohnhäuser in Assur (The Private Houses at Assur), WVDOG 64 (1954); idem, Vorwort, Einleitung und der Abschnitt über Gruft 45 (Foreword, Introduction and the section on Tomb 45) in: Arndt Haller: Die Gräber und Grüfte von Assur (The Graves and Tombs at Assur), WVDOG 65 (1954); idem, Vorwort-Überblick (Foreword and Summary): Die Raumformen assyrischer Paläste (Room Shapes in Assyrian Palaces) in: Conrad Preusser: Die Paläste in Assur (The Palaces at Assur), WVDOG 66 (1955); Arndt Haller, Die Heiligtümer des Gottes Assur und der Sin-Šamaš-Tempel in Assur (The Shrines of the God Assur and the Sin-Shamash Temple at Assur), with a contribution by W. Andrae, WVDOG 67 (1955).
31 W. Andrae – W. Bachmann, MDOG 53, 1914, 41 ff. – See also T. Eickhoff, Kār Tukulti Ninurta, Abhandlungen der Deutschen Orient-Gesellschaft 21 (1985); R. Dittmann – T. Eickhoff – R. Schmitt – R. Stengele – S. Thürwächter, MDOG 120, 1988, 97 ff.
32 W. Andrae, Hatra I. Allgemeine Beschreibung der Ruinen (Hatra I. General Description of the Ruins), WVDOG 9 (1908); idem, Hatra II. Einzelbeschreibung der Ruinen (Hatra II. Individual Description of the Ruins, WVDOG 21 (1912).
33 See MDOG 40, 1909, 1.
34 See Catalogue Nos 132, 133; Mem. 180 ff., and J. Renger op. cit. (see Note 24) 168 f.:
'Both Meissner and Zimmern particularly emphasize in their recollections Delitzsch's part in the production of the historical pantomime ›Sardanaplus‹. It seems that this production left special impressions on Assyriological contemporaries. The material for ›Sardanaplus‹ has been repeatedly used in opera since 1698 (F. Stieger, Opernlexikon III, 1975, 1084). The pantomime ›Sardanaplus‹ dates back to a ballet in four acts by Peter Ludwig Hertel, who was Court Composer from 1858 and Director of Royal Ballet Music from 1860. The ballet was originally performed on the 24th of April 1865 at the Royal Opera in Berlin; it then found favour with Wilhelm I. (Information kindly provided by Prof. Güterbock of Chicago)
The new production and transformation of the historical pantomime would not have come about without the personal interest of Kaiser Wilhelm II, who was known for his interest in historically accurate operatic staging. He says of it: ›I got my friend Graf Hülsen-Haeseler, the brilliant theatre manager, to set the play ›Assurbanipal‹, and this was done, after long preparation, by the German Oriental Society. I did this because I realised that assyriology, which occupied so many worthy men of both religious persuasions, still did not appreciate the value of agreement in their interpretations.‹ (Kaiser Wilhelm II., Ereignisse und Gestalten aus den Jahren 1878–1918 (Events and Figures, 1878–1918), 1922, 169.)
Delitzsch reformed Hertel's ballet, with Paolo Taglioni's choreography, into an historical pantomime. The ballet scenes were enhanced by recitations by allegorical figures such as ›Knowledge‹, or ›The Assyrian Past‹.

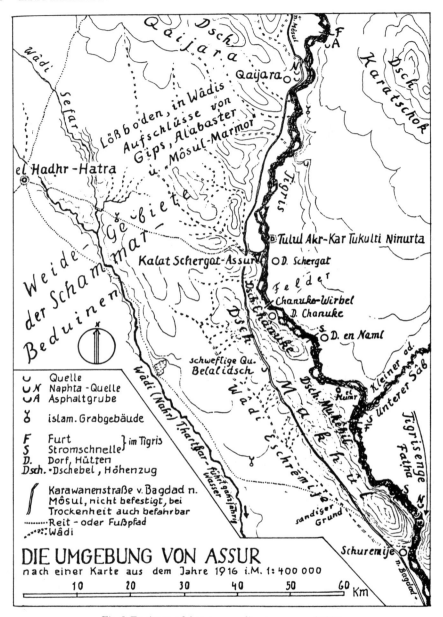

Fig. 8 Environs of Assur, according to a map of 1916

rian dynasty in Nineveh and the Kaiser had wanted the set to be historically accurate. The excavator of Assur was considered the most suitable person for the job. The scenery-painters converted watercolours prepared at Assur into a full opera-set in three scenes, with all the details. Andrae would hardly have mentioned this episode in his autobiography on account of the set-designs alone, but he realised with what close interest Wilhelm II had followed Koldewey's achievements at Babylon, and also his own at Assur from 1904 onwards. The Kaiser had painstakingly acquainted himself with the

---

Far away in Assur, W. Andrae had to draw stage-sets and costumes. Wilhelm II took part personally in the staging and rehearsals. The play opened at the Royal Opera at Unter den Linden on the 1st of September 1908 (F. Stieger, op. cit. 1084); according to those present it was deadly boring. The production was repeated often at the Kaiser's behest. The house was empty every time (G. Güterbock-Auer, unpublished memoirs, 187)! At the grand opening the King of Siam was present. The denouement at least, with Nineveh in flames, must have made a realistic impression, because when the Emperor of Siam awoke from his snooze he wondered aloud why no-one had called the fire brigade (information kindly provided by Prof. Güterbock of Chicago).

On the evening of the production the Kaiser decorated Delitzsch with the Order of the Red Eagle, 3rd class (Berliner Lokal-Anzeiger, 2. 9. 1908, 2). The assyriologists invited specially for the production – Dieulafoy from Paris, V. Schmidt from Copenhagen, M. Jastrow from Philadelphia, Rev. Patterson from London and Hommel from Munich praised it to the skies the following day in the ›Berliner Lokal-Anzeiger‹. A somewhat unusual state of affairs was associated with the name Dieulafoy. Grethe Güterbock-Auer, who was at the opening night herself, says: ›Gaiety was not altogether lacking that evening, for there was a special entertainment for the initiated. The French archaeologist Dieulafoy turned up with his wife and colleague, a slim little person who was in the habit of dressing as a man, no doubt from a habit acquired on excavations. This lady had occupied the Court Administration the entire day, trying to keep her at all costs from being seen by the prudish Empress. So a Court Official was assigned to her to accompany her with great skill only to places where the empress would definitely not appear. And now this creature of ill-fortune entered the opening night house of the State Opera – in a tail-coat. Mrs. Dieulafoy was quickly installed in a box right next to the Kaiser's, where she could only be seen from the Royal Box if someone leaned right out. The gentlemen of the Court Administration and the Royal Attendants never had a more anxious time, but luckily it did not occur to the Kaiser to think of his foreign guests during the interval – he spoke almost entirely with the gentlemen of the Oriental Society – and even less to peer into the neighbouring box.‹ (G. Güterbock-Auer, 188)

A whole string of highly critical reviews appeared in the press. The ›Berliner Tageblatt‹ said: ›Naturally the pantomime was well received yesterday. The Kaiser was there in his box and enjoyed the production, in which he had had an active hand himself, and nobody disagreed. But anyone who judged from anything more than the volume of the applause ... could see that the public was bored to death ... One concludes from the collaboration of Friedrich Delitzsch that such elevation ... to the realm of academia is utterly and entirely misconceived.‹ (Berliner Tageblatt, 2. 9. 1908, 2 f.).

Elsewhere we find that: ›The author (Friedrich Delitzsch) of the new ›Sardanaplus‹ fostered the notion that art should consider itself ›fortunate to be allowed to serve Learning‹. One cannot misjudge the soul and purpose of Art more severely than with these words.‹

›Vossische Zeitung‹ reports: ›All that propped it up was what was left of the earlier ballet‹ (Vossische Zeitung, 2. 9. 1908, morning edition, 3). The ›Berliner Tageblatt‹ resumes in a leading article: ›From what one hears and reads the Assyrian ballet ›Sardanaplus‹ is so boring that anyone who lasts to the end receives the Order of the Crown, third class.‹

(Ballettpolitik, in Berliner Tageblatt, 7. 9. 1908, 1.) It seems as though Delitzsch had trespassed upon ground that brought him no fame – apart from a decoration – but rather mockery and accusations of ›Byzantine‹ behaviour. But it would be wrong to let this circumstance detract from his academic service during his time in Berlin, for it probably had more to do with his personal standing with the Kaiser. More detail on the matter is required.'

Frau Dr. M. Srocke was kind enough to give the following information: 'The Staatsbibliothek (National Library), SPK, has the notes. This was a great historical ballet in four acts and seven scenes, composed by Peter Ludwig Hertel (Choreographer Paul Taglioni) with stage design by W. Andrae (original production Berlin 1. 9. 1908). The composer wrote some ballet music.'

historical and dynastic problems – it was as though the voice of fate were warning him of the future. But according to Andrae, 'whatever there was to learn did not have any real effect on his attitude. The play told of a dangerous coalition of Assyria's enemies, and the fall of both dynasty and empire, and there was meant to be a moral here, not just for those with their own dynasties and empires to worry about. The tragic background was certainly lost on all those concerned.'[35]

In 1912 Andrae went to the State Museums at Berlin to see the animal reliefs sent there from Babylon, where they had been reconstructed. Apart from these there was an immense number of glazed fragments which conservators in Berlin now had to put together following the example of the Babylon team.[36]

Our supposedly unsophisticated 'man of the desert' found himself proudly presented with their latest creation, a completely flawless lion. Perfection had been achieved by filing down the broken edges to fit exactly, and gaps in the glaze were filled in with oil-colours, so the whole effect was rather of an animal wearing a coat of varnish. The Museum Directorate considered this lion far superior to the one put together at Babylon, which showed the actual positions of the breaks. While at Babylon Andrae had developed a different attitude to the handling and restoration of ancient works of art, and expressed his opinion forcibly. This occasioned much excitement with the old conservators and with the Director, Richard Schoene.[37] He must have mentioned the young man from Babylon to the Kaiser, for the latter sent for both of them. He looked at the lions, both the filed-down one and the one restored at Babylon. Andrae stated his opinion once again, and Wilhelm II also preferred the Babylon lion. At this point Andrae set off for Assur, and in the Museum lions continued to be reconstructed as before. However, progress was so slow that Andrae was able, as Museum Director 24 years later, to find enough material to fulfill his own interpretation.

In 1914 the excavation at Assur was closed down. All the most important areas had been carefully investigated, all noted, drawn, listed. 700 large chests of finds with inventories had to be transported to Basra, 1,000 km away, and they had to go by water. The Tigris is an unpredictable river, especially upstream of the Jebel Hamrin. Andrae was acquainted with its temper, for in 1908 he had navigated a steamboat from Baghdad to Assur, through all the shallows, rapids and gravel banks.[38] The only available transport for the heavy boxes was the local keleks – flat-bottomed rafts, which were built in Mosul and could only go downstream.[39] They were made of inflated goatskins, onto which branches were built, so that the latter remained above water and the cargo stayed dry for as long as the goat-skins held. Raft-travelling experience suggested that the cargo could in fact be transported dry about as far as Baghdad. Andrae decided to allo-

---

35 Mem. 182.
36 See Nos. 2 and 80; catalogue entries for No. 80 and Mem. 196 ff.
37 5. 2. 1840–5. 3. 1922.
38 See the detailed report in MDOG 42, 1909, 63 ff.
39 See Mem. 218 f.

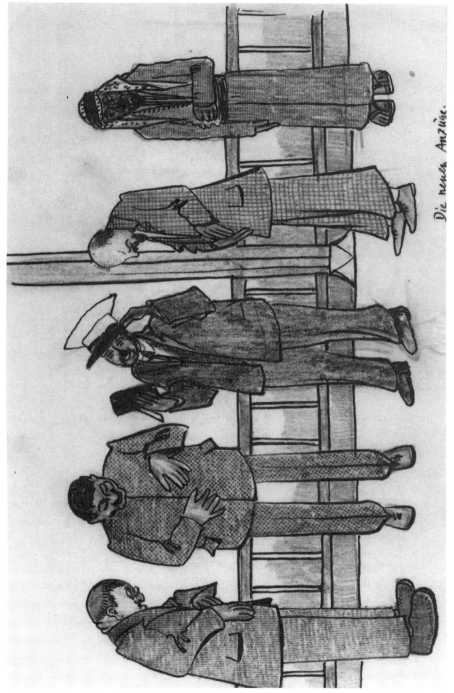

Die neuen Anzüge.

Fig. 9 Assur. 'The excavators of Assur in new suits.' From left to right: Paul Maresch, Walter Andrae, Julius Jordan, Conrad Preusser, and the somewhat bemused Ismain ibn Jasim, c. 1908

cate an overseer or one of his colleagues to each individual raft. He was aware of what had happened to Botta during the last century when he had tried to transport the great stone-reliefs from Khorsabad downstream from Mosul by kelek: the finds ended up in the Tigris, and despite various attempts to raise them, have never been found.

Andrae's plan worked out well. Not till they reached Baghdad did the keleks get so low in the water that it would have been up to the boxes the following day. In Baghdad the cargo was lifted by steam crane onto barges of the British Tigris Navigation Company. The boxes arrived at Basra and were loaded into a ship bound for Istanbul. Andrae himself wanted to get back to Europe as quickly as possible.[40] He travelled with a British line from Basra via Karachi, Bombay and Aden (Nr. 112) to Port Said, where he changed to a British torpedo boat on courier service between Egypt and Brindisi. Thus he caught the quickest connection to Europe, albeit less comfortable than the passenger steamer from Aden to Naples. While they were in the Red Sea the captain told them over the loud-hailer in the dining-room that the Austrian Archduke and Duchess had been assassinated in Sarajevo. They discussed the matter on the torpedo-boat: quasi casus belli? – would this mean war? Andrae was not much affected. The express from Brindisi to Vienna brought him to Villach, and the wedding arrangements were finalised. Three days later Austro-Hungary and Serbia were fighting. The honeymoon took them straight into the First World War, to Dresden, to where Andrae was called to his regiment with the rank of captain.

What of the steamboat with the finds from Assur? When war was declared it was near Lisbon, as the captain had been instructed by telegraph to find the nearest neutral port. In 1916 Portugal entered the war, and both ship and cargo became forfeit.[41]

The War 1914–1918

Back in 1912 Koldewey had foretold that his colleague's days as a field-archaeologist were drawing to a close.[42] The occasion was a postcard from the beautiful Austrian province of Carinthia, which Andrae sent to Babylon when on leave. Koldewey answered by asking what he had found to occupy himself in a region already so well-charted? Could he be engaged to be married? That was in fact the case. Koldewey thought it impossible for a good excavator to be married. His saying 'mulier taceat in excavationibus' (women should have no voice in excavation) occasioned smiles at the time, but he was right: Andrae never dug again after 1914. He concerned himself rather with reconstruction, synthesis, and the task of communicating to others the conclusions to be

40 See Mem. 220 f.
41 See Mem. 219.
42 See Mem. 196.

Fig. 10 On the Euphrates between Meskene and Baghdad: in the cabin of the barge Safineh, 20. 1./7. 2. 1916

drawn from the traces of earlier cultures. From 1914–1920 war service kept Andrae from doing this. In 1915 he was company commander in the trenches near Laon. He describes his own appalling wartime experiences in France only briefly in his memoirs.[43] He never spoke of them.

During 1915 Andrae (No. 2), was seconded to the service of Field Marshal von der Goltz,[44] who was engaged in trying to stabilize the Turkish Front in Mesopotamia. So he returned to the East, and took part in events which, as one who had come to love that region, caused him great sorrow. He went down the Euphrates to Baghdad via Aleppo by boat (fig. 10), stopping also for a time at Mosul (No. 167).

His wartime duties made no sense to him after hard but rewarding years at Babylon and Assur. There are pictures done at the time (nos. 144–192, 194–198). In one or two dating to 1917 and 1918 (of Turkey, Iraq, Syria and Palestine) we find a technique that was new to Andrae, one used by the Impressionists: the artist tries to bring out the effect of light by means of contrast between crayon and coloured paper. Examples of these attempts are No. 167 done in Mosul in 1917 and No. 181–182, of Nazareth. Andrae says these were the result of meeting Georg Lührig (later director of the Dresden Academy of Art)[45] in Baghdad and Aleppo.

The German offensive of 1915 was successful, due to the personality of the old Field Marshal. He spoke Turkish, and had spent a year in Western Turkey as advisor to the Turkish army. The Turks respected him, and did all they could for him on this, his first visit to Baghdad. A few former Mesopotamian archaeologists were given him as advisors. Andrae compared the two members of the Supreme Command with whom he had dealings thus: von der Goltz took advice, informed himself thoroughly, convinced his subordinates, and was successful. Von Falkenhayn,[46] who was in command in 1917/18

---

43 See Mem. 223 f.

44 Wilhelm Leopold Colmar Freiherr von der Goltz, Field Marshal, Pasha, 12. 8. 1843–19. 4. 1916. Mem. 228 ff: 'When Turkey entered the war in 1914 on the side of the Central Powers, the old Field Marshall v. d. Goltz went to Constantinople, where he had been for many years instructor to the Turkish army. In 1915 he took command of the Turkish forces on the Iraq front and collected us archaeologists to his staff from various places. For he did not know Asiatic Turkey at all and he needed advisors. His staff consisted of a motley collection of cavalry officers, who had not the first clue about the Orient. So those of the old Koldewey collection were ordered to Berlin, assigned to his staff, and set off in 1915 across unified Hungary and Bulgaria to Turkey. Eventually former archaeologists from Syria and Mesopotamia gathered themselves into very diverse positions, not all close to the aged Field Marshal. His army consisted of 12 staff officers, their subordinates, a junior paymaster and an orderly, while the Turkish troops were commanded by their officers. The old Field Marshal was the most engaging personality in Baghdad by a long way. More philosopher than soldier, one able to appreciate and judge men well, and therefore well loved and respected by the Turkish army as well as the populace.'
See also Th. Wiegand, Halbmond im letzten Viertel (Crescent Moon on the Wane) 1970, 175. 277; General Pertev Demirhan, Field Marshal Colmar Freiherr von der Goltz (1960); Hermann Teske in Neue Deutsche Biographie (New German Biography) 6 (1964) 629 ff.

45 *26. 1. 1868. See Thieme-Becker 23 (1929) 449 f.

46 Erich Georg Anton Sebastian Reichsfreiherr von Falkenhayn, Prussian Colonel General, 11. 11. 1861–8. 4. 1922. See Th. Wiegand op. cit. 260 f. 263 f. 267. 274; Friedrich Freiherr Hiller von Gaertringen in Neue Deutsche Biographie 5 (1961) 11 ff. see von Falkenhayn under 1. – Mem. 238 f.:

in Syria and Palestine, and was replaced by Liman von Sanders,[47] did the opposite: he knew everything better than his staff, and his subordinates followed him reluctantly or not at all.

Andrae was supposedly language-expert to the staff, though he had in fact only picked up the local speech of the peasants of Kuwairish and Shargat. So in eastern Jordan he was a modest counterpart to his colleague Thomas Edward Lawrence,[48] who had been a participant in the excavations at Carchemish, near Jerablus, since 1914. In 1912 Andrae had visited this excavation, which lay at the point where the Baghdad Railway crossed the Euphrates, without meeting Lawrence. As is well-known, Lawrence managed to unite the Arabian tribal leaders against the Turks. The railway line from Damascus to Medina, known as the 'Hejaz Railway', built under Meißner Pasha (No. 190)[49] and vital to the Turkish war effort, was sabotaged by Arab bomb-squads led by Lawrence. In 1918 Andrae was sent south by this railway to the region of Ma'an.[50]

He had been posted to Aleppo, where a First Lieutenant Erdmann was preparing a map of the town and surroundings under his direction (Fig. 11), when Nazareth was taken by the British in a bold surprise attack on 20th September 1918. The German Supreme Commander Liman von Sanders had to retreat.[51] In October one of the last trains of German soldiers travelled back along the Baghdad Railway through the Taurus Tunnel under Andrae's command. British ships were already in the Sea of Marmara.

'It was with a heavy heart that I took up the new order to Aleppo and then to Nazareth to the unit Yıldırım, commanded by General von Falkenhayn. He belonged to that strange breed of Generals who always know everything in advance, and in this was the antithesis of von der Goltz. In handling the Turkish mentality he encountered opposition rather than obedience. It was already rumoured that he had been placed in an impossible position as an excuse for replacing him. And in 1918 Liman von Sanders took over the command in a very brusque fashion.'

47 Otto Liman von Sanders, Prussian General and Turkish Pasha, 18. 2. 1855–22. 8. 1929. See also Th. Wiegand, op. cit. 167. 204. 274. 279; Franz Menges, Neue Deutsche Biographie 14 (1985) 563 ff. see Liman v. Sanders.

48 Thomas Edward Lawrence, archaeologist, Colonel, 15. 8. 1888–19. 5. 1935. – See also Wiegand op. cit. 213. 263. 278; T. E. Lawrence, The Seven Pillars of Wisdom; idem., Revolt in the Desert; A. W. Lawrence, Lawrence by his Friends.

49 Heinrich August Meißner Pasha, Chief Engineer of the Baghdad and Hejaz Railway and its branches in southern Palestine, lecturer at the Technical College Ayas, 3. 1. 1892–14. 1. 1940. See also MDOG 48, June 1912, 22; Wiegand op. cit. 263.

50 See Mem. 245 f.:

'I was instructed to escort a chest of Turkish gold pounds, struck in Germany, to Transjordan, where ›Little Jemal Pasha‹ was supposed to lead a contingent of Turkish troops against hostile Arabs east of the Dead Sea. That was so I would have the necessary cash – at the same time I was to hang onto it as long as possible! It was the barometer of trust among our allies. The train journey on Meißner Pasha's Mecca railway was otherwise lonely, but I saw from the window the ruins of Mshatta ›in plena solitudine‹ (in splendid solitude), but without the façade. This had already been presented to Kaiser Wilhelm by Sultan Abdulhamid, and taken by Bruno Schulz to the Kaiser-Friedrich-Museum in Berlin. I could count myself lucky that my Mecca train was not wiped out by one of the many explosives strikes of the Desert Revolt, organised by my counterpart T. Lawrence. Their traces were clearly to be seen, and had occasioned much bloodshed.'

51 Liman von Sanders, Fünf Jahre Türkei (Five years in Turkey), 1920, 354 ff.

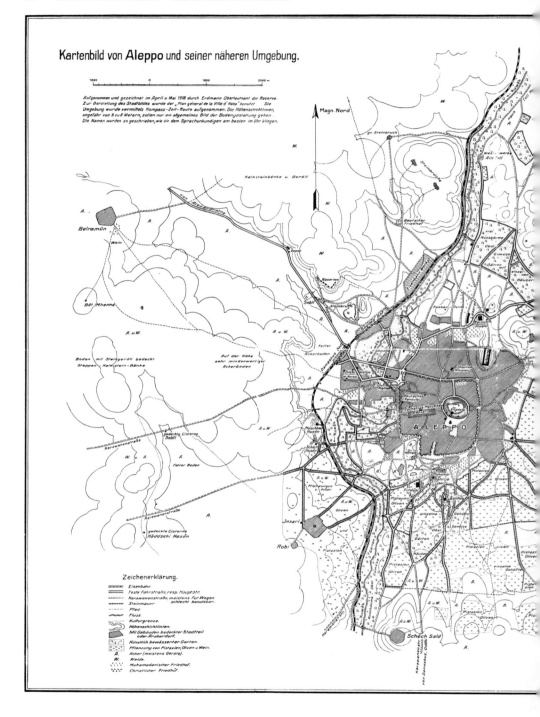

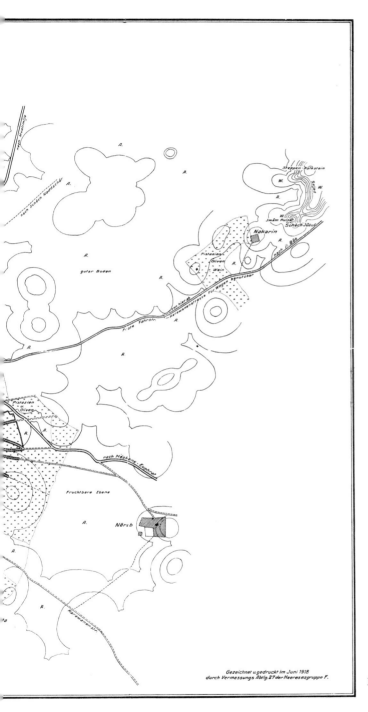

Fig. 11 Map of Aleppo and its environs.
Executed by First Lieutenant Erdmann under
Andrae's direction, 1918

The remnants of the German Eastern Army were interned on empty German ships which had been anchored in the Bosporus since 1914. That included Andrae with 960 men, on the 3,000 ton coalsteamer 'Patmos' (No. 198, Fig. 12). The boat left Constantinople in February 1919 under the English captain Moses (No. 197) and arrived in Cuxhaven in March.

Lake Constance 1919–1921; Berlin 1921–1956

While on leave in Europe in 1918 Andrae had bought an old, somewhat delapidated farmhouse at Hemmenhofen am Untersee, near Konstanz. His wife and son lived there. Now unemployed, Andrae began writing up his work at Assur, and toyed with the idea of becoming a professional artist. In 1921 he succeeded Koldewey as Curator of the Near Eastern Department of the State Museums at Berlin, and after his formal appointment to the post began lecturing in Near-Eastern, Egyptian and Byzantine Architecture at the Technical College (Technische Hochschule) at Berlin-Charlottenburg.[52] Meanwhile he began working on the Mesopotamian finds in the Museum.

In 1925 Andrae made a start on the Museum's 'foreign affairs'.[53] The German consul in Lisbon, Dr. Stüwe, had managed to persuade the Portugese government to give back the impounded Assur finds. However, by the time Andrae arrived in Portugal to take charge of them the government had been overthrown. It was until spring 1926 that further negotiations by the German chargé d'affaires Herr von Voretzsch met with success. Andrae had the bones loaded onto a German ship,[54] and they travelled by water from Portugal via Hamburg right to the Museum Island in Berlin. Other boxes had fallen into the hands of British troops at Basra during the war and been acquired by the British Museum. In 1923 Andrae got a little of this material back.[55]

Towards the middle of 1926 a message arrived in Berlin from Miss Gertrude Bell to say that the Iraqi regime wanted to return the boxes of antiquities which had been impounded at Babylon since 1917. They contained among other things about 300,000 fragments of glazed bricks from the Kasr Mound.[56] Would Berlin care to send a delegation to Babylon for hand-over?

Shortly beforehand an important decision had been reached in Berlin. The new Museum building begun by Messel[57] and continued by the municipal councillor Hoffmann,[58] had the south wing of the Near Eastern section still available. This was because

---

52 J. Renger op. cit. (see Note 24) 187.
53 Mem. 252.
54 See W. Andrae, MDOG 65, 1927, 1 ff. with Fig. 2; Mem. 219. 258. 260 f.
55 Mem. 255 f.
56 Mem. 258. 261.
57 Dr. Alfred Messel, Government Privy Councillor, Architect to the Berlin Museums, 22. 7. 1853–24. 3. 1904.
58 Ludwig Hoffmann, Dr., Development Privy Councillor, Municipal Development Councillor to Berlin, 1896–1928, 30. 7. 1852–11. 11. 1932.

Fig. 12 The ship's carpenter on the 'Patmos', March 1919

Heinrich Schäfer[59] preferred to leave his Egyptian collection in the Stühler building (which was completely destroyed in the war of 1939–1945 and never rebuilt). With the finds from Assur, and now those from Babylon offered by Miss Bell, there now occurred the possibility of reconstructing certain ancient Mesopotamian architectural elements on a large scale, some even at original size. This happened in 1930 under Andrae's direction (compare Nos. 81–84) at about the same time as the completion of the Galleries of Hellenistic Architecture in the new Museum building, which came to be known as the Pergamon Museum.

  Because Gertrude Bell's return of the finds was of decisive importance, her encounter with Andrae is described here. The name Gertrude Lowthian Bell is found in the guestbook of the Babylon Expedition for 1. 4. 1909 (Fig. 13). She wrote beside it a one-line remark in Arabic script. Gertrude[60] was also at Assur[61] at around that time. She payed

---

59 Prof. Dr. Heinrich Schäfer, Director of the Egyptian Department of the Berlin Museums, 29. 10. 1868–6. 4. 1957.

60 A. J. Arberry, (Professor at the University of Cambridge) in: Gertrude Bell, Persische Reisebilder, Hamburg 1949 (Original: Persian Pictures, London 1947) 178 ff.:

'Gertrude Lowthian Bell, daughter of Sir Hugh Bell and granddaughter of Sir Lowthian Bell, Bt., was born at her grandfather's residence in Durham on the 14th of July 1868. In 1885, Gertrude went up to Lady Margaret Hall, Oxford, and two years later took a brilliant First in History. In 1891, her uncle Sir Frank Lascelles being appointed British Minister in Teheran, she began to learn Persian; and when in the following spring she accompanied Lady Lascelles to Persia she had the great advantage of being able to speak and write the language of that country. She recorded her experiences and impressions during that visit in her diary, with no thought of giving them to the world; but Mr. Bentley, the publisher, was anxious to have them, and her familiy seconded the proposal, so that she eventually consented, with much diffidence, to publication, stipulating, however, that her name should not appear. So in 1894 the sketches came out as *Safar Nameh. Persian Pictures. A Book of Travel.* The book was well-received at the time, but than forgotten; it was not reprinted until 1928, when Messrs. Ernest Benn published it with its shorter title, *Persian Pictures,* and with a preface by the late Sir Denison Ross.

The generation which read the first edition knew Gertrude Bell as an accomplished young lady of good family and brilliant intellectual gifts. The second edition came after the unexpectedly early close of a life of outstanding service not only to her country, but to humanity at large. Twenty years later, when the book is coming a third time before the public, Gertrude Bell is to the younger generation a name and a legend, best known as the writer of charming and intimate letters. But she was infinitely more than that; for it may be truly said of her as can be said of few even among the famous, that she shaped the course of human affairs in an important part of the world.

After her visit to Persia, Gertrude Bell never again had commerce with that country; her Persian episode closed with the publication in 1897 of *Poems from the Divan of Hafiz,* a remarkable monument to her schorlarship and literary gifts; though some twenty hands have put Hafiz into English, her renderings remain the best. It was the Arab world that claimed her chief interest and whole devotion thereafter; from her first visit to Jerusalem in 1899, until her death at Baghdad in 1920, she passed the greater part of her life among the Arabs.

Archaeology was the primary motive of her extensive travels in the Desert and the Sown; her journeys brought her a wide and detailed knowledge of Arab tribes and politics, and led to her being summoned by David Hogarth to join his Arab Bureau at Cairo in 1915. From that time onward she was the close associate and loved colleague of men whose names will live in the history of the Near East, men like Lawrence, Cox, Wilson, Dobbs, Philby, Storrs. In 1916 she joined the staff of Sir Percy Cox at General Headquarters, Basrah, and accompanied him to Baghdad the following spring; she was his Oriental Secretary, and his successor's as High Commissioner for Iraq, Sir Henry Dobbs; apart from attending the Peace Conference at Paris in 1919 she continued at her post to the end of her days. Despite her preoccupation with political affairs she did not neglect her first love; in 1921, she was appointed Honorary Director of Antiquities, and founded the Iraq

two visits there, and was well-received. Andrae describes her visit thus: 'One of the most noteworthy personalities among the visitors was undoubtedly Miss Gertrude Lowthian Bell, who came to Assur twice. She wanted to know absolutely everything, and crept with me tirelessly into every hole and corner of the excavation. Her coura-

---

Museum. She died at the height of her fame, and in the full maturity of her powers, on the 12th of July 1926; she was buried in Baghdad.

Her premature death, two days before her fity-eighth birthday, was rightly regarded as a calamity; it was the occasion of a rare Ministerial tribute in the House of Commons by the Colonial Secretary, Mr. L. S. Amery ...'

Perhaps the most memorable protrait of Gertrude Bell at the height of her career is due to V. Sackville-West in 'Passenger to Teheran':

'I felt that her personality held together and made a centre for all those exiled Englishmen whose other common bond was their service for Iraq. ... Whatever subject she touched, she lit up: such vitality was irresistible.'

61 Gertrude Lowthian Bell, Amurath to Amurath (1911) 221 ff.:

'We rode down into the ruin-field and found one of Dr. Andrae's colleagues at work in the trial trenches. He directed us to the house set round with flowers, as I had predicted, wherein the excavators are lodged. There Dr. Andrae and Mr. Jordan made me so warmly welcome that I felt like one returning after absence into a circle of life-long friends. They had grave news to give me, news which was all the more disquieting because it was as yet nothing but a rumour. Constitutional government had foundered suddenly, and it might be for ever. The members of the Committee had fled from Constantinople, the Liberals were fugitive upon their heels, and once more 'Abdu'l Hamîd had set his foot upon the neck of Turkey. So we interpreted the report that had reached Asshur, but since there was no means of allaying or confirming our anxieties we turned our minds to more profitable fields, and went out to see the ruins.

A site better favoured than Kal'at Shergât for excavations such as those undertaken by Dr. Andrae and his colleagues could scarcely have been selected. It has not given them the storied slabs and huge stone guardians of the gates of kings with which Layard enriched the British Museum; they have disappeared during the many periods of reconstruction which the town has witnessed; but those very reconstructions add to the historic interest of the excavations. Asshur was in existence in the oldest Assyrian period, and down to the latest days of the empire it was an honoured shrine of the gods; there are traces of Persian occupation; in Parthian times the city was re-built, walls and gates were set up anew, and the whole area within the ancient fortifications was re-inhabited. Valuable as are the contributions which Dr. Andrae has been able to make to the history of Assyria, the fact that he is bringing into the region of critical study a culture so shadowy as that of the Parthians has remained to us, in spite of its four hundred years of domination, adds greatly to the magnitude of his achievement. His researches in this direction have been pursued not only at *Asshur,* but at the Parthian city of Hatra, a long day's journey to the west of the Tigris, where the famous palace is at last receiving the attention it merits ...

As Dr. Andrae led me about the city, drawing forth its long story with infinite skill from wall and trench and cuneiform inscription, the lavish cruel past rushed in upon us. The myriad soldiers of the Great King, transported from the reliefs in the British Museum, marched through the gates of Asshur; the captives, roped and bound, crowded the streets; defeated princes bowed themselves before the victor and subject races piled up their tribute in his courts. We saw the monarch go out to the chase, and heard the roaring of the lion, half paralyzed by the dart in its spine, which animates the stone with its wild anguish. Human victims cried out under nameless tortures; the tide of battle raged against the walls, and, red with carnage, rose into the palaces. Splendour and misery, triumph and despair, lifted their head out of the dust.

One hot night I sat with my hosts upon the roof of their house. The Tigris, in unprecedented flood, swirled against the mound, a waste of angry waters. Above us rose the zigurrat of the god Asshur. It had witnessed for four thousand years the melting of the Kurdish snows, flood-time and the harvest that follows; gigantic, ugly, intolerably mysterious, it dominated us, children of an hour.

'What did they watch from its summit?' I asked, stung into a sharp consciousness of the unknown by a scene almost as old as recorded life. ›They watched the moon‹, said Dr. Andrae, ›as we do. Who knows? they watched for the god.‹ I have left few places so unwillingly as I left Kal'at Shergât.'

62 Mem. 174; mentioned in a report of 27th April 1909: MDOG 42, 1909, 34.

geous independent journey into Asiatic Turkey had not only political purpose and background, but was also undertaken out of a passionate interest in archaeology. We had long conversations on both subjects, about which she was very frank. Her connections in diplomatic circles in England and her many travels had given her an unusally broad view of peoples and places and destined her later to play a leading role in British Oriental politics during the First World War. At the time of her visit to Assur she had surveyed the Arab desert fortress of Ukhaidher (north-west of Kerbala). She presented me with a copy of her splendid report, inscribed with a friendly dedication. Her linguistic ability was marvellous, even allowing for the fact that her particular circumstances had been favourable to its development. She had close relatives in high positions in the British Foreign Service, for example in Berlin, Teheran, and India, and as their guest she was able to acquaint herself with the local languages when young. So she liked to speak German with us and only reverted to English when necessary. On the second visit she must already have had a diplomatic mission in Mesopotamia, and made friends with various sheikhs, something ordinary British officials were unable to do. The effect was felt during the war, when the Mesopotamian sheikhs made Emir Faisal king in accordance with the wishes of the 'White Queen' – Miss Bell!'

For her own part, Gertrude mentioned her meeting with Andrae at Assur in a letter (1913 or 1914): 'He is a big, strong, silent man, who has spent the best part of fifteen years digging in Mesopotamia, and until you have seen them at it you can scarcely guess what labour and self-denial that means. There is no guesswork here at Assur, and no scamping, but observation so minute that nothing can escape it.'[63]

King Faisal I was the son of the Emir of the Hejaz who led the Arab Revolt in the 1914–18 war and had T. E. Lawrence as his advisor.

Andrae's remarks about his accession referred to the fact that Gertrude managed to persuade the most influential sheikhs and notables of the newly-created Iraqi state to put Faisal on the throne in 1921. Faisal had been called upon to become King of Syria in 1920, but had been driven out by the French mandate. In Iraq the British had comitted themselves to gradual independence, and at critical points of Arab authority there were British advisors. With her exceptional knowledge of the country Gertrude was the most important of these – also the most important of her compatriots, though she remained in the background. She founded the Iraq Museum in the early twenties and directed it until her death in 1926 (compare note 53). After the occupation of Baghdad in 1917 she immediately took under her protection the Babylon Expedition house and all the finds and equipment stored there. In a generous and exemplary gesture of scientific co-operation she had the doors walled up and the compound placed under guard.[64] The new Antiquities Law of the Iraqi state required that finds made by foreign workers had to

---

63 Elizabeth Burgoyne, Gertrude Bell from her Personal Papers 1889–1914 [London 1958] 267 in: Deutsche Orient Gesellschaft (1984) 21; see further Note 60, especially the beginning and end concerning the complimentary qualities of these two persons, who had so much in common.

64 Mem. 263 and Note 66 below.

Fig. 13 Gertrude Bell in front of her tent at Babylon, 1909

stay. Apart from duplicates, which could be removed with the special consent of the Antiquities Service, all finds had now to stay in the country. Gertrude knew about the brick fragments from Babylon, and she realised there was no hope of desalinating and reconstruction them in Baghdad, so they ought to go to Berlin.[65] This was the right decision, for otherwise the material would have been eaten away by salt, have fallen to pieces and been lost forever. Walter Andrae mentioned this in his memoirs: 'The Babylonian Galleries of the Berlin Museum are partly due to Miss Bell' (Mem. 175). In return

---

65 Mem. 175: 'Shortly before her death – she was then in charge of the Museum of the newly-founded Iraqi state – she had given the order that the boxes of relief-fragments from the Processional Way which were still at Babylon were to be given back to the Berlin Museum.'

a reconstructed lion and a selection of baked bricks had to go back to the Iraq Museum later (Mem. 263).

The Prussian government delegated to Andrae the job of taking possession of the antiquities in Baghdad and arranging transport from Babylon. He chose as his assistant Dr. Julius Jordan, one-time colleague at Assur and excavator at Uruk. While still in Lisbon Andrae heard of Gertrude Bell's sudden death.[66] Would the arrangement hold good? He decided to go on. Gertrude's word survived her, and the handover went smoothly.[67] What proved more difficult was dealing with the actual boxes, which were now rotten.[68] The entire former staff of the Babylon Expedition was still there, and came to help: the old foreman, the water-carrier Ali Jamus (Ali 'Water-Buffalo' –

---

66 See Note 52, Mem. 174. 261.

67 Mem. 262. – For the whole story see W. Andrae, MDOG 65, April 1927, 7 ff.:

'Journey to Babylon for the division of the Babylon finds: After correspondence between the Honorary Director of Antiquities for the State of Iraq, Miss Gertrude Bell, and the German Oriental Society (DOG), it has been decided that finds left in Babylon by Koldewey from the excavations of the German Oriental Society and the Berlin Museums should be divided according to the new antiquities law. The DOG suggested me as delegate, the General Director of the State Museums gave his permission and the Iraqi regime, through Miss Bell, accepted the suggestion. Autumn 1926 was settled on for the undertaking. I had asked for an assistant, after my experience with transporting the Assur finds from Portugal, and the Iraq regime had no objection to that either. The Minister for Science, Art and Popular Education agreed to provide the means of getting the Babylon finds back. The German Oriental Society appointed Dr. Jordan to take part in carrying it out. Miss Gertrude Bell's unexpected demise at the end of June did not after any of the arrangements. Her instructions, as we later discovered, remained unchanged with the authorities in Baghdad.'

See also Mem. 262 f.:

'On Sunday the 15th of October 1926 we went via the Adjutant Captain Holt to the High Commissioner Sir Henry Dobbs, who after a few friendly words of greeting passed us on to the Honorary Dietor of Anti-quites Mr. Cooke, Miss Bell's successor in the post. We made an appointment with him for the following day, the 16th, for our journey together to Babylon to start on our task. We cast an eye over Miss Bell's newly installed Iraq Museum in the Government Press building on the road to the old bridge, where Abdul Qadir Pachachi, our old representative at Assur was Curator. His assistant Selim Levi came with us to Babylon.

On the 16th of October we laid a wreath at Miss Bell's grave. We left at 8 o'clock and were at Babylon at 11. We discussed with Mr. Cooke the necessary arrangements to be made on the spot, and received his assurance that we might take the glazed brick fragments to Berlin. And the unbaked clay objects. The Iraq Museum was to have a reconstructed lion and a choice of baked tablets. The Expedition House was placed at our disposal, likewise the official guard and what was left of the furniture. Mr. Cooke had brought beds for us with him.'

68 MDOG 65, 1927, 12 ff.; Mem. 263 ff.:

'The Expedition House was placed at our disposal, likewise the official guard and what was left of the fur-niture. The old house which contained the finds had been walled up on Miss Bell's instructions, but was still accessible via a primitive ladder. We hacked open one door to the ›Museum‹ and took in the hopeless state of the unpacked finds. They were mixed up, strewn about, and partly soaked through from the leaking roof. Some bits were scattered wildly in other rooms. It seemed as though many hostile or ignorant hands had been at work here. The bookcases had been brought into the dining room, the only place still water-tight. Kolde-wey's room was empty, the roof fallen in. The open hall in the courtyard contained about 500 packed boxes, mostly bits of glazed brick. Mercifully the English had covered over the fallen roof with corrugated iron. Innumerable bats, pigeons, sparrows, wasps, hornets and white ants were nesting in the abandoned rooms. In the courtyard young palm trees were growing, which had not been there when Koldewey left in 1917 and owed their existence to discarded date-kernels. Among them was one whose crown already reached the 8 m high roof and filled much of the yard with its great fronds. Thick layers of dust lay over everything, and, as in a nature reserve, one saw little trace of the men who must have disturbed the idyllic peace of this walled-up castle over recent years. The impression was not very different from that you might have on opening an ›intact‹ Egyptian tomb to find that someone had after all been there before you.'

Fig. 14), and the artisans of Kuwairish (Fig. 15) and Hilla.[69] A small raft of boats was rigged up and Kurdish porters transferred the boxes from the house to the boat, which then stuck in the mud. A dash by car to the Hindiya Barrage, then an arrangement with the British official there provided the Hilla branch of the Euphrates with more water.[70] So the boats floated again and conveyed the boxes to Hilla to the crane on the narrow-gauge Baghdad-Basra railway. Goods wagons were waiting, and soon they proceeded to Basra. They were held up a little while longer in a storeroom at the harbour, and were finally conveyed by the German ship 'Trautenfels' from the Shatt al-Arab to Hamburg, thence to Elbe, Havel and Spree, and finally to Berlin. On the 20th January 1927 a total of 536 chests arrived from Babylon, of which about 400 were filled just with fragments of glazed brick.[71]

One result of Andrae's negotiations in Baghdad was the re-opening of a German expedition to Uruk-Warka, and in 1928 the work which had originally begun in 1913 started up again. Andrae supervised it from Berlin.

After Otto Weber's premature death in 1928 Andrae became director of the Near Eastern Department of the National Museums (Fig. 16), and remained so until 1951. This was a post that had traditionally always been held by a philologist. The governing body of the State Museums was supposed to suggest a candidate to the Prussian Ministry of Culture. Kurt Regling, director of the coin collections suggested that, in view of the intended arrangement of the Near-Eastern department in the New-Museum building, an architect would be an appropriate choice this time, one who had been familiar with the objects on exhibition from the moment of their discovery. The governing body and the Minister followed his suggestion.[72]

In the following years Andrae took on labours that provided even more tribulations than the excavation used to. After Koldewey's death on 4. 2. 1925 he became responsible for the publication of Babylon as well as working on the finds from Assur. At the end of 1927 intensive work began on putting together the Babylonian reliefs. Andrae used the pillared hall of the National Gallery on Museum Island as his workplace. A wall was put up between the pillars, with windows glazed at the top. Organised in se-

---

Men. 266:
'Towards the end of the job Abdul Qadir Pachachi, the Curator of the Iraq Museum appeared in Babylon to oversee the division and transport and ease the passage with the necessary documents.'

69 Mem. 264 f. V MDOG 65, 13 ff.

70 Mem. 267 f. = MDOG 65, 17 ff.

71 Mem. 268 f.:
'Eight wagons in all were loaded for Basra and four for Baghdad. 536 boxes were bound for Berlin, 93 for Baghdad. The actual quantity is of course no measure of the real division. Over the last 14 years of work Koldewey had collected about 400 boxes of glazed brick fragments whose fate depended entirely on whether they were allowed to go to Berlin or not. There the first part was already being worked on and built up into decorative elements and relief animals. It is definitely something to be thankful for, the fact that the Antiquities authorities in Iraq allowed this work to continue, the only sensible solution that could be found! The other objects were shared according to number and value with the Iraq Museum, as the new Antiquities law required.' = MDOG 65, 20 f.

72 Mem. 258 f.

quence, the work began: cleaning, desalinating, conservation, and sorting into animal, plant, or decorative forms, and finally putting the pieces together according to the Babylonian marks on the bricks.[73] In order to compare the basic architectural elements

---

73 W. Andrae, MDOG 13, 1902, 1 ff. and MDOG 66, 1928, 20 ff.:

'A first shipment, sent to Berlin by Koldewey in 1903, had already been almost worked through by the sculptor Scheschonka and the Inspector Otto, under the direction of the Near Eastern Department. According to an agreement with the General Director of the Stamboul Museum of Antiquities half of everything that was reconstructed had to go to Constantinople. So it is one of each pair of lions, bulls and dragons, which now decorate the walls of the Oriental Gallery of that Museum. At the end of 1927 I was made responsible for the new shipment from Babylon, which had arrived in the spring of 1927. In the meantime they had been worked on by Prof. Rathgen in the chemical laboratories of the Museums and were largely desalinated and impregnated with paraffin and generally ready for reconstruction. This task began in 1928 and was given over to the conscientious sculptor and moulder Struck, who, together with 6 to 8 assistants and the patience of a angel arranged the hundreds of thousands of pieces according to findspot and to type of animal or decorative motif.

Then he started trying to put them together into single bricks, and finally into complete animals: lions, buls and dragons, and then by stages into the various decorative elements that went with them. From all this one can work that the Lion Street in Babylon, according to Koldewey's reckoning, must have had at least 60 lions on the band of decoration on the one wall, so 120 lions in all. One could not expect that this vast number, or anything like it, could be put back together. The attentive reader of Koldewey's excavation reports and particularly of his book on the reconstruction of Babylon will remember in what sorry state Arab brick-robbers had left the walls of the street and most of the baked-brick palace of Nebuchadnezzar, to whom we owe this coloured ornament. In trying to put the pieces together we find joins from find-spots up to 100 m apart, easily explained by the activities of later robbers stirring up the spoil after large or small brick fragments.

One look at Struck's infinitely long work-table shows what a painstaking job this joining is. On it everything is arranged according to type, for instance all pieces with a lion's eye or with the right forepaw of a left-facing lion are arranged together. We know that all 60 lions on one side of the street come from one and the same mould, that is, each of the fifty-odd bricks of about 33 cm length and 10 cm height, which make up one lion, out of one mould, and likewise the other 60 lions, which are distinct from the others in that they march in the opposite direction and connect differently. The same applies to the two kinds of bulls and dragons. In addition there are colour differences among all six types of animal. On top of that one must reckon with the fact that the baked bricks from the walls had not been gently handled and came to us split. This splitting occurred mostly in the places where in Nebuchadnezzar's factory the moulders pressed lumps of clay together into the moulds. Their finger impressions show clearly how they carefully layered six or seven little lumps into the mould. Women and children must have been engaged in this, for the fingers are often quite little. These lumps have not always stayed stuck together. In firing a hair-line crack would remain, and the relief surface has almost always split along it. So we always get about 6–7 fragments for one relief-face of a brick, and the reconstructor must look for two flat bits that fit out of perhaps hundreds of possibilities. In fact, it succeeds, and only when further searching is hopeless is reconstruction resorted to, naturally in perfect imitation by the antiquaries.

I need scarcely say a word to the reader of this report about the terrific expense, both of labour and cash. We are committed to placing the result alongside the great sculptures of Pergamon and the Mshatta façade, and consider ourselves the guardians responsible for a great historical treasure, which we are bound to treat with the greatest care. The result will speak for itself and more than repay every effort.'

See in conclusion the relevant work at the chemical laboratory of the Berlin Museums and Friedrich Rathgen (2. 6. 1862–19. 11. 1942) in H. Otto, Das chemische Laboratorium der Könglichen Museen in Berlin (The Chemical Laboratory of the Royal Museums in Berlin), Berliner Beiträge zur Archaeometrie 4, 1979, 55: 'Even greater was the effort needed to rescue the many glazed bricks from the famous Processional Way and Ishtar Gate at Babylon, which contained about 1% common salt and in drying out led to the danger of the glazing crumbling. Soaking to remove the salt content took place in 200 great vats, for which undertaking a separate hut had to be constructed. After a year and a half they could be taken out.' 64 ff. 76 f. – See also L. Jakob-Rost – E. Klengel – R. B. Wartke – J. Marzahn, Das Vorderasiatische Museum (The Near Eastern Museum), 1987 Fig. 141.

Fig. 14 Ali Jamus 'the water-buffalo': one-eyed
water-carrier to the Babylon excavation, 1926

of the reconstruction, the portions of brickwork with simple decoration, or even none
at all, had also to be filled in. Andrae's efforts at three ceramics factories in Berlin culmi-
nated in the simultaneous re-invention of the Babylonian glazing technique.[74] As his
plans took shape on paper, the relevant officials saw the incredible quantity of brick

Fig. 15 Carpenter nailing up a
transport chest. Babylon, 1926

---

74 Mem. 274: 'For this purpose I persuaded three Berlin workshops to each try in their own way to reproduce as nearly as possible the six Babylonian colours, and that of Frau Helene Körting was the best by a long
way'.

fragments still lying on the long tables in the colonnade.[75] It was not easy to make them imagine the as yet unseen result. Andrae describes how he succeeded in doing this (Mem., p. 274 ff.): 'We had to arrange with the building management for reasonable modification of the shell of the exhibition's new home, which had been put up without consulting us. The entire southern wing had been presented to us rather like a fancy-dress costume which did not fit properly. We had to try to make the best possible use of the various dimensions of the walls and rooms. I tried to 'help along' the somewhat limited imagination of the Museum architects with the colours and perspectives of a few watercolour sketches. The Ministry giving the money had to be helped along too, by the most easily comprehensible means, that is, in life-size! Wille, the building counsellor, was so impressed with my perspective drawing of the Ishtar Gate that he had it made in wood and paper, and got the scenery painters of the State Opera to paint onto it my bulls and dragons, true to life down to the shadows – it was a comedy to watch.[76] The ministerial officials – who had previously only wanted a single pair of each type of animal, because they were 'all the same', were so taken with this theatrical model that they immediately agreed to everything. I extolled the building counsellor. His name was Wille, and henceforth I called him 'Good Will(e)', and I blessed the scenery painters and their big brushes.

There was nearly another mishap: the Ishtar Gate did not stand quite four-square, and that of course would not do in a Prussian national building. Nothing could be done, however, because in the next gallery the famous Miletus Gate had already been built, and access had to be maintained, leading through the Ishtar Gate, against which it stood back-to-back. Ludwig Hoffmann, Alfred Messel's successor, and creator of the new building, wanted to give the Miletus Gate a different central axis from that of the Ishtar Gate Gallery, to make the ground-plan 'more interesting'. Quite out of the question, of course: I let slip the dry observation that 'King Nebuchadnezzar didn't have his Ishtar Gate standing four-square at Babylon'. The building was thus saved, and for evermore participants in the procession along the Lion Street will all look through the Ishtar Gate at a slight angle.'[77]

In the late twenties and early thirties the construction of the Department was continually held up by economic difficulties, which Andrae had to overcome by constant negotiations with the Prussian Ministry of Finance.

More animal representations were put together from the pool of brick-fragments than were actually necessary for the Ishtar Gate and Processional Way. A few examples were given to the Iraq Museum, but Andrae managed to sell the rest to museums in Europe and America.[78] According to the law the proceeds from the sale of State prop-

---

75 See the photographic figure in W. Andrae, MDOG 66, April 1928, 19 ff.; J. Renger op. cit. (see Note 24) 161 Fig. 17; H. Otto, Berliner Beiträge zur Archäometrie 4, 1979, Figs. on p. 64–66.

76 MDOG 66, April 1928, 23 Fig. 9.

77 See his sketches Nos. 81–84 with accompanying text.

78 Mem. 277 f.

Fig. 16 Walter Andrae, portrait by Irmin Grashey-Straub, 1952

erty belonged to the Ministry of Finance. Thanks to certain Ministry officials with an appreciation of the arts, Andrae was able to use the not inconsiderable proceeds for the completion of the Department. And that did not follow as a matter of course in a time of such stringent financial crisis in Germany.

Andrae was reponsible for various expanding spheres of museum work: for working on the finds that came in from Uruk-Warka from 1928, for the publications, for building up the Department in the Museum, and for teaching at the Technical College (Technische Hochschule) in Berlin. He could not have done all this without the numerous helpers he found, or who found him.

Andrae returned to the East twice after 1926–7. In 1932 he travelled through Syria and Iraq, and visited the current excavations there, particularly to observe progress at the dig at Uruk. An archaeological congress in Turkey enabled him to visit Boğazköy, where Kurt Bittel had begun digging. To sum up the remaining years, one might mention that Andrae taught at the Berlin Technical College (Technische Hochschule) as supernumerary professor. And from 1946 to 1951, now over seventy (No. 3), he was Professor-in-Ordinary of architecture and architectural history at the same institution, which had meanwhile become the Technical University. On being made Professor Emeritus in 1952 he became an honorary senator of the same (Fig. 16). In 1914 he was awarded the silver Leibniz medal of the Prussian Academy of Science, and in 1951 the Order of Merit of the Federal Republic.

An appreciation based on personal experience of a man's character can say more than a summary such as the foregoing, and for this reason the reminiscences of Ernst Heinrich,[79] Andrae's pupil, colleague and successor, are included here.[80] In fact, nothing more apt has been said or written about the man. Heinrich spoke thus in memory of Walter Andrae at a meeting of the Koldewey Society in 1957. Andrae was a founder-member of this special school of architectural research.

---

79 15. 12.. 1899–28. 3. 1984

80 E. Heinrich, in: Neue Ausgrabungen im Nahen Osten, Mittelmeerraum und in Deutschland (New Excavations in the Near East, the Mediterranean and in Germany) in: Bericht über die Tagung der Koldewey-Gesellschaft in Regensburg vom 23.–27. 4. 1957 (Report on the assembly of the Koldewey Society in Regensburg from 23rd to 27th April 1957), 7 ff.

An appreciation by Ernst Heinrich

THE LIFE AND ACHIEVEMENTS OF WALTER ANDRAE

I first heard of Andrae from my teacher Daniel Krencker, an inspired and inspiring individual, who told us all about him and his work at Babylon and Assur. He showed us Andrae's drawings, which at the time were displayed in a room of the old Museum. There I saw for the first time the life-size watercolours of the brick-reliefs from Babylon and the delightful reconstructions of the buildings at Assur: scenes from a strange land, and difficult for us to fathom. Then Andrae himself came to see us. He had just settled in Berlin after his ten years in the field. This was after the war, which he spent mostly back in the Near East as an army officer, and after a short period of reflective peace at his farm at Hemmenhofen am Untersee. He came across as healthy and robust, a strikingly tall and imposing figure. While without the least pretension, he gave an impression of inner serenity, of self-confidence. He said little – in fact merely answered Krencker's questions – but what little he did say brought his pictures so much to life that we were fascinated. He was very serious and matter-of-fact, and this first impression of him, which stayed with me for a long time, awakened deep respect without hinting at the warm heart within.

Once I began to work under his supervision, our relationship was much the same: I would almost call it cool and impersonal. He was not readily approachable. Heinrich Lenzen and I started work on the Babylon and Assur finds at about the same time, in the summer of 1928. The way Andrae dealt with us says a lot about him. In fact, he did not deal with us at all. We had each taken on a really difficult subject, without knowing the first thing about it. We were handed the plans and inventories and shown whereabouts in the Museum store the relevant finds were kept, then left to get on with it. I am convinced to this day that Andrae did this on purpose, not out of lack of interest. He considered that methodology and familiarity with the literature were not unimportant, but were essentially tools which everyone has to learn to use for himself. Anyone without sufficient stamina, will, and application, soon found himself ready to give up, and this seemed to Andrae just as it should be. He only began to make corrections when our work was in its final draft. Of course, by working in this way we meandered somewhat – at least I did – and could be said to have 'wasted' a lot of time. In fact, for what we were to go on to do, it was all to the good, and Andrae possessed a character trait which has become rare today: he could always wait till the time was right. I never saw him lose his patience, even when the building of the new Museum, the new exhibition of the Near Eastern department, publication, teaching commitments both in the Technical College (Technische Hochschule) and in the Museum, looking after expeditions in the field and committee work really amounted to terrific pressure. He never appeared flustered, even for a moment, even when swamped by deadlines to be met. I never heard from his lips the well-worn phrase 'I haven't time'. Where chaos threatened, his persuasive calm restored order at once. We never heard him raise his voice, or talk 'off the top of his head', as they say. He corrected mistakes calmly, and minor offences such as other people might take to heart he ignored or treated with apt but never vicious irony. He never bore an offender any grudge, because such things were trivial to him and he forgot them at once. If, however, an ill-wisher managed to transgress on a particularly sensitive spot, or misused his trust, then he would sever relations altogether. And there would be no going back.

There was only one thing Andrae insisted upon, and he convinced himself that we approved: anything we did had to be executed with the greatest thoroughness and accuracy, no matter whether it was important or comparatively insignificant. He applied the same rule to himself. This is worth emphasizing, because many know him mainly from his later works, in which he sought to synthesize on a broad basis without much reference to the particular. It is easy to overlook the fact that he was primarily a master of painstakingly patient and eloquent detail. Putting together the brick-reliefs from Babylon, his own project from the start, is proof of that. His 'Archaic Ishtar Temples at Assur (Archaische Ischtartempel in Assur)' which appeared in 1922, was a milestone in our field, as it was the first publication of a careful stratigraphic excavation. It provided the first application of excavation technique to ancient Mesopotamian chronology and art history, and the results still stand today. I often observed him working on such minutiae when the Assur and Babylon finds came back from Lisbon and were being prepared for publication and exhibition. He applied the same patience whether involved in mending a simple storage jar or restoring a great sculpture from countless fragments. For weeks he and the master-moulder tried this and that until he was familiar with the positions of the figures in the big water-basin of pieces from Assur and was as sure as possible of the correct reconstruction. He went about the planning of the new Museum galleries and the exhibition of the finds with the same care and calm, never over-hasty. Every detail, every technical matter, down to the arrangement of individual cases, was thought out in advance. He knew good, honest craftsmanship and how to appreciate it. He always guarded against the mere collection of individual items or even restriction to the pursuit of knowledge in the fields of art, culture, and art-history. For him these were only stages on the way to a particular goal, of which I shall say more shortly. The precision in his work, which he both practised and demanded, was not just a working method, one without which no result could be considered certain. It came rather from an unusually highly-developed respect for the legacy of ancient peoples, be it represented by the simplest pottery vessel or by some great work of art. He treated even the most unprepossessing pieces with tenderness, and never allowed trivial explanations for unknown and puzzling phenomena. Even these were to him witnesses to a vanished way of life, one which he did not consider dead and isolated, but as something to be held in the highest esteem as being precursor to a part of our own lives. Esteem. That was a sentiment which he breathed. It is often said that one should only lay hands on the remains of an ancient culture with respect, but it is not always done. With Andrae this ideal was upheld to the letter, and instilling it into his students and colleagues was one of the basic precepts of his teaching.

The way he left us entirely to ourselves to begin with might give the impression that he had neither talent nor inclination for teaching. In fact the opposite was the case, for all that he did was designed to influence the people around him, to educate in the real sense of the word. It was just that he went about it in an unusual and unsystematic fashion. To begin with we were guided only by his example, but that changed as we got to know him better. His colleagues had increased in number, and almost every mid-day he emerged from his office to spend an hour with us in the drawing-office. Conversation would follow, in which Andrae naturally took the lead. He was a wonderful raconteur, and the talk often turned itself to the East and what he had done and experienced there. The countryside with its steppe and desert, its two rivers and mountain ranges, its towns and inhabitants, Kurd and Arab – all these we heard and learnt about, until when we actually encountered them they were no longer foreign. Then there were tales of everyday life on an excavation, its trials and rewards. Andrae had a well-developed sense of humour, and much that had probably pained him greatly at the time was now recounted in a way that brought forth gales of laughter. Thus we learnt the basic theory of excavation. At the same time a whole host of personalities became vividly real for us: Gurlitt and Koldewey, Andrae's teachers, for whom he kept all his life a warm heart and an almost fanatical regard; his colleagues at Babylon and Assur, then influential people in the academic, administrative and economic worlds. What we learnt in this way of persons and characters was very useful to us later. However, Andrae did not linger on such subjects, and soon the talk would come round to what we were involved in at the time. For him the most important thing after the exhibition of the collections was the preparatory work for 'The Origin of Building in the Near East (Urformen des Bauens im alten Orient)', and later for 'The Ionic Column: Structural or Symbolic? (Die Ionische Säule, Bauform oder Symbol)'. Andrae was living through a transformation in working methods. Towards the end of his life he described this stage, which he considered not only right for him personally but as the general culmination of every scientific endeavour, thus: 'Once something has been worked through at the material level and more or less grasped from the emotional and psychological point of view, then it must be thoroughly worked over and fulfilled at a spiritual level'. Many of you know this quotation from our eightieth birthday dedication volume, and Andrae explained more in subsequent sentences. This meant that in our conversations a subordinate role was played by matters like whether finds should be arranged according to chronology or state of preservation. For him this kind of thing could and should be left to the realm of good honest craftsmanship, and he took it all for granted. His aim was to discover the spiritual aim behind the outward form of an object. Once this was achieved it became of more than mere antiquarian interest to Andrae, and represented a particular stage of physical existence. Its relationship in turn to the metaphysical then had a bearing on his own development and self-awareness. I know Andrae would not really have agreed with the way I am trying to express something that was so fundamental to him, but I can only use my own words to describe what we experienced at the time. I felt that Andrae epitomized all the timeless ethical qualities of scientific knowledge. The basic precepts of his teaching were: 'Find yourself in that which you find in antiquity' and 'Build on your knowledge and live by it.' I still remember how astonished I was in 1928 when I heard his first lectures, after he had asked me to assist him with his teaching and practicals at the Technical College (Technische Hochschule). Virtually no material was referred to – that was left to me in the practicals – rather, he led his audience from the nature of objects to the nature of human beings, as he saw it, and thence to the darkest secrets of metaphysics. Even when he became Professor in Ordinary for History of Architecture, after the Second World War, he taught in the same way. No-one else would really have dared to, but the students followed him eagerly, and his pupils still speak of him as an unusual colleague, mostly with enormous gratitude. His facility for leadership came very much to the fore in almost all that he did. His lectures in the Museum bore witness to it, even the way the finds were exhibited. A casual visitor saw only a chronological arrangement of the usual kind, and admired most the great architectural remains of Babylon and Assur, for which, along with the Pergamon Altar, the Berlin Museum was and is particularly famous. But Andrae saw therein an exposé of the stages of man's development, which one should recognize and allow to act upon one. We know too that the arrangement and choice of the objects, the pictures on the wall, taken from his own paintings, even the colours of the walls, of the ceilings and of individual decorative elements were all calculated down to the last detail.

It was not always easy to follow Andrae's train of thought, and not all of what he said and wrote during his last 25 years passed without criticism. Even our discussions in the Museum could become heated, and I have witnessed persons of academic standing and broad mind who were in fact good friends disagreeing vehemently at his lectures. Andrae's basic tenets definitely rested on very precise and individually influenced concepts of a religious and philosophical nature. It has been said that he projected his own convictions into the interpretation of his finds, instead of questioning the evidence, as scientific method requires. Andrae would not perhaps have considered such an insinuation as criticism. Firstly he did not make a distinction between the two areas. Secondly, along with intuition, what he called 'perception' had the same legitimacy in interpretation of reality. Such a working method can hardly be recommended to everyone. Anyone else would come to grief by it, even if he had as many decades of experience in objective, unbiassed observation and the same thorough classical education as Andrae. But with him the combination of the researcher's observation and the poet's intuition – for that is what it seems to me to boil down to – led to results and conclusions entirely peculiar to him, and of real and immeasurable value, even if some have been superceded or will become so. And his endeavours have had a beneficial effect even on those who could not or would not follow precisely in his footsteps. He was sufficiently generous of spirit to tolerate ways of thinking other than his own, as long as objectivity and honesty could be demonstrated. For these he both demanded and revered.

To know Andrae well one had to see him at home with his children, and with his wife, who not only saw to his physical well-being but was also his spiritual companion. He was a good father, made time for his children, drew enchanting picture-books for them, and in summer went out nearly every Sunday with the whole family to one of the lakes to spend the day enjoying the sunshine and water. Moreover, this was not out of step with his psyche. Pleasure in nature, in his children, in his friends, in his work, were all in harmony with him. Lying in the meadows or in a boat on Sundays his 'musings' filled many notebooks. His paternal concern was not restricted to his family either. Anyone in his circle of acquaintance who was in trouble could come to him for advice, and if necessary for help, which I suspect he often gave at considerable personal sacrifice. His circle was wide-ranging. His lectures and tours were famous in Berlin, and created a following of visitors who knew each other and even became friends. Outside the sphere of our Museum there was another circle with which Andrae had connections through his religious convictions. His relationships therefore with his colleagues, professional and otherwise, were broadly-based and for the most part extremely cordial. But the core of his life remained the Museum circle, which he built up himself, whose academic principles he had created from scratch and in a curious way still managed. He had reason to be proud of his colleagues as he went from one to the other, discussing their daily work with them, from his two faithful secretaries, his old friends and co-workers from Assur and Babylon, to us young architects, the philologists, the archaeologists, to the library, the two photographers, the old departmental overseer, the people in the stores, in the casting workshop, in the stone and carpentry workshops. His energy, his care, his sense of purpose, held all this together. The best thing about it was that no-one felt under any coercion. Wherever he appeared there was no sudden rush to be seen to be working, no interruption if a meal was in progress, no task set suddenly aside. Although he enjoyed the highest respect, no-one feared him as a superior, and when he chanced along eyes were bright and faces happy. He made us all one big, happy family, and among ourselves we considered him a father.

The war brought great unhappiness to Andrae, in his family life and in his profession. His circle of friends was destroyed, the Museum badly damaged and robbed. He got to work straight away, and started many things over again from the beginning. At the Technical University he took on greater responsibilities than before with the post of Professor of Architecture and History of Architecture. Then he began to have trouble with his eyesight, and as this became an increasing handicap, he began to withdraw from his official duties. All the same, as long as he lived he was the fulcrum of all our endeavours. He helped the new director of the Near Eastern department. Without any thought for himself, he remained at the service of his Faculty as Professor Emeritus, he presided over the meetings of the German Oriental Society with stature and wisdom, he advised the comittee of the Koldewey Society and concerned himself with the outstanding volumes of publication of the German Oriental Society. He died when the last volume of architecture from Assur had appeared, and his life's work was finally fulfilled. I was able to take part in the service of blessing conducted according to the rites of his sect, on the day before the funeral with its customary mourning, pomp and eulogies. Yet at his house there was no mourning. No tears were shed and no words spoken except those of the liturgy. It was a grateful leave-taking of a truly fulfilled human being, one who had literally finished his work, who was a blessing to so many, who had loved and been loved in return, and who has now passed on before us. And it is with gratitude that he lived, and lived among us, that we shall hold his memory in honour.

CATALOGUE TO PLATES 1–128 (NOS. 1–198)

(Unless otherwise stated the background is plain paper or plain cartridge-paper. All measurements are in centimetres.)

1 1908 – Coloured chalk on tinted paper – 23.0 × 18.8
Self-portrait, Assur.

2 1915 – Oil-painting by Johann Walter-Kurau – 87.0 × 79.0
Walter Andrae as a captain, in front of one of his first sketches of a lion from the Processional Way at Babylon. Note the signature "AW 1899" near the lion's right paw, and compare No. 80.
Deutsches Archäologisches Institut, Baghdad Dept.
Artist: Thieme-Becker 35 (1942) 133 has: Walter-Kurau, Johann, Painter, 4. 2. 1869–1932. The same painter is also responsible for the large wall-painting of the Kasr at Babylon in the Vorderasiatisches Museum at Berlin. See L. Jakob-Rost – E. Klengel – R. B. Wartke – J. Marzahn: Das Vorderasiatische Museum (1987) 91.

3 1948 – Oil-painting by Otto Jäger – 63.4 × 50.0
Walter Andrae.
Deutsches Archäologisches Institut, Baghdad Dept.
Artist: H. Vollmer, Allgemeines Lexikon der bildenden Künstler des XX. Jahrhunderts 2 (1955) 522 has: Jäger Otto, Dr. of philosophy and medicine, German painter, born 21. 8. 1900.

4 18. 12. 1898 – Watercolour – 17.6 × 25.3
In the harbour at Alexandria.
See RK 97 ff.

5 21. 12. 1898 – Watercolour – 18.8 × 25.5
Port Said.
See RK 100 f.

6 22. 12. 1898 – Pencil – 18.5 × 27.5
The 'Nettuno' at Jaffa (Caption 'Saturno' subsequent and incorrect).
Berlin, Staatsbibliothek, SPK, Andrae Bequest 15/2.

See RK 101 ff:

'Sailing along the Palestinian and Syrian coasts, with no ports, was quite different from the voyage along the North African coast. One is put in mind of the ancient Phoenicians, plying the Mediterranean coastline up to the pillars of Hercules with their wares, without really having a home base. What pass for harbours here are only really suitable for sheltering small craft and fishing vessels against the breakers thrown up by the westerly storms of this north-south coast. The old ›Nettuno‹ was like a steam-powered and rather grubby Phoenician, and like its ancient counterparts, and their pupils, the Hellenic Greeks, kept nice and close to the shore. It did not venture into the ›ports‹, even Beirut.'

7 22. 12. 1898 – Watercolour and pencil – 18.0 × 26.9
   Jaffa. View from the vessel.
   RK 102:
   'The Palestinian coast is distinctly unattractive. As you come into Port Said a low and even range of hills obscures the view of the interior. It stretches from north to south, brown in colour. The great historical secrets of the land are kept hidden from the seafarer. One cannot see much at Jaffa, ancient Joppa, either, when steamboats are moored. Often enough it is not possible for the steamboats to dock at all and let their passengers disembark. These are then taken on a detour to Cyprus or back to Port Said, usually in difficulties until they can alight.'

8 22. 12. 1898 – Pencil – 27.2 × 18.4
   Aboard the Nettuno off Jaffa (see Nos. 6 and 7). Robert Koldewey with the Arabist Dr. Bernhard Moritz (see Mem. 32). Bernhard Moritz had already accompanied R. Koldewey in 1886/7 on his first visit to Mesopotamia (Surghul and al-Hibba). See RK 38.96. As Director of the Khedive's Library in Cairo he took part in the Baalbek exploration, though for only eight days, as the Arabic inscription which interested him proved to be out of reach.
   See RK 101.

9 23. 12. 1898 – Pencil – 27.5 × 19.0
   View of Beirut.
   Berlin, Staatsbibliothek, SPK, Andrae Bequest 15/3.
   See RK 104.

10 23/26. 12. 1898 – Watercolour – 34.7 × 24.8
    Beirut, view of the Hotel Bassoul.

11 28. 12. 1898 – Watercolour – 17.0 × 25.0
    Baalbek, general view (temple area).
    Berlin, Staatsbibliothek, SPK, Andrae Bequest 15/4.
    See RK 96. 106 ff. and Mem. 29 f.:
    'After the voyage, landing in Alexandria and, staying in Damascus over Christmas 1898 we finally reached our goal, Baalbek, on the 30th of December 1898. Robert Koldewey was required by the Kaiser to make a preliminary investigation of the ruins with a view to later excavation. The great temple (of Jupiter) had 19 columns along and 10 across. Now there are just 6, 19 m high, with a mighty cornice (see illustration) on mighty foundations. Of the small temple (of Bacchus) there remain the cella and about 20 columns of 1.8 m diameter and

5.2 m circumference (Nos. 13 and 14). The architecture reminds one of Baroque, with mighty niches on the inside, always two one above the other, ornamented, always constructed of the mightiest blocks. One column has fallen in the earthquake and leans on the cella wall. The whole thing was reinforced in the 13th century by Saladin's successor, made into an impregnable fortress, with maximum defensive cunning. It is actually a separate masterpiece, this time of Islamic architecture, with glorious cross-arches and stalactite niches, trapdoors, arrow-slits and bridges (Nos. 16 and 17). Unfortunately these later additions have damaged some of the lovely ancient parts; but one can easily see the overall plan.

For an artist the ruins are a real treasure. You would not believe how golden the mighty limestone pillars gleam against the blue sky, with behind them the brilliant peaks of the Lebanon and Antilebanon, which are at their highest here.

The snows are melting now in the valleys, and the fertile Beka'a plain is red again, a deep red-brown with patches of green. In the evening it is particularly lovely – an unaccustomed feast of colour for the eye. The Antilebanon is a glowing rose coloured reflection of the setting sun, the valley cloaks itself in the blue and violet gloaming, and the sky changes from minute to minute (No. 12). Then the clear shining moon climbs out from the snowy peaks and lights up the nocturnal landscape so brightly that you can read and write by it. From our room we can see the whole side of the ghostly ruins with white Sannin (3,200 m high) in the background. The air is lovely here, for we are 1,200 m above sea-level.'

'My work is very interesting, and absorbs one completely in the scheme of the great plan. And I draw and paint for all I'm worth, for the landscape is absolutely glorious. From the battlements of the Arab fortification wall, which is built round the temple precinct, one has a fine view over the reddish plain of the Beka'a and of the mighty snow-clad Lebanon, which glistens in the sunlight (Nos. 11, 14). And in the evening, when the sun sinks behind the snowy peaks, you can turn round and watch the alpine glow on the Antilebanon (No. 12), at the foot of which the ruins lie.'

12 2. 1. 1899 – Watercolour – 19.5 × 17.8
   Baalbek, dusk over the Lebanon range.
   See notes to No. 11.

13 16. 1. 1899 – Watercolour and pencil – 35.3 × 25.3
   Baalbek, at the temple of 'Bacchus'.
   See notes to No. 11.

14 Jan. 1899 – Watercolour – 35.3 × 25.3
   Baalbek, temple of 'Bacchus'.
   See notes to No. 11.

15 Jan. 1899 – Pencil – 34.0 × 24.3
   Baalbek, in the forecourt of the temple of 'Jupiter Heliopolitanus',
   detail.
   See notes to No. 11.

16 1. 1. 1899 – Pencil, coloured pencil – 33.5 × 24.2
   North Baalbek, at the Arab bastion.
   See notes to No. 11.

17 1. 1. 1899 – Pencil – 18.5 × 27.3
Baalbek, first floor of the Arab bastion.
See notes to No. 11.

18 February 1899 – Pencil – 24.00 × 33.5
Aleppo, Tekke (Dervish mosque). See No. 154: Takiya al-Shaikh Abu Bakr and No. 228.
Berlin, Staatsbibliothek, SPK, Andrae Bequest 15/6.

19 22. 1. 1899 – Pencil – 27.7 × 18.6
Iskenderun, Market.

20 22. 1. 1899 – Pencil – 27.1 × 18.5
Iskenderun, path leading up the Amanus mountains.
Described thus by W. Andrae, around 1950 (unpublished): 'On landing in the little harbour
we were caught by native viceconsul in a very primitive taverna. There were four of us, and
we had come from Beirut in the tiny Austrian vessel ›Nettuno‹. Now we were beyond European culture. A tortuous bazaar-alley served this little Turkish town. But we had to get into a
three-horse Landau with our luggage. And thus we travelled over the Bailon Pass of the
Amanus, taking three days to get to Aleppo.'

21 1. 1. 1899 – Pencil – 17.3 × 20.6
Baalbek, the innkeeper Perikli Mimikaki (Hotel Palmyra).
See RK 106.

22 February 1899 – Pencil – 24.4 × 14.4
Aleppo, 'Ain at-Tell. Picnic with Frau Koch. From right to left: three diplomats (probably
the German Consul Zollinger, the British Consul Barnham, and the British Vice-consul
Falanga, see Mem. 37), Mrs. Koch, R. Koldewey, two unidentified persons. See RK 114 ff.;
Mem. 35. 229:
'I had not the experience to be much use at organising the caravan. Help came from another
quarter, and without it the 14 day stopover would certainly have stretched to three weeks.
Martha Koch, wife of the trader Carl Koch, saw to all that was necessary. All Aleppo seemed
to be at her service. She knew where to get the best and cheapest mules and pack-horses, the
most reliable drivers, servants, and cooks, the best tents, covers, sacks, provisions, lanterns
and riding horses. She possessed dignity and authority, experience in the endless haggling
over the price and the energy to combat over-charging. In short, the entire caravan drama
was staged at ›bet Madame Koch‹ (Madame Koch's house), known to every child in
Aleppo.'
See also No. 160.

23 10. 2. 1899 – Pencil – 18.6 × 27.5
Derhafa: beehive baskets (between Aleppo and Meskene). Mem. 37 f.:
'On the 9th of February we proceeded towards Derhafa across flat cultivated plain. Since the
so-called road has become ›safe‹ over the last few years, fields have appeared from the desert,
at any rate near to the road. However, despite the fertile ground nothing is truly productive,
because wherever anything profitable appears the government lays hands on it and either

confiscates it or imposes high, almost impossible taxes on the natural produce. The villages here look like colonies of mole-hills, proper domes of unbaked brick, crowned with chimneys, every village a little fortress.'

24 11. 2. 1899 – Pencil – 18.5 × 27.3
The Euphrates valley at Meskene (caravan), Mem. 38 f.:
'On the third day we started along the Euphrates, which for three weeks was our constant companion and water-provider. The entire landscape is quite extraordinary, even bizarre – a natural undisturbed exhibition of geological history. A mighty Tertiary formation, over it even alluvium (brecchia, conglomerate), stretches over the entire land of the two rivers, the Euphrates and Tigris. Under the conglomerate is the Tertiary, then marl, then chalk, and limestone right at the bottom. At Meskene the marl stands to 30–40 m. The whole system is alluvial, broken through and torn and bruised by the stream-bed, and at the edges one can observe an almost mathematical section through the whole unlikely layering. The alluvial area consists mostly of the well-known fertile Euphrates mud, which is often 3–5 m deep, and is of greasy clay. The Euphrates winds through this in countless meanders, making numerous islands and mudbanks. The shores are almost vertical, even with concave sides, and a lot of destruction takes place. We often heard in the desert stillness a loud thunderous report as one of these clay walls fell into the water. In today's economic climate the fertility is but latent, and there is settlement in increasingly fewer places. Nothing is done to get the water up from the river, i.e. to make irrigation channels, even though that would benefit the regime, in the person of the highest mortal in the land. All land and its inhabitants belong to the Sultan, and he can treat them as he pleases. Anyone can take a barren piece of land and work it, but if it produces anything he must prove possession over a number of years' occupation or produce receipts for the purchase, which of course is never possible, or it can be taken from him. Unpopular persons find themselves preferentially swindled in this way. Now it is mainly tamarisk bushes or brambles and sometimes grass which dominate. We have only seen occasional fields, and their green is the more refreshing.'

25 11. 2. 1899 – Pencil – 16.5 × 18.2
Qal'at Baalis (Barbalissus), Byzantine Praetorium.
Sarre-Herzfeld I 123 ff. III Pl. 23.
See Mem. 40.

26 12. 2. 1899 – Ink – 13.5 × 18.8
Qal'at Djabar, 5th – 14th century.
There is a photograph taken about ten years later by Bell, AtA, Fig. 50. The present state of preservation can be seen in A. Mahmoud, Land des Baal (1982) Fig. 77.

27 14. 2. 1899 – Pencil – 9.0 × 18.2
Tell Menachir, between Ḥammàm and Sabḥa, a 'crown formation' mound (M. Freiherr v. Oppenheim's term ›Kranzhügel‹). For similar see Moortgat-Correns, Die Bildwerke vom Djebelet al Beda in ihrer räumlichen und zeitlichen Umwelt (1972) 26. 34 ff.; H. Kühne in: R. M. Boehmer and H. Hauptmann, Beiträge zur Altertumskunde Kleinasiens. Festschrift für Kurt Bittel (1983) 299 ff. According to Dr. Kay Kohlmeyer this is not a 'crown formation' mound as assumed in our first edition but an extinct volcano.
For basalt-deposits in this area see No. 141, No. 142 and the text of No. 222.

28 15. 2. 1899 – Watercolour – 16.4 × 24.5
The Euphrates at Tibne, see Nos. 140–142.
See Mem. 41.

29 15. 2. 1899 – Pencil – 9.3 × 18.5
Halebiyeh (Zenobia), Byzantine city gate. There is photo of Halebiyeh taken by Bell about
ten years later, AtA Fig. 46.
See also Sarre-Herzfeld I 166 ff., II 365 ff., III Pls. 72–75. RK 125 f.:
'To my knowledge Halebiyeh has not been worked on since E. Herzfeld and F. Sarre. It lies
in the narrow part of the Euphrates valley, the sides of which climb a good 100 m, and start
at the top with a great covering of volcanic basalt lava at the Ledscha. There is so much of
the black basalt in the landscape that it gives an impression of gloominess, against which the
bright buildings of the spectacular town on the slope fit uneasily. They are made of silver-
grey transparent gypsum or alabaster, worked by careful masons into gateways, city-walls
and churches as well as the Pallas inserted into the city wall. What one saw had been done in
Byzantine times. The city was named after the well-known Palmyrene queen Zenobia. At the
top of the high plain lies a small acropolis, falling steeply away on all sides, from which the
two diverging city-walls drop down to the river, along which runs an embankment wall
with sluices. On the other side there is a small town now called Zelebiyeh, the remains of
which were less imposing, and which we were not able to visit.'

30 19. 2. 1899 – Ink – 23.5 × 34.2
Qal'at ar-Rakhba, Seljuq ruins, 13th century, Sarre-Herzfeld II 382 ff., III 79.80; present
condition: A. Mahmoud, in: Land des Baal (1982) Fig. 76 (pencil sketch for the picture in
Berlin, Staatsbibliothek, SPK, Andrae Bequest 15/9.
RK 127; Mem. 42:
'The following day I rode with Dr. Koldewey and two soldiers to the ruins of the Arab castle Rakhaba, which was situated on a completely impregnable cliff surrounded by a 40 m
deep ditch. It had high walls of baked brick and stone, and was once the citadel of a great city
which streched from there to Meyadin with gardens and fields. Now it is totally barren.'

31 20. 2. 1899 – Watercolour and pencil – 33.8 × 24.3
The cliff at Khan Kalessi (Dura Europos).
See Sarre-Herzfeld II 386 ff. III Pl. 81–83; RK 122. 125 f.:
'Koldewey arranged the caravan journey so that we took in two important sites and were
not only able to see them, but to draw and quickly plan them too: Halebiyeh and Islahiyeh
(Khan Kalessi), ancient Dura Europos, which he mentioned in the letter above. The latter
site was worked on later for several years by a French-American expedition and published.
For me it was my first attempt at planning in Mesopotamia. Koldewey took me on a
methodical tour of the whole city area. The enclosure wall was well-preserved in two deep
gulleys, with the ›neck‹ of the fortress between them with a huge arched gateway. The acropolis, decimated by a terrific rock-fall, forms the steep slope down to the valley bottom of
the Euphrates. The view up and down the valley from the castle makes an unforgettable
impression.' Mem. 42:
'On the 20th of February we planned the hitherto unknown ruined city of Khan Kalessi
(Blood Castle), which lies half an hour's journey from the Euphrates. It has a wall of ala-

baster, but almost entirely fallen away. The interesting thing is that one can work out the ground-plan of the houses and streets from the ground surface.'

32 24. 2. 1899 – Watercolour – 35.0 × 25.0
Ana, entrance to the village. On the right along the bank, a water wheel on the island now submerged by the Haditha dam. Mem. 42:
'At Ana I saw the first date-palms, and what date-palms! Here the river forms a narrow, winding oasis in the yellow limestone cliffs and hills, stretching 20–40 days' journey to the right and left. Ana itself is three hours' journey long, with palm-trees all the way. We are lodging at the Saray, right under the great fronds of the palm-trees, by the burbling Euphrates, with the fertile island opposite. The na'urs (primitive water-wheels) creak gently, the shining moon is rising, and a deep bright stillness covers this lovely valley. I was writing down my impressions by moonlight, it is so bright here.'

33 24. 2. 1899 – Coloured pencil – 14.5 × 22.4
Ana, view from the Euphrates island.
Compare No. 32 and the photograph taken by Bell about ten years later, AtA Fig. 51.

34 24. 2. 1899 – Watercolour – 25.3 × 35.3
The Euphrates below Ana. In the foreground a post, throwing a shadow; in the background na'urs (water-wheels, as can be seen in Bell's photograph taken about ten years later, AtA Fig. 49 and No. 165. 166).
Compare No. 32.

35 26. 2. 1899 – Pencil – 33.9 × 24.6
Haditha on the Euphrates. On the near bank na'urs. (compare Nos. 32, 34, 165 and 166).
(An inked version of this picture Berlin, Staatsbibliothek, SPK, Andrae Bequest 15/4).

36 28. 2. 1899 – Watercolour and pencil – 24.4 × 34.0
Hit, tombs outside the town (a similar picture Berlin, Staatsbibliothek, SPK, Andrae Bequest 15/17). Compare Bell's photograph of about ten years later, AtA Fig. 54. Mem. 43:
'The glorious moonlight made up for the rigours of the day's riding during the following days too, till on the 28th of February we got to Hit (Herodotus' ancient Is). Six hours before we arrived we saw the smoke of the bitumen wells of Hit, known to the ancients. The spring is now dry, covered by a layer of bituminous limestone, worked in tiny holes by the locals in a most unrational fashion. The stench of salt water and sulphuric acid make the place a bit like Sodom and Gomorrah, particularly when the lit by the setting sun. Hit is on an ancient Tell (ruin-mound) and is a good example of the way such Tells build up. There are also many beautiful palm-trees by the river.'

37 10. 3. 1899 – Ink – 13.8 × 22.3
Baghdad, the 'Dragon Gate' or Talisman Gate (Bab el Tilism), Seleucid. Compare Bell, AtA 190 f. Fig. 114 f.; Sarre-Herzfeld III Pls. 10, 11 and 49; T. Jawad al-Janab, Studies in Mediaeval Architecture (1982) 46 Pl. 6.

Bagdader

Holz keilchen-
Kapitelle.

19.3.99.

> abra muss rubba -

N Kómas - Arbeit.

Fig. 17 Capital to a wooden pillar, Baghdadi style, March 19th 1899

38 March 1899 – Watercolour – 18.6 × 25.7
Baghdad, Kadhimain, mortuary mosque of the brothers Kadhim. Mem. 44:
'Baghdad! What you see first are the golden domes of Kathimein (pronounced Kathmen, with English th), which shine out in the sunlike two golden stars on the horizon, visible four hours before you get to them. The domes are covered with pure gold leaf, as thick as a finger nail: a great Shiite shrine!' The tombs themselves are at present in one of the domed rooms, each of which has two minarets.

39 15. 3. 1899 – Pencil – 22.0 × 13.6
Baghdad, Khan Mirjan (Seljuk, 760 aH/1359), Sarre-Herzfeld II ff. 111 Pl. 51; T. J. Al-Janab op. cit. 140 ff. Pls. 134–140,
Figs. 30–35.

40 7. 3. 1899 – Pencil – 13.4 × 9.1
Baghdad, alleyway (To accompany his first letter to his parents).

41 March 1899 – Pencil – 22.4 × 13.6
Baghdad, Berk house, court.
See AK 131 f. and Mem. 38, also Fig. 17.

42 1900 – Pen and ink – 17.6 × 27.5
The village of Kuwairish, view from Babylon.

43 1901 – Watercolour – 23.4 × 16.4
Babylon. Kuwairish, village street scene: children playing with astragals
(cf. R. M. Boehmers – N. Wrede, Baghdader Mitteilungen 16, 1985, 399 ff.).

44 1900 – Watercolour – 14.0 × 24.7
Babylon. Village street in Kuwairish after a thunderstorm.

45 1901 – Watercolour – 35.0 × 25.0
Babylon. Kuwairish, banks of the Euphrates south of the Expedition House.

46 1899 – Watercolour – 35.3 × 25.3
Babylon. Palm garden near Kuwairish.
Mem. 59 f:
'We now have the most wonderful, honey-sweet ripe dates. Something different from the sticky cardboard pulp that passes for dates in Europe. Here there are a hundred different sorts: yellow, grey, red, black, big, small, and all have different names. Now also begins the season for date-stealing, and day and night there are guards everywhere, often armed with old blunderbusses, but mostly just to demonstrate the existence of a guard. Now and again soldiers came and carry off a few datethieves, but it does not come to anything. The palm-gardens are a wonderful sight now. The dates are the purest golden yellow, surrounded by the deep green graceful palm fronds and brown and white trunks against the deep blue sky.'
Mem. 77:
'I must now add something of my experience with these stubborn date-palms. These plants – they are not actually trees, even if they do get to 20 m high and more – force the artist again

and again to his easel. To re-create them from colour alone gives an inevitable poor result and demonstrates neither their spirit nor their appearance. So if one does not wish to paint purely in the abstract then one must be resigned to patiently putting in each frond with all its tiny leaves, in other words to paint with a fine brush.

When you live for four years with the palms, see them sprout, bloom and fruit, and finally live off their sweet fruit, you feel obliged as a painter to do them justice, without abbreviation or charicature. You learn to respect them. You know what care they need and how richly they repay it. You understand why ancient man honoured them as almost divine and incorporated them into his symbolism as almost no other plant.'

47 1899 – Watercolour – 25.5 × 17.9
Babylon, Kuwairish. Koldewey's tent on the evening of the Babylon Expedition's arrival in the courtyard of the future Expedition House.
Mem. 38:
'Cases, saddlebags, flint and pistols, cartridge belt and camp stool, a place was found for everything. There was even room found for the table in the middle, and we dined at it on camp stools, extremely cosy and pleasant. Table and stools are made of bamboo, and so light that you can pick up the whole lot with one hand.'

48 1899 – Watercolour – 25.7 × 17.7
Babylon, Kuwairish. The Babylon Expedition House seen from the west across the river.

49 1900 – Watercolour – 25.0 × 17.5
Babylon, courtyard of the Expedition House in its first building phase, with finds.

50 1901 – Watercolour – 25.2 × 35.2
Babylon. View from the roof of the Expedition House into a neighbouring courtyard.

51 1901 – Watercolour – 9.3 × 12.1
Babylon, Expedition House. View of the courtyard after alterations.
Mem. 54 f.:
'Shortly after starting the excavation we also began alterations and additions to the house we had rented from Habib al Alaui, the sheikh of the village. I wrote thus to my grandfather in Dresden: ›The building work is a dreadful sight in our usually quiet courtyard. About 20 men are employed on it, none of whom can be quiet for a minute, but must be screaming, shouting, complaining, encouraging, even when it's not necessary. However, it is like an ant-heap with everyone puffing and panting with an iron determination for 10 hours at a time without letting up. The entire ground floor has been completed in a mere 8 days. Little boys, who earn 2 piastres (35 Pfennig) a day, bring the Teen (mud) to the building site, while two men standing the whole day up to their knees in the stuff make it up, mixing water with adjacent earth. That is the mortar. In critical places, like over an arch, gypsum can be used too, with one stone stuck to another, the gypsum sets so quickly that the arch is ready in half an hour and can be walked over. There is no scaffolding, and the stairs are built up the outside and are massive. They are made of baked bricks, each step out of three complete Nebuchadnezzar-bricks. It is a very successful operation, very interesting for me to watch as it goes on.‹

Over the building presided the master builder Ustad Emin, that is ›Master Emin‹. He came from the local centre of Hilla, measuring with his staff, planning, and keeping the workmen busy. He was a worthy man, with a big turban, carrying in his pocket only a pattern-book with secret building-codes. He fulfilled his masters' every wish in building. He drew out the required plan on the ground with his staff and began at once to lay mud-mortar and bricks directly onto it, then to carry on upwards till the desired object was attained. He also cast the brick ornamentation at the main entrance and worked it up in front of our eyes, all on the ground, which he first smoothed out with his hands. He worked the modern yellow-fired bricks with a pad-saw, laying them on the ground in all kinds of geometrical figures and stars according to the secret pattern-book, then filled them in with gypsum plaster and reeds to form a great ornamental frieze which could then be stuck on the wall over the door. In Koldewey's room he created a combination of stairs to the roof, niches, windows and a bench with a view of the Euphrates where Koldewey could have his siesta and smoke the local chibook. The new ›castle‹ waxed splendid and was finished with gleaming gypsum plaster, and became known to the Arabs as Kasr al-abiad, ›the white castle‹. It also became free of fleas, which did not like the snow-white gypsum walls and preferred to creep into the old mud rubble walls. But the wily Ustad Emin plastered these too and immured the fugitives alive.'

52 1902 – Watercolour – 25.2 × 35.3
Babylon, Expedition House, view of the courtyard.

53 Summer 1901 – Watercolour – 35.5 × 25.5
Babylon, Expedition House. A loggia on the upper floor, with a servant bringing coffee.
Berlin, Staatsbibliothek, SPK, Andrae Bequest 15/18.
Unpublished description by Andrae, about 1950:
'Shortly after excavations began the director, Robert Koldewey, had the Expedition House altered to include some European features. It lay at the north end of the village of Kuwairish in the courtyard of the village headman Habib el Alaui. During the alterations the four team members (Koldewey, Meißner, Meyer and Andrae) lived in the headman's mudif, that is the winter audience room (in summer people collected in the courtyard along the mud walls). The changes and additions meant the gain of an upper storey with living quarters, dining-room, bathroom, and 'museum'. In the courtyard there was a stall and an open hall for the finds. The mudif served the Turkish Representative Bedri Bey as living quarters, with a side-room for valuable finds which were separated and packed in boxes. The kitchen was under the living quarters on the ground floor. Later an outer courtyard in the palm garden was added, in which a further stall was made, and on the upper floor more living accomodation, which became known as the ›cavalier wing‹, as the younger members of the Expedition lived there. The picture shows the verandah of the old upper storey with the servant Murad wearing the traditional garb of a Baghdadi. He was a Chaldaean Christian.'

54 1899 – Coloured-in pencil drawing – 21.1 × 33.3
Babylon. W. Andrae in his room in the Expedition House.
Mem. 56 f.:
'I wrote letters home even in the July heat now setting in: ›Now that we have two hot, windless July days behind us people are at least telling us that it has been hot, and we are very

happy, for it was quite amusing. The whole world sweats, even the oldest folk. When it becomes warm they lose their energy, let everything flop, drink water and think of nothing but the heat. We always find ourselves something to do, slowly, as every bodily exertion costs a great deal of sweat. But by the end of the day we have always managed something, and we have much to do. Luckily the sun does not rise here until 5 and goes down at seven, even on the longest day. The nights are still pleasant. I am sending you one of the products of the hot days: an accurate picture of my room, with me sitting and sweating at my desk, dressed lightly and surrounded by the day's finds, with the 'decorated' wall behind. The carpets are not yet there, so the Eratonen flag is the only ornament, the little German flag and the round leather cut-out on the shaft being presents from Frau Koch, Aleppo; below there is a bookcase, with the library consisting almost entirely of sketch-books. There are lovely brown cupboard doors of Indian wood, brown ceiling of palm-trunks, table and side-table of white wood, and a pot-stand on the right – all the work of our carpenter in Hilla. On the left is the cupboard, with my shirt hanging on it to dry, as it was soaked with sweat, and above is the lamp and suitcase; below is the mysterious bag with the finds I have already drawn. The chest contains more of the same. On the right is the old grey trunk. at present being the Expeditions's strong-box, containing 2 to 3,000 marks apart from stored winter things. The cupboard in the wall contains toilet articles, and all kinds of paper, bits and pieces, and shooting materials; the hand-towel is drying too. The snake-like object hanging further along the wall, is twine, which is used a great deal. Below, in the palm-leaf basket is what I still have to do today. Then you see one of the windows with home-made curtain, the water-jar, and the yellowish thing is the teapot wrapped in wet towels, then the water-bucket, and my beloved rifle. The floor consists of monumental flag-stones; just another 40° warmer, and that will be that.'

55 1900 – Watercolour – 18.0 × 25.8
Babylon. Evening on the roof of the Expedition House. The servant is bringing the water-pipe.

56 1899 – Ink – 19.0 × 9.5
Babylon, Expedition House. A window in W. Andrae's work-room. See No. 61. In the background the chird (compare Nos. 61–63).

57 Babylon, 1899 – Pencil – 21.7 × 14.2
Babylon, loggia on the upper floor of the Expedition House.

58 1927 – Ink–
Babylon, Expedition House, inner courtyard.
After RK Fig. 18

59 1927 – Ink –
The Expedition House at Babylon on the Euphrates.
After RK Fig. 19

Fig. 18 Babylon. Inner courtyard to the Expedition House, 1927

60 1901 – Watercolour –
Babylon, Euphrates: View over the Babil mound, the north part of the ruins, from the Expedition House. Probably from R. Koldewey's window. Alter a storm. See No. 206.

61 1899 – Watercolour – 25.5 × 14.0
Palm-garden on the Euphrates with water-drawing device (compare Nos. 62 and 63), from W. Andrae's window in the Expedition House, in Babylon (see No. 56). See photograph in: R. Koldewey, Das wiedererstehende Babylon. 5th ed. (1990) Fig. 9.

62 April 1900 – Watercolour – 35.3 × 24.4
Babylon, water-drawing device by a nabuk tree: Zizyphus spina Christi, see Michael Zohary, Pflanzen der Bibel (1983) 154 f. with figures; D. Zohary and M. Hopf, Domestication of Plants in the Old World (1988) 178 f. (reference thanks to U. al-Sadoon). Compare Nos. 61 and 63.

63 1902 – Watercolour and ink – 28.8 × 45.2
Babylon, Euphrates. Cleaning the slipway of an animal-driven water-drawing device (chird): the animals pull up the water-buckers or sacks, which are then emptied by hand. For similar see e.g. B. H. E. Wulff, The Traditional Crafts of Persia (1966) 256 ff. and R. Koldewey, op. cit. (No. 61) 30. For the workmen, ibid. fig. 10.

64 1902 – Pencil with watercolour – 22.5 × 28.5
Babylon, boys fishing in the Euphrates with basket traps.

65 1901 – Watercolour and ink – 22.0 × 28.0
Babylon: Arab fishermen near the Expedition House at Babylon. The drag net is being let

Fig. 19 Expedition House on the Euphrates at Babylon, 1927

out from the boat. One man drives the fish upstream into the net by shouting and beating the water with a long stick.
Berlin, Staatsbibliothek, SPK, Andrae Bequest 15/15.

66 1900 – Ink – 13.5 × 22.0
Babylon, on the Euphrates.
Berlin, Staatsbibliothek, SPK, Andrae Bequest 15/12.

67 1900 – Watercolour – 35.5 × 24.5
Palm-trees on the Euphrates. Dawn, before sunrise, after a storm in the night.

68 1901 – Watercolour – 35.5 × 21.5
Babylon. Dusk over the palm-gardens of the Euphrates.
Berlin, Staatsbibliothek, SPK, Andrae Bequest 15/20.

69 July morning 1901 – Watercolour – 35.5 × 25.5
Babylon, in the palm-gardens near Kuwairish.
Berlin, Staatsbibliothek, SPK, Andrae Bequest 15/23.

70 1902 – Watercolour – 35.0 × 25.2
Babylon. Euphrates near Amran hill.

71 1901 – Watercolour – 24.9 × 17.6
Babylon. Dusk on the Euphrates.

72   1900 – Ink – 14.2 × 27.5
Islamic tombs on Tell Amran ibn Ali.

73   1901 – Watercolour – 24.5 × 35.0
On the Baghdad-Hilla road near Babylon.

74   January 1900 – Ink – 16.5 × 33.0
Babylon. The Kasr from the north-east.
Berlin, Staatsbibliothek, SPK, Andrae Bequest 15/11.

75   Undated – Watercolour – 16.0 × 24.0
Spoil heap of the excavation at Babylon.
Berlin, Staatsbibliothek, SPK, Andrae Bequest 15/32.

76   1899 – Watercolour – 9.3 × 6.4
Habib al Alauwi, the one-eyed sheikh of Kuwairish. (To accompany a letter of W. A. to his parents); G. Buddensieg. MDOG 42, 1902, 53 ff.

77   1902 – Pencil and watercolour – 26.5 × 19.3
Jum'a ibn Barakli.
Mem. 315:
'Jum'a means Friday. He was a cheerful, rather shabbily clothed lad with a big friendly grin. This young man was universally popular, but met an untimely death. Shortly after I had drawn him he stood too near to one of the Europeans who was handling his rifle carelessly, and accidentally shot and killed the boy. One can imagine what a furore such an event caused among the Arabs. If compensation were not made at once then revenge in kind would be exacted, taking no heed of the fact that the European had not done it on purpose. As leader of the Expedition, Robert Koldewey had to treat both with the local Turkish authorities and the village sheikh of Kuwairish to settle blood money for the parties concerned. The guilty European had to disappear from Babylon as fast as possible.'

78   1900 – Ink – 16.6 × 16.0
Babylon. Young Arab in a field-railway truck.
Mem. 57:
'The day before yesterday our railway for moving spoil arrived. It has taken two months from its arrival in Baghdad to get here, seven months to get here from Germany.'

79   1901 – Watercolour – 17.7 × 25.0
Men of Kuwairish dancing.
Mem 68 ff.:
'We have now lived through the 3-day Mohammedan festival with which the fasting month of Ramadhan concludes. It consists of general gluttonous swilling (one can scarcely call it eating), with song, dance, gunfire, drums and every kind of ear-besieging racket. They have been looking forward to it for a week and have reminded us so constantly of the customary Baksheesh which everyone must have for the festival that in the end we could not avoid paying it. For the festivities themselves everyone puts on new and splendid costumes, many in

silk and silver cloth, with the most brilliant reds and yellows preferred. The old women like dark blue and black from head to toe, and only the young women wear the piercing purple. Every man, indeed every boy over eight years old, bears firearms, at least a pistol, which he knows how to use.

The dances seem distantly related to the Hungarian, with lots of stamping and waving of red handkerchieves, altogether quite sedate. The music comes from a single double-flute, with a windsack as backing, and a negro drum. The main attraction seems to be the length of the dance, in which only men take part. We made our state-visit to the Kaimaken in Hilla for the festival and on the way there and back met a colourful procession of pilgrims going to Tell Amran to say their Suras (prayers). From Babylon to Hilla there was an uninterrupted stream of men, all in their Sunday best. You can hardly imagine the gay effect, it had such a splendid impression on the sparkling bright grey of the canal banks and waste desert earth, with the matt white-ish green palms in the background. Here the most ugly colours seem to glow. Fashion is always bringing something different, or rather, the latest shipment from Manchester or somewhere in Europe does. A sulphur-yellow head-cloth was in fashion just now, grass-green or Lincoln-green shirts, fire-red skirts, orange velvet jackets and similar ensembles. Everything glitters, nothing offends the eye, as long as you do not see it too often close up. Our Chaldaean Christian servants Murad, Rasuki and Abdallah had their best things on too: sky-blue waist-coats with gold stripes, gold or lemon-yellow shirts and gold-embroidered belts, with carmine pointed slippers of local make, which all wealthy folk wear for the festival.'

80 1899 – Watercolour – 17.0 × 27 (= 1/9th actual size)
First representation of the lion of the Processional Way at Babylon
Berlin, Staatsbibliothek, SPK, Andrae Bequest 15/79.
RK 90:
'Babylon was taken on (for excavation), specifically because of Koldewey's supposed brick reliefs. Koldewey often emphasized that [Richard] Schöne [General Director of Berlin Musems] had been responsible for recognising the value of the glazed work and for working energetically to push through the decision to investigate Babylon. Since the brick reliefs have been reconstructed in the Near Eastern Department, a small case on the wall shows the three unprepossessing fragments which Koldewey brought home from the preliminary expedition to Babylon and showed to Schöne. It is to Schöne's undeniable credit that he recognised from such small clues the unique worth of the destroyed art of Babylonian glazing and courageously supported such a long and expensive undertaking.'
Mem. 96:
'At the end of February [1901] I was finally able to write home ›Dr. Koldewey has now been digging for a week at Birs. In the meantime I have had much to do in Babylon, as our work has produced a large number of glazed bricks which I am obliged to reconstruct and which seem to come from three exclusive objects. More of that later! Because I have to do it all alone – every day there are three big chests of fragments to sort out, wash and number, then group and fit into the sketches – it takes up most of my day. I cannot let anyone else do it. But in spite of all the dirty work the results make it a worthwhile job! Every day a new and greater understanding is to be had from the reconstruction‹.'
R. Koldewey, MDOG 3, 1899, 4 ff. 10 ff.; F. Delitzsch, MDOG 6, 19, 15 f.:
'Painstakingly restored by Koldewey and Andrae, with the advantage of being fully and

entirely put together from original fragments, their reconstruction available to all members of the German Oriental Society, it is the ›Lion‹ of Babylon which prove beyond doubt the highest mastery of the artists of Nebuchadnezzar, at least in making lions.'

Mem. 275 ff.:

'As reported, the ground and first floors of the south wing of the new building were already promised to the Near Eastern Department in 1926. In 1928, when Otto Weber's untimely death took him from his family and the Museum and I became his successor, the whole situation changed at once. I became reponsible for all decisions over spatial disposition and internal building in the big exhibition halls on the upper floor. In particular it became essential to speed up the reconstruction of the Babylonian animal-reliefs, which was going ahead in a haphazard fashion, not according to my wishes, and downright incorrectly. I immediately acquired the right materials and a big workroom for the job, and employed the skilled mason Willy Struck, who got about 30 helpers and in two years had the amazing total of 72 relief-animals, big rosettes and ›decorative‹ bands ready. Then I persuaded three Berlin ceramics factories each to try in their own way to reproduce as nearly as possible the colours of Babylonian glaze, and Frau Helene Körting's turned out the best.

Between summer 1928 and summer 1930 we had 30 lions, 26 bulls, 16 dragons, 2 parts of the throne-room facade and the Parthian palace-facade made ready and set up in the south wing. The Processional way and the Ishtar Gate were opened for the Museums' centenary in 1930, along with the Pergamon Altar.'

Mem 279: on the further preparation of the coloured relief animals:

'I was able to send a few examples of these animals as presents to the museum of Antiquities in Istanbul and the Iraq Museum in Baghdad. Others I offered, with the approval of the Ministry, to museums within and without the country. They went to Vienna, Paris, Copenhagen, Gothenburg, Chicago and other museums in the USA, and finally to Dresden and Munich.'

81 1927 – Watercolour – 35 × 24.5

Working sketch of the reconstruction of the Processional Way in Berlin, Near Eastern Museum: view toward the Syrian Hall.

Berlin, Staatsbibliothek, SPK, Andrae Bequest 15/82.

Mem. 278:

'The ›art of the museum architects‹ had let us down, in that our street was only 8 m wide instead of 16. Only the height of the two defensive walls on either side, along which the lions ran, was right. One felt a sense of occidental enclosure, instead of oriental space. This was especially felt by those who came from Babylon and cursed the cramped museum rooms.'

82 1927 – Watercolour – 35 × 24.5

Working sketch for the reconstruction of the Processional Way in Berlin, Near Eastern Museum: view toward the Ishtar Gate.

Berlin, Staatsbibliothek, SPK, Andrae Bequest 15/81. See Mem. 277.

83 1927 – Watercolour – 37.5 × 27.0

Working sketch for the reconstruction of the throne-room facade in Berlin, Near Eastern Museum. To the left the Ishtar Gate, to the right the facade of the Parthian Palace.

Berlin, Staatsbibliothek, SPK, Andrae Bequest 15/80.

84 1927 – Watercolour – 24.5 × 35.0
Working sketch for the reconstruction of the Ishtar Gate in Berlin, Near Eastern Museum.
Berlin, Staatsbibliothek, SPK, Andrae Bequest 15/83.

85 c. 1901 – Watercolour – 28.7 × 45.3
Babylon, Kasr, n-w corner.
Berlin, Staatsbibliothek, SPK, Andrae Bquest 15/27.

86 2. 6. 1902, evening – Watercolour – 25.2 × 35.2
Babylon, al-Kasr mound from the east.
Unpulished description by W. Andrae, about 1950:
'From the east one could take the whole Kasr mound for a long range of hills stretching up
to the edge of the excavation, if you had come through the loveliest and only occasionally
watered plains of the city precincts at the right distance. From the right, that is from north,
palm gardens reach right up to this range of hills.'

87 1902 – Watercolour – 25.5 × 35.5
Babylon. Excavation in the northern palace of the Kasr, down to groundwater, with the
Lion of Babylon. Compare Bell's photo taken about 7 years later, AtA Fig. 104.
Berlin, Staatsbibliothek, SPK, Andrae Bequest 15/26.

88 July morning, 1902 – Watercolour – 17.0 × 35.0
Babylon. Amran ibn 'Ali mound from the north.
Berlin, Staatsbibliothek, SPK, Andrae Bequest 15/24.

89 1902 – Watercolour – 24,5 × 34,9
Babylon. Excavation in the Ninmach Temple, after a coloured photograph.

90 22. 6. 1902, morning between 5.30 and 7 o'clock. – Watercolour – 20.0 × 35.5
Babylon. Babil hill from the s-e.
See Mem. Fig. 33.
Berlin, Staatsbibliothek, SPK, Andrae Bequest 15/25.

91 1901 – Watercolour – 25.2 × 35.3
Borsippa (Birs Nimrud), remains of the ziggurat E-ur-imin-an-ki with the temple of Ezida in
the foreground. On the walls of the latter are the excavators' tents.
Mem. 90:
'On Sunday I made myself scarce, as there were so many visitors. I undertook a little Sunday
outing consisting of 7^{1}/2 hours' riding and 3 hours' climbing. On this occasion I had got permission from the consul to visit the ruins of Borsippa, modern Birs Nimrud. This came via
Constantinople and was granted with the proviso that I enjoyed the ruins with my eyes only,
and not with pencils or any other dangerously cultural device. In Hilla, where I visited the
new Kaimakam, I obtained an official who was to watch over me, and did so; he was in addition to our armed policeman, and I had brought with me two of our own Arabs on donkeys,
who were armed in a festive manner, each with double-barrelled shotgun, double-barrelled

pistol, dagger and cudgel. We could have dealt with a hundred enemies, if there had been such. I got to Birs by midday and rambled about the ruins. There is the temple of Ezida and the stage-tower E-uriminanki, and nearby the inhabited tell of Ibrahim ibn Khalil, named after a small domed tomb there. The temple was excavated by Rassam about 20 years ago (1879/80), and was therefore easy to see. The tower is still very impressive, mainly made pyramid-shaped by the dumps which level it off. At the summit there is still a great chunk of baked brick about 15 m high, its top being about 90 m above plain level. There would be a wonderful view from the top, if there were anything to see. But all is as flat as a pancake, with marsh to the north, looking like a great lake with occasional palm-gardens. Otherwise the horizon is as straight as a ruler, and the sky a perfect bell-shape. By around 8 o'clock in the evening I was back in Babylon.

A month later, at the end of November, Koldewey moved to Birs to start a new excevation there…'

See further Mem. 91 ff. 96 ff!

92 26. 3. 1901 – Watercolour – 18 × 25.5
    Courtyard of the caravanserai Imam Jasim.
    Berlin, Staatsbibliothek, SPK, Andrae Bequest 15/16.
    Mem. 81 ff.:
    'Diwaniyeh is the seat of the Mutsharif, to whom the Kaimakam of Hilla is answerable. The road to Imam Jasim, about half way between the two, is straight and flat, passing for a long way between palm groves and gardens, fields, and canals with bridges. Eventually the land becomes quite desert-like the further one gets from the Euphrates, which makes a bend here. Imam Jasim consists of a little mosque with a few houses and a coffee-house which serves mainly as staging post. The dome is high and visible from afar, while the accomodation is as comfortable and plesant as usual for an old oriental village, with quite unnecessary filth, in a medley of donkeys, mules and horses, cursing soldiers and yelling Arabs, and the inevitable fleas. I installed myself on a long bench in the coffee-house, fully dressed with a bundle of cloths for a pillow, but did not succeed in sleeping: the flea attack was not to be repulsed even by the most energetic applications of insect-powder. The best part of such a stopover is when dawn begins to appear, when one can get out. The other sleepers are mainly in the same hurry to leave.'

93 1902 Watercolour and charcoal – 25.0 × 18.0
    Coffee-house at Kifl.
    Berlin, Staatsbibliothek, SPK, Andrae Bequest 15/29.
    Kifl is on the road from Hilla to Najaf (Fig. 5), and during Andrae's time Jews lived in the little town, where the tomb of Ezekiel is honoured. 'According to Goldziher Dh'ul-Kifl is a second name of Ezekiel as is the case with four other prophets who have two names, such as Ya'qub: Isre'il; Yunus: Dhu'l-Nus; 'Isa: al-Masih; Muhammad: Ahmad. Other modern researchers also suggest that Dhu'l-Kifl is the Arabic and Islamic from of Ezekiel.' (Tariq Jawad al-Janabi, Studies in Mediaeval Iraqi Architecture [1982] 97.) In 1950 W. Andrae described the coffee-house thus: 'The coffee-house looks like all country coffee-house in Iraq, that is blackened by the open hearth used to make the coffee. The roof consists of reed-matting more or less in tatters, the wooden benches are antique and you sit on them cross-leg-

ged. There are no tables, and the landlord doles out the coffee a few drops at a time as required by the customer. Waterpipes are very popular with it.'

Compare also Mem. 114 on the coffee-house at Imam Jasim (No. 92): 'I repaired to my usual
coffee-house, the same black cave which I had the opportunity of describing on the first
journey to Nippur. I rested on a metal bedstead in the shade of this cave, and gobbled coffee,
tea, chicken, eggs, bread and cucumbers while the heat of the sun burned away outside, and
even somewhat inside. At any rate it was expressed in the limp state of the people who sat
around. In their loose hanging clothes they look a bit like wilted flowers, though the com-
parison ill fits the dark-brown to violet blue of their sweat-glistening skins. And one sees
something never seen before, which normally occasions great shock, the removal of the
head-cloth. The effect is not ennobling, and one sees mostly strangely pointed heads to
which the head-cloth usually adds something of an imposing quality. Outside the sun scor-
ches down on the harness of the stamping donkeys and horses and up on the rough black
palm-fronds of the roof, under which the smoke of the coffee-house collects, sit the sparrows
with gaping beaks.'

94 26. 3. 1901 – Watercolour – 25.0 × 17.5
Domed tomb of Imam Jasim.
See No. 92.
Unpublished description by W. Andrae, c. 1950:
'The dome of the grave of Iman Jasim stands solitary on the road from Hilla to Samawa. In
The evening light the rays of the setting sun give simple building a sot of halo. There is
nothing under the dome except the cenotaph of the dead priest. There are many such imams
in the countryside. The surrounding area is referred to by the same name as the deceased.'

95 27. 3. 1901 – Watercolour – 17.0 × 25.0
Diwaniyeh, Euphrates landing place.
Berlin, Staatsbibliothek, SPK, Andrae Bequest 15/22.
See No. 96.

96 27. 3. 1901 – Watercolour – 17.6 × 25.0
Diwaniyeh, pontoon bridge, Khan and Saray.
See Nos. 95, 97 and 98.
Mem. 82 f.
'The second day brought me to Diwaniyeh. The road is desert, though not without the
occasional field. The nearer I came to Diwaniyeh, the more desolate it became. The ground
is only a few centimeters above sea-level and can easily be irrigated, but lies fallow. The first
meftul (fortress) was sited on the bank...
We reached Diwaniyeh towards mid-day. A few houses on the right, most to the left of the
Euphrates. The two banks are linked, that is to say the Jezireh, the island between the Euphrates and Tigris is linked with the rest of the world, by one of those marvellous (dung-
strewn) pontoon bridges that one cannot look at without feeling dizzy. I dismounted at the
new Khan by the bridge, where I obtained a tolerable room on the upper floor with a nice
view of the bridge and the Euphrates. Painting was not easy (see No. 95), as I was continually interrupted by curious Turks or Arabs, or ran with sweat, or flies tickled my nose or got
in the paint, or the hot wind dried up paper and brush. Art under strain!'

97 27. 3. 1901 – Watercolour – 25.0 × 17.0
The Euphrates above Diwaniyeh, meftul (fortress) and Sarifehs.
See No. 96.
Berlin, Staatsbibliothek, SPK, Andrae Bequest 15/21.
Mem. 84:
'For the Sultan to get his money it is often necessary to batter down the meftuls (fortresses) of sheikhs unwilling to pay. This is about the only contact between ruler and subject. The Arabs call the meftuls their strongholds. They live round and about them in mere sarifehs, that is in huts of reeds or reed-mats (see also Nos. 105 and 106). If there is an attack by a hostile branch of the family or the government, then all those able to bear arms, that is all the men-folk, go into the meftul. This usually consists of no more than a hollow round or square tower of mud, with an amazing number of loopholes facing all directions. Access is through a small hole in the ground, and a narrow staircase leads up to the firing gallery and the battlement. The whole region is speckled with these warlike buildings.'

98 29. 3. 1901 – Watercolour – 18.0 × 25.5
A settlement on the Nahr Jeliha in the mash area round Afaj, with two meftuls (see No. 97) and Mem. 84 ff.

99 1. 4. 1901 – Watercolour – 17.7 × 25.0
Najaf, view of the town from the Kufa road.
Mem. 87 ff:
'The journey from Kufa to Najaf lasts about 1 1/2 hours over clean desert gravel, among which various dried-up spring-plants are to be seen just now. Najaf is surrounded by a turreted fortification wall and consists of a maze of little alleys around the contrasting gold and faience shrine…'

100 2. 4. 1901 – Watercolour – 17.3 × 24.5
Najaf, view from the city gate to the pilgrim's path tombs.
Berlin, Ernst Heinrich Bequest.
See No. 99.

101 2. 4. 1901 – Watercolour – 25.0 × 17.5
Najaf, entrance to the Bazaar and the mosque of 'Ali
See No. 99.

102 4. 4. 1901 – Watercolour – 25.5 × 35.5
Kerbela, mosque of Hussein.
Berlin, Staatsbibliothek, SPK, Andrae Bequest 15/19.
See Mem. 89.

103 4. 4. 1901 – Watercolour – 25.0 × 17.5
Kerbela, mosque of Hussein.
See Mem. 89.

104 4. 4. 1901 – Watercolour – 25.0 × 17.7
Mosque of Abbas at Kerbela.
See Mem. 89.

105 1903 – Pencil – 31.0 × 22.3
Reception in the mudhif, in the reed house of a sheikh near Fara.
See Mem. 121 f.

106 1903 – Coloured chalk – 27.5 × 22.0
Reception in the mudhif, in the reed house of a sheikh near Fara.
Berlin, Staatsbibliothek, SPK, Andrae Bequest 15/68.
See Mem. 121 f.
Unpublished description by W. Andrae (c. 1950): 'In southern Iraq building material comes
from the giant reed jungles of the flood plain of the Euphrates. Reeds over 4 m tall are bun-
dled up and planted in two rows in the earth, then tied together at the top to form an arch.
Stability is achieved by adding bundles longways, and a good solid roof-covering is made of
woven mats of reed, to offer shelter from heat and rain. The sheikhs have built great hall-like
structures like this to serve as meeting places, in which one can sit near one of the two
entrances and be well entertained with coffee. The guests sit along the sides of the hall. A
Somali Negro left over from slaving times serves the coffee.'

107 1903 – Watercolour – 35.2 × 25.2
Landing stage at Kut el-Amara on the Tigris.
See Mem. 128.

108 1903 – Pencil and coloured crayon – 17.0 × 26.0
The stupa of Sanchi, India.
See Mem. 134 f.

109 1903 – Watercolour – 25.0 × 35.0
Taj Mahal near Agra, India.

110 1903 – Watercolour – 25.0 × 35.0
The Purana Killa gate at Indraput, India.

111 1903 – Watercolour – 30.0 × 22.0
Delhi, view from the gate of a mosque.
Berlin, map collection of the Technical University, 7730.

112 1903 – Watercolour – 25.2 × 35.0
Aden, seen from aboard ship. (Detail: the sea in the foreground has been left out.)
Mem. 137.

113 1908 – Coloured chalk on tinted paper – 44.7 × 30.2
Tigris valley south of Assur. Straits of Fatha. The dark flecks in the foreground suggest leaking bitumen.

114 1909 – Coloured chalk on tinted paper – 31.0 × 25.3
Assur, the north face, with the Wadi Umm es-Shababit (Mother of Carp), which is rich in fish, from east to west, see Mem. 168.

115 1909 – Mixed medium, watercolour, coloured chalk and pen – 30.5 × 25.7
Assur, north face in evening light, from west to east.

116 c. 1908 – Ink, brush – 9.2 × 13.3
View across the Assur plain and the Tigris north of Assur.

117 c. 1906 – Coloured chalk on tinted paper – 25.1 × 31.0
View of Assur towards the south. Sunset over the Tigris gorge.

118 December 1910 – Pencil and coloured pencil – 15.7 × 22.8
Banks of the Tigris at Assur.

119 c. 1904 – Watercolour – 24.6 × 35.6
Retreating storm over the Tigris east of Assur.

120 1904 – Watercolour – coloured chalk on tinted paper – 29.3 × 21.6
Assur: retreating storm over the Tigris south of Assur.
See Mem. 170.

121 1904 – Coloured chalk on tinted paper – 29.7 × 22.7
Assur, view to the south, evening over the Tigris.

122 1904 – Watercolour on tinted paper – 22.0 × 26.0
Assur ziggurat in evening light.

123 1908 – Watercolour – 17.0 × 25.0
Assur, Watchman's hut at the Anu-Adad temple excavation (see No. 129), full mid-day sun (Caption "Abend/Evening" subsequent and incorrect).
Berlin, Staatsbibliothek, SPK, Andrae Bequest 15/31.

124 1906 – Coloured chalk – 21.6 × 29.5
Assur. Shargatis' hut and two spoil-heaps at the edge of the excavation.

125 1906 – Coloured chalk – 25.5 × 31.0
Workers from Shargat preparing to swim the Tigris.
Mem. 170:
In the spring the Tigris rose to 'six or more metres above its bank and pushed around thick slurries of mud, combined with the melting snows coming down from the Kurdish mountains. Then it became audibly spiteful with its rolling gravel-banks and pushed its bed around as though generally dissatisfied. It then became three km wide at Assur, and made the crossing from the opposite bank almost impossible for our workers. But the brave ones were not afraid of high water or even of ice, which was also present in cold years. The thick-skinned ones arrived, the brave swimmers emerging stark naked from the freezing water

with their inflated goat-skins which served them as swimming floats, and their clothes
wound round their heads, and went off fresh and cheerful to their workplaces.'

126 1937 – Ink –
   Assur, northern face.
   After W. Andrae, Das wiedererstandene Assur, Fig. 2.
   8.2 × 26.5.

127 1937 – Ink – 8.2 × 26.5
   Assur gorge from the north.
   After W. Andrae, Das wiedererstandene Assur, Fig. 1.

128 1937 – Ink – 32.5 × 41
   View across Assur toward the north, published in:
   W. Andrae, Das wiedererstandene Assur, Fig. 24.
   Berlin, Staatsbibliothek, SPK, Andrae Bequest 15/85.

129 1908 – Ink – 16.5 × 24.5
   Assur. Anu-Adad-Temple. Attempt at reconstruction.
   Here Andrae still reconstructed the ziggurat with the way up winding round, a theory which
   he later retracted. See for instance Nos. 126, 127, 130 and 131, and his essay on the question
   of the approach in W. Andrae, Das wiedererstandene Assur p. 92 f.
   Deutsches Archäologisches Institut, Baghdad Dept.

130 1923 – Charcoal – 31.0 × 44.5
   Assur. View from the Festival Hall toward the city. Attempt at reconstruction.

131 1923 – Charcoal and chalk – 30.0 × 49.5
   Assur. View from the ziggurat over the temple and palace complex toward the Festival Hall.
   Attempt at reconstruction. – See also the contemporary suggestion for the reconstruction of
   Sham'al, Fig. 20.

132 1907 – Watercolour – 31.5 × 44.9
   Sketch for stage-set I, 'Sardanapalus'.
   Courtyard of an Assyrian temple with a view of the god's portrait.
   Mem. 180 f.:
   'Then I had to take part in the rehearsals and production of the French pantomime 'Sarsa-
   naplus', as ordered by Kaiser Wilhelm II in Berlin. You can think what you like about the
   artisitc quality of the performance – opinions were divided then too. But the Kaiser's idea of
   furnishing the play with the latest knowledge of true Assyrian style certainly had a charm
   about it and deserved the attention of us Orientalists and excavators. I had been comissioned
   early in the year at Assur to design three stage-sets, so that the architecture looked authentic.
   In Berlin they stuck rigidly to all three sketches, and I nearly fell over backwards when I saw
   my little coloured pictures at full stage size at the State Opera. In the meanwhile Friedrich
   Delitzsch had to see to it that the entire court of Nineveh, men and women alike, could

appear on this stage in proper Assyrian hairstyles and clothes, and that the furniture and fine vessels were accurate. Kaiser Wilhelm attended the rehearsal personally. It seemed so easy, with so many Assyrian representations available from the orthostats of Calah, Niniveh and Khorsabad, to copy for the stage the costumes of the king, the courtiers, the soldiers and servants. But there were all kinds of problems which could not be solved from the Assyrian representations and resort was had to decisions based on modern intuition rather than Assyrian art. The archaeologists could have learned a lot.'
See further ibid. 181 f. and No. 129 here for the ziggurat staircase in the background.

133 1907 – Watercolour – 29.0 × 45.3
Sketch for stage-set II, 'Sardanapalus'.
Treasure house of an Assyrian palace.
See No. 132.

134 1912 – Watercolour and pencil – 30.4 × 22.9
Assur. The Expedition House garden.
Mem. 157:
'In our dry lunar landscape the little garden in front of the house drops down to the Tigris in concave fashion, especially when we succeeded in planting a real vineyard. An ancient Assyrian spring provides water, and Sultan the gardener, father of innumerable children, sees to the mallow, almonds, pumpkins and other vegetables.'

135 5. 4. 1908 – Coloured chalk – 22.7 × 31.5
Tell Afer.

136 5. 4. 1908 – Coloured chalk – 30.7 × 21.8
Near Tell Afer, view toward the Sinjar Mountains.

137 6. 4. 1908 – Coloured chalk on tinted paper – 18.5 × 31.7
'Ain Ghazal (between Tell Afer and Sinjar, see for instance W. Andrae, MDOG 20, 1903, 11).

138 8. 4. 1908 – Coloured chalk on tinted paper – 26.0 × 32.1
Tell Shemsani on the Khabur.

139 9. 4. 1908 – Coloured chalk on tinted paper – 26.2 × 31.8
Suar on the Khabur.
See Sarre-Herzfeld I 177 ff.

140 11. 4. 1908 – Watercolour and chalk – 31.5 × 23.0
Edge of the Euphrates valley in spring, near Tibne. See No. 222: text.
Mem. 194.

141 11. 4. 1908 – Coloured chalk on tinted paper – 26.2 × 32.0
Basalt formations near Tibne. See No. 222: text.

Fig. 20 Sham'al – Zincirli, 'reconstructed view of the city', 1923

142 11. 4. 1908 – Coloured chalk on tinted paper – 25.8 × 31.3
     The Euphrates near Tibne (see No. 28). In the middle foreground a cemetery.

143 1908 – Mixed medium, watercolour, coloured chalk and pencil – 30.9 × 21.0
     Samos, the harbour at Vathi.
     Berlin, map-collection of the Technical University, No. 7732.

144 21. 6. 1917 – Coloured chalk – 20.6 × 25.9
     Istanbul, the Golden Horn.

145 1915 – Coloured chalk – 25.9 × 21.1
     Istanbul, the Golden Horn.
     Berlin, Staatsbibliothek, SPK, Andrae Bequest 15/60.

146 24. 12. 1915 – Coloured chalk and pencil – 14.5 × 22.5
     Istanbul, view toward Pera.
     Berlin, map-collection of the Technical University, No. 18349.

147 1918 – Coloured chalk on tinted paper – 30.6 × 22.7
     Istanbul. Boulevard in Pera: now Tepebaşı caddesı in Beyoğlu.
     Foreground far left, the Hotel Bristol (K. Bittel).

148 19. 4. 1917 – Coloured chalk on tinted paper – 21.1 × 26.0
     Istanbul. Café garden in Pera.

149 June 1917 – Coloured chalk on tinted paper – 20.0 × 25.8
     Istanbul. Pera, Petits Champs (Café chantant).

150 Sketch 1912, actual production 1922 – Coloured chalk – 18.6 × 29.4
     Istanbul, view of the town from the Bosporus.

151 1916 – Coloured chalk on tinted paper – 12.3 × 15.2
     Afyon-Karahissar in Anatolia, the castle and town.

152 1918 – Coloured chalk on tinted paper – 20.9 × 26.0
     Pass through the Taurus mountains.

153 1917 – Coloured chalk on tinted paper – 16.5 × 25.5
     The Gulf of Iskenderun/Adana.

154 1918 – Coloured chalk –16.1 × 10.5
     Dervish mosque (Tekke) near Aleppo: Takiya as-Sheikh Abu Bakr, see H. Glaube – E.
     Wirth, Aleppo, Beiheft 58, Tübinger Atlas des Vorderen Orients, Reihe B (1984) 160.408 –
     For the precise identification of this picture and Nos. 156, 158 and 169 we are grateful to
     H. Gaube.
     See Nos. 18.228

Unpublished description by Walter Andrae (c. 1950):
'On a slight rise before the gates of Aleppo, there is the dome of a small monastery with living quarters for dervishes (monks), and its courtyard includes a giant stone-pine, whose dark crown contrasts piercingly with the bright surrounding walls. In the evening gloaming the reddish-brown of the ploughed fields takes on a violet hue, while the chalky-white house-walls seem to mirror the last rays of daylight as though touched with magic light. A moment's impression!'

155 1917 – Coloured chalk on dark paper – 30.5 × 22.4
Mosque. Aleppo region (?)
It is not possible to identify the exact location of the mosque. A description written in pencil on the back of the dark paper is completely faded. Those of my colleagues familiar with Syria, A. Becker, H. Kühne, M. Meinecke, E. Strommenger and T. Ulbert could not identify it, nor K. Bittel. This leads one to wonder if the building is still extant today. David Oates – likewise Boehmer – concludes that it is in northern Iraq and sums up his impressions of the building as follows: 'The structure in the background suggests that the mosque (?tomb) is on the building opposite the entrance and beyond the dome – the river flows on its western side, and seems to be flowing approximate from *south* to *north*. The gallery of the minaret looks to me West Syrian or possibly South Turkish – compare, although it is on a very much larger scale and octagonal in plan, the gallery of the south-western minaret (AD 1488) of the Great Mosque in Damascus. The dome also looks to me rather western in style than Mesopotamian.' (Letter of 28th November 1988).
Andrae was in Aleppo in 1917. The building in question seems to be related in position and structure to those in Nos. 18 and 154 showing Tekkes near Aleppo. The description 'Aleppo region' would seem therefore to be approximately correct.
Tübingen, Altorientalisches Seminar (previously in possession of A. Falkenstein).

156 1917 – Coloured chalk – 29.5 × 22.5
Mosque on the outskirts of Aleppo: Madrasa al-Firdaus, see H. Gaube – E. Wirth op. cit. (No. 154) 87. 98. 150. 411.
Berlin, Staatsbibliothek, SPK, Andrae Bequest 15/78.

157 1918 – Coloured chalk – 30.5 × 23.0
Aleppo. View of a courtyard (with dog).
Berlin, Staatsbibliothek, SPK, Andrae Bequest 15/76.

158 1917 – Coloured chalk – 22.4 × 30.3
Aleppo by night, view of the citadel. Burial ground outside the town: cemetery of the el Jubaila district (H. Gaube).
Berlin, Staatsbibliothek, SPK, Andrae Bequest 15/75.

159 1918 – Coloured chalk on grey card – 10.0
Twilight with full moon over a small village with 'beehive' houses and a Tell, near Aleppo. Coloured sketch made while passing in the train.
On the Quwaiq stream.
Berlin, Staatsbibliothek, SPK, Andrae Bequest 15/69.

160 1918 – Charcoal and coloured chalk on tinted paper – 60 × 43
View of the 'promenade' on the Quwaiq stream near Aleppo.
Berlin, plan collection of the Technical University, No. 18347.
Unpublished description by W. Andrae c. 1950:
'On the outskirts of Aleppo, near to Karl Koch's house, which the folk of Aleppo call bet
Madame Koch, there flowed a narrow stream in a flat depression. It came from a powerful
spring a few kilometres away and watered the fertile valley bottom. On either side arose flat,
barren cliffs which weathered away to reddish-brown soil leaving bright, bare planes of
limestone. If you can imagine the whole region of Aleppo being like that then you will
understand how the little valley of the Quwaiq with its gentle waters became a favourite
promenade place for the folk of Aleppo. You could see them dressed in their best clothes,
the women in costumes as gay as parrots and the men in red fez, strolling under the blessed
shady pistachios and other trees through the fresh green of the vegetable and corn fields.
Seen from the balcony of Mr. Koch's house it was a very cheerful sight. It is probable that
little of it remains, as the fairly large Aleppo railway station is planned for nearby, and the
main road to it goes through the Quwaiq valley.' See also catalogue entry for No. 22.

161 1918 – Coloured chalk on tinted paper – 10.4 × 16.5
View of Aleppo.

162 1917 – Coloured chalk – 30.0 × 22
Aleppo. Cemetery.
See also No. 158, right foreground.
Berlin, Staatsbibliothek, SPK, Andrae Bequest 15/77.

163 7. 2. 1916 – Coloured chalk – 14.0 × 21.5
Euphrates above Ana.

164 7. 2. 1916 – Coloured chalk on tinted paper – 21.0 × 27.7
Euphrates above Ana.

165 11. 2. 1916 – Coloured chalk – 14.0 × 21.0
Water-wheels (na'urs) of birchwood at Zawije.
Berlin, Staatsbibliothek, SPK, Andrae Bequest 15/67.
Unpublished description by W. Andrae, c. 1950:
'In Syria on the Orontes and on the middle Euphrates the local water-drawing devices of
Arab manufacture are made of a variety of crooked branches skillfully bound onto a central
hub. The edge of the wheel is bound with equally crooked bits of wood. On the edge of the
water-wheel they fix clay pots, which serve both to weight the wheel and set it in motion,
and when filled with water to move it upwards. Thus the water is lifted from the surface of
the Euphrates to a considerable height, i.e. to that almost equal to the diameter of the mighty
wheel. The clay jars are so arranged that they empty themselves sideways when they get to
the top. The water then falls into the irrigation canal, which at this point is on a sort of
bridge, and then flows down to irrigate the fields. Part of the hub is made of hard wood, and
when the wheel turns it emits a dreadful complaining squeaking noise, which tells the owner
of the na'ur that his wheel is working. Every na'ur has its own melody.'

166 11. 2. 1916 – Coloured chalk on tinted paper – 40.3 × 53.3
Water-wheels (na'urs) of birchwood by night, on the Euphrates at Zawije.

167 1917 – Coloured chalk – 30.2 × 23.2
Mosul. Courtyard of the German Vice-Consulate.
For Andrae's stay in Mosul see Mem. 233 ff.

168 30. 12. 1917 – Coloured chalk – 12.0 × 18.1
Water-wheel (na'ur) near Hama, Syria.

169 1918 – Coloured chalk – 30.0 × 23.0
Damascus. Courtyard of the Dervish Mosque: Ottoman Tekke Sulaimaniyeh (H. Gaube)
with plane trees and the corner of a waterbasin. The latter was supplied from the mountain
river Barada.
Berlin, plan collection of the Technical University, No. 7731.

170 1917 – Coloured chalk – 23.5 × 30.7
Turkish camp followers at a watering place in the Yarmuk valley.

171 Spring 1918 – Coloured chalk – 10.5 × 17.0
Orchids in bloom in the Yarmuk valley.

172 23. 1. 1918 – Ink drawing re-touched with coloured crayon – 22.1 × 14.0
Nazareth. View of the town from above.
See Mem. 242 f.
'From the plain of Jezreel one climbs steeply into the hills of Galilee. Here hidden in a hollow is Nazareth, climbing up the mountain in a semi-circular formation like a theatre
(No. 164). There are gardens round about, protected by hedges of prickly pear (No. 173),
with oil-bearing trees, fruit trees and cypresses (Nos. 179, 180, 183 and 185). The Franciscans
have the most beautiful, peaceful garden on a knoll (Nos. 178. 183–185). It is February 1918,
the beginning of spring. Lonely paths takes me through the blooming, sweet-scented rocky
landscape on either side of the gardens. I can no longer hear the bustle of the town-centre.
Outside in the loneliness the orchids, cyclamen and apricot blossom speak to me, thriving
from the reddish-brown earth between the sheer limestone cliffs (No. 180). The dark cypresses seem sombre amid this splendour, and fresh, clean, newly-rolled clouds from the sea
hang large and close.'

173 1918 – Coloured chalk – 40.5 × 29.0
Nazareth. Path to the town, between hedges of prickly pear.
See ref. to No. 172.

174 1918 – Coloured chalk – 27.8 × 40.0
Nazareth, view of the town.

175 1918 – coloured chalk – 18.5 × 12.2
Mosque at Tiberias, built of basalt.

176 1917 – Coloured chalk on tinted paper – 40.1 × 28.3
     Nazareth. Minaret of the mosque.

177 19. 1. 1918 – Coloured pencil and ink – 13.3 × 9.9
     Nazareth. Alleyway down into the town.

178 15. 1. 1918 – Coloured pencil and ink – 13.4 × 9.9
     Nazareth. View from the town towards the Franciscan monastery.
     See ref. to No. 172.

179 Spring 1918 – Coloured chalk – 26.0 × 21.0
     Nazareth. Donkey in an orchard.
     See ref. to No. 172.

180 January 1918 – Coloured chalk – 23.5 × 30.2
     Nazareth. Path up to a knoll, with almonds in bloom.
     See ref. to No. 172.

181 January 1918 – Coloured chalk on tinted paper – 30.3 × 23.7
     Nazareth. Gate of the Franciscan monastery.
     See ref. to No. 172.

182 1918 – Coloured chalk on tinted paper – 28.0 × 21.0
     Nazareth. On the road to the Chapel of the Virgin Mary.
     See Mem. 245:
     'Legend has it that the Nazarenes wanted to throw Him from the mountain, being angry at
     the truths which He told them. But He floated down unharmed, and Mary fainted on the
     way down the mountain from where He had been thrown, following Him fearing for His
     life. A chapel stands at this point at the end of the gardens. And here it all began to get lively
     and happy for me.'

183 1918 – Coloured chalk – 38.8 × 28.0
     Nazareth. In the garden of the Franciscan monastery.
     See ref. to No. 172.
     In 1917/18 the Franciscan monastery on a rise above the town of Nazareth was inhabited and
     worked by only two monks, both of German origin – one came from Biberach in Upper
     Swabia. A large garden belonged to the monastery. The sketch shows cypresses and almond
     trees and the two monks.

184 1918 – Coloured chalk – 28.8 × 40.9
     Nazareth, dusk.
     See ref. to No. 172.
     Berlin, plan collection of the Technical University, No. 7728.

185 Spring 1918 – Coloured chalk on tinted paper – 40.0 × 28.5
Nazareth, At the Franciscan monastery.
See ref. to No. 172.

186 1918 – Coloured chalk on tinted paper – 15.7 × 10.0
A merchant of Aleppo.

187 1918 – Charcoal – 17.5 × 13.1
Aleppo. Portrait of Omer, a Turkish soldier.

188 1918 – Coloured chalk on tinted paper – 16.0 × 10.0
Aleppo. Two old men.

189 1918 – Coloured chalk – 11.2 × 8.0
A vendor from Aleppo. See also No. 232.

190 1916/17 – Pencil – 9.9 × 15.0
Baghdad. The chief engineer on the building of the Baghdad and Hejaz railway, Meißner
Pasha.

191 1918 – Coloured chalk – 10.6 × 16.4
Aleppo. Arab merchant, distinguished by the Royal Prussian Service Medal for wartime
service.

192 1918 – Charcoal and chalk – 13.8 × 17.9
Aleppo. Flute-playing dervish.
Unpublished description by W. Andrae (c. 1950):
'The beggar attracts his alms-giver with an off-key wind instrument, and is of well-nour-
ished appearance. He clearly has good standing in the beggars' guild. Beggars and thieves in
Aleppo have a sheikh as their chief. If something was stolen you could get it back from the
sheikh of the thieves. A special fee was payable.'

193 12. 8. 1906 – Coloured chalk on tinted paper – 29.0 × 22.0
Assur. Abdullah in festive dress.
Berlin, Staatsbibliothek, SPK, Andrae Bequest 15/34.
Unpublished description by W. Andrae (c. 1950):
'Abdullah was employed to help around the Expedition House, and had been behaving
exceptionally well in order to earn a reward. The reward consisted of a festive costume to
wear with pride for the great sacrificial feast, the Korban-Bairam, in order to elicit suitable
admiration from his relations. The costume also had a shirt with sleeves that trailed along the
ground.'

194 1816 – Coloured chalk on tinted paper – 13.8 × 9.0
Baghdad. Portrait of a fellow soldier.

195 19. 6. 1916 – Coloured chalk – 23.8 × 16.9
Baghdad. Portrait of the staff-surgeon Dr. Ludwig Külz. See also Fig. 21.
Mem. 231 f.
'A staff of German majors and captains and lieutenants of cavalry was in Kasr-i-Shirin by
1916, trying to organise a flank attack against Persia. The region is most interesting from an
archaeological point of view, but was riddled with infectious disease. The funeral caravans
of Shiites from all over Persia, which I told of in Babylon, were all caught up here in danger
of disease when the Turks declared quarantine and closed the border. So cholera, typhus,
pestilence, malaria, spotted fever, and other interesting infections all collected together. The
German doctors who should have been treating them fell victim to them without exception,
and lay at death's door. I met Ludwig Külz, with whom I had shared a table at Grimma, this
time as a staff surgeon suffering from cholera. He had been a government doctor in Came-
roon. He considered his present position as trying in the extreme, but lived to tell the tale.'
See further: W. Litten, Persische Flitterwochen (1925) 303. 335.

196 1919– Charcoal and chalk on tinted paper – 26.0 × 18.2
Istanbul. Bektasi dervish in the monastery of Camlica.
Unpublished description by W. Andrae (c. 1950):
'On a mountain not far from the Anatolian shore of the Bosporus dwelled a kindly old dervish who made his living as proprietor of a coffee-house. He was meditative and philosophical over war and the stupidity of man. He enjoyed the broad view over the fertile plain at the
foot of the mountains, far from the life of the big city. His bright, layered felt hat, his ice-grey
beard and his light brown dervish coat lent him a priestly appearance. It was good to listen to
his clear Turkish speech delivered in short sentences.'

197 1918/19 – Coloured chalk – 25.6 × 17.8
Istanbul. Captain Moses, the British captain of the 'Patmos'. (Another almost identical picture in Berlin, Staatsbibliothek, SPK, Andrae Bequest 15/54: Captain Moses with his eyes
closed).
See No. 198.

198 1918/19 – Coloured chalk on tinted paper – 34.8 × 27.2
The steamer 'Patmos' on the Bosporus off Istanbul. Haidar Pasha in the background. In
Mem. 247 ff. Andrae writes thus of the 'Patmos':
'The rest of the German Eastern Army arrived in Haidar Pasha near Istanbul in October
1918. We were still 10,000 strong, but the allied fleet now lay in the Sea of Marmara, so we
might as well have been in a mousetrap. The war was about to end, but no-one wanted us as
prisoners of war: what was to be done with us? So we were imprisoned in small German
merchant ships lying at anchor in the Sea of Marmara off Istanbul. I and 960 men were put
on a 3,000 ton coal-steamer of the Levant Line, which went by the unusual name of ›Patmos‹. Bunks were improvised in the ship's big loading areas, four deep, two by two, all in
the smallest possible space. Wooden stairs led down to the flooded hold of iron planks. The
machinery was old and did not work properly. On the deck was an ›exercise area‹, a room
about 8 m square. In our bunks there were two individuals, a medium-sized one and a short
fat one. The latter had to stay in bed more or less all the time, or the others were unable to
move. We suffered most from lack of news from home, for the victors had impounded our

Fig. 21 Dr. med. Külz. Baghdad, 15. 5. 1916

mail. Our relatives back home did not know which of us were still alive. Being only human, none of this did anything to prevent us from re-living and dwelling with bad feeling on the grim experiences we had been through.

When we had been two and then three months in the Sea of Marmara the general mood became dangerous. Clever souls devised all kinds of gambling games. As there was no possibility of physical movement, the only way to counteract this activity was in the intellectual realm, with poetry, calculation and other exercises. The simple fact of being cooped up in a small space gave rise to a sort of paedagogium. There were archaeologists and excavators among the officers, and a couple of orators, though nothing special. But each gave of his best, and it was probably due to these efforts that the ›Patmos‹ arrived in Hamburg six months later without a full-blown revolution. Still those months of claustrophobia did not suffice, in the inevitable process of mental analysis of wartime experiences, to convince that such barbarity must never happen again. When did we start thinking about a second war? The physiognomies of my companions interested me, and I tried to compose portraits without pretension to likeness. Most of them I gave away. The most impressive character was the English captain, Moses, who was handed the ship as a British ›garrison‹, entirely alone and unarmed, when we weighed anchor in March and set off for Germany (No. 197). One could not but admire the simple British self-inspired courage of a man alone among 960 ›enemies‹. We had of course been disarmed, but there were still a few firearms hidden aboard, which we later used to dispose of mines in the North Sea. But Moses was simply one of the companions fate had thrown together. We had changed from ›enemies‹ to human beings, as is fitting when a war is over.

Captain Moses abandoned us in the North Sea after landing in Rotterdam had been denied us and we had to continue through the mine-field to Hamburg. Former comrades who had been on much faster ships and had reached home via Genoa ahead of us, had affectionately informed our waiting relatives that the ›Patmos‹ could not possibly make it home – such an unseaworthy vessel, with no lifeboats, with so many on board, sailing right round Europe through dangerous mine-fields!

But the Patmos was quarantined in Cuxhaven at the end of March 1919, and three days later entered Hamburg harbour in a dead calm.'

E. W. A. – R. M. B.

CATALOGUE OF TEXT FIGURES

1 1902 – Pencil – 23.0 × 15
   Babylon. Self-portrait.
   Mem. Fig. 5.

2 Mesopotamia and Syria/Palestine according to a map of 1918.
   Drawn by Corinna Maschin. The writing of the names looks very much like Andrae's.

3 15. 2. 1899 – Pencil
Halebiyeh.
Mem. (lst Edition) Fig. 10.

4 22. 2. 1899 – Pencil – 24.4 × 33.4
East of Kishla Kaeen.

5 1917 or later – Ink –
Environs of Babylon, according to a map of 1917.
Mem. Fig. 14.

6 1902 – Ink – 13.5 × 14.6
Map of the environs of Fara and Abu Hatab.
See also 2nd impression of 1903 in E. Heinrich, Fara (1931), facing p. 2.

7 1903/1904 – Pencil – 22.8 × 15.3
Dresden. Self-portrait.

8 1916 or later – Ink
Environs of Assur, according to a map of 1916.
Mem. Fig. 34.

9 c. 1908 – Ink drawing, coloured in – 12.5 × 20.0
Assur. 'The excavators of Assur in new suits.'
From left to right: Paul Maresch, Walter Andrae, Julius Jordan, Conrad Preusser, and the somewhat bemused Ismain ibn Jasim.

10 20. 1./7. 2. 1916 – Coloured pencil – 14.2 × 22.8
On the Euphrates between Meskene and Baghdad: in the cabin of the barge Safineh (see Nos. 24 and 26).
Mem. 227 f. and W. Andrae (unpublished, c. 1950):
'In 1916 I was alotted the task of travelling from Aleppo to Baghdad down the Euphrates, to reconnoitre the possibilities of river transport. For this purpose a marine station had been installed near Carchemish, with the forlorn hope of organising downstream traffic. Lieutenant von Zitzewitz, Lieutenant von Gosern and a Turkish captain were detailed to this venture, of which nothing could possibly come. We were given a pair of floating boxes tied together, with a flimsy room built above, quite habitable, with three beds and a table. Outside the room were two rudders before and two behind. The passage followed the current of the river, and the helmsmen's only task was to keep us going and to push us through the various currents. They were not obliged to speed us up. The journey therefore took a month, instead of the usual 18 days. If the wind blew we could not move at all, but just lay by the bank'.

11 1918 – Ink – Original 1:25,000
Map of Aleppo and its environs. Executed by First Lieutenant Erdmann under Andrae's direction.

12 March 1919 – Charcoal and chalk – 34.8 × 26.3
The ship's carpenter on the 'Patmos', see Nos. 197 and 198.

13 1909
Gertrude Bell in front of her tent at Babylon.
S. Hill, Gertrude Bell (1976) Fig. 1.

14 1926 – Pen – Dimensions not known.
Ali Jamus 'the water-buffalo': one-eyed water-carrier to the Babylon excavation.
MDOG 65, April 1927, 13 Fig. 5.

15 1926 – Ink – 9.5 × 7.7
Carpenter nailing up a transport chest.
MDOG 65, April 1927, 15 Fig. 8.

16 1952 – Watercolour, charcoal and chalk – 40.0 × 30.0
Walter Andrae, portrait by Irmin Grashey-Straub, for many years illustrator with the Leip-
ziger Illustrierten. J. Renger in: Berlin und die Antike (see Note 24), 185 Fig. 21.
Berlin, Staatsbibliothek, SPK, Andrae Bequest 15/38.

17 19. 3. 1899 – Pencil – 21.6 × 13.3
Capital to a wooden pillar, Baghdadi style.
See Nos. 41, 52, 53 and 57.

18 1927 – Ink – 7.8 × 16
Babylon. Inner courtyard to the Expedition House.
Sketch for No. 58.

19 1927 – Ink – 8.8 × 14.8
Expedition House on the Euphrates at Babylon.
Sketch for No. 59.

20 1923 – Charcoal and Chalk – 19.5 × 33.6
Sham'al – Zinçirli, 'reconstructed view of the city'.

21 15. 5. 1916 – Coloured chalk on tinted paper – 23.5 × 16.5
Baghdad. Dr. Külz (with Iron Cross 2nd Class and Royal Prussian Service medal for wartime
service). See also No. 195.
Berlin, Staatsbibliothek, SPK, Andrae Bequest 15/44.

PREFACE TO THE SECOND EDITION

INTRODUCTION

In producing a second edition of this book, the Baghdad section of the German Archaeological Institute has departed from its usual practice, for a particular reason. While the first edition is out of print, a Babylon Exhibition by the Berlin Museums (SPK) is currently in preparation. This is to be shown at several locations throughout Germany, and will include some of Walter Andrae's pictures. It was felt that visitors to the exhibition should be given an opportunity to appreciate the beauty of Andrae's work at home too. So a second edition has been prepared, in conjunction with Mr. Ernst Walter Andrae and publishers Gebr. Mann.

For these pictures show much that has fallen victim to 'progress'. Since the building of the Baghdad railway (see Andrae on No. 233) the Orient has endured so many vicissitudes, with the ups and downs of economic power, the all too brief respites of peace, then political disintegration coupled with arms escalation. These pictures, then, are witness to a world that existed just a short time ago, a world whose traditions go right back to the culture which Andrae spent his life researching.

The new edition has 24 new plates and 4 text illustrations. In all there are 42 pictures more. The majority come from the Andrae family's own collection, but there are some from the Berlin National Library (Staatsbibliothek), SPK, and from the Berlin Near Eastern Museum, of the Berlin National Museums (SPK). We are grateful, as before, to Dr. Brandis and Dr. Stolzenberg for permission to publish, and for the first time to the Director of the Near Eastern Museum, Dr. L. Jacob-Rost: pictures from there were not available to us before the re-unification of Germany.

The layout of the first edition has been retained for reasons of cost. Additional illustrations follow on Plates 129–152, their descriptions on pp. 194.

By his eightieth year Walter Andrae was almost completely blind (see p. 2), yet to his inner eye images of his life were as clear as ever. He dictated an unpublished piece entitled 'The Beautyful – the Good – the True' (Das Schoene – das Gute – das Wahre, heareafter SGW). In order that the reader may better understand Andrae, a glimpse has been afforded into this mental world of his closing years. The first part of this manuscript has therefore been reproduced as the following extract plus two further passages, these pertaining to Nos. 210 and 224. The characterisation of Meissner-Pasha, builder of the Hejaz Railway (see No. 233), comes from an unpublished portion of Andrae's memoirs (LE).

Berlin, August 8th, 1991   R. M. B.

WALTER ANDRAE

DESCRIPTIONS OF INDIVIDUAL PICTURES

On No. 46, from SGW, 12.4.1954

Phoenix dactilifera: Among the palm-trees too there twinkles an unexpected delight, for eyes which the relentless burning of the white mid-day sun has driven to despair, believing all beauty burnt and shrivelled away. Now the glowing orb inclines toward the edge of the night, followed in the sky by all the hues through to purple, like footmen. A tender pink settles behind the palm-fronds. These threatened by day like bundles of naked swords, but now sway softly in the breeze like so many harmless feather-dusters. Below, the ripening dates begin to glow like purest gold, and even the earth-grey stumps of old stems play along in this colour symphony. On the ground the gently fragrant mimosa and licorice foliage, with its carefully restrained green, joins in inaudibly. By the Euphrates, in the evening shadows already figures shimmering brown and blue are at work with spades, leading the canal anew to the bucket conveyor. At the lower edge, the warm, yellow Euphrates rounds off this peaceful picture.

On No. 79. From SGW, 30.4.1954

Kurban bairam: On this day of the sacrificial Muslims feast the midday sun beats down on the colourless earth-grey courtyard of the village huts. It is thronged with men in festive garb, yellow and red and snowy white glinting from under their brown cloaks, and new red or blue cloths held to the head by their agals. They arrange themselves into a dance, and form a snake which proceeds on red pointed slippers. At the front of the snake, in the lead, is Murad, chief servant in the 'palace' of the Europeans who dig at Babylon. He ist wearing a red fez and waving a red handkerchief. His jacket is of the brightest blue, canary yellow his long silken shirt, and a girdle of woven gold trails at his side. The double flute plays on continuously, in eighth-note performed on the long bones of a gazelle, brought to each dancer by the bowing musician. The lady of the house, shyly admires the spectacle, her black cloak pulled over her head. She draws it daintily before her nose at every male glance, covering the silver discs in the wings of her nose. The Europeans look on in equal amazement, for in Europe the beauty of the dance is treasured in a different way.

The sun sets, and with it the heat of the day, and from out of the twilight comes a distant gentle *brekekex,* accompanied softly and sonorously by *koax koax.* A gentle crescendo builds up to a chorus. You suppose it to be a lullaby. Well, you're wide of the mark! Anyone acquainted with the frog and his neighbour will understand why each has to sing louder than any who would outsing him. Such is the will of the unseen conductor. And thus it goes: the lullaby becomes a male choir, and then a roar, with sudden pauses followed by fresh starts, the noise swelling and waning like the surging of the sea, assaulting the ears. And there is no finale. The moon rises, the long night abates, but the volume of the accompaniment abates not. Not until the morning sun appears. The only respite is flight!

On No. 101–103, from SGW 13.4.1954

The golden mosque: For the saint who once, a thousand years before, kindled the thoughts of men like sunshine, brightening their hearts with colour, piety has erected this tomb. The dome bedecked with purest gold, the gateway splendid in gold and colour, the many arches of the courtyard – all this that his immortal presence might yet shine as sunlight, might yet bring tender colour to the lame hearts of men.

Now so many of the gay tiles have been taken from the wall by greedy hands, carried off somewhere and parted from their original purpose. Still what has been left retains its beauty, and if there are still hearts that can open, they would open wide to the heart-prayer of this saint.

For this is not beauty for its own sake! It has as much to do with good and truth. Otherwise the golden dome, the golden sun-star guiding the traveller across the empty fields all hours of the day, all were in vain. The star is no mere mortal guide!

On No. 109, from SGW, 19.3.1954

The Taj Mahal: The unbounded love of a noble human couple placed its monument here: of peerless, great, and spotless purity, of white marble in noblest form, in a setting of well-ordered nature. Where else is there a memorial of such greatness, yet not great enough for its content of human love, given and returned? It stands like a snow-capped mountain against the starry firmament, the moon glazing the dome and the slender towers, the whole reflected in orderly marble pools, set round with roses and palms. In the dark foliage the nightingale plies her sweet song. Like a veil of the finest silk it threads its way round the still paths. Like clouds of incense it threads its way up to the marble dome, as though the dead empress embraced still the parting gift of her bride-groom, he who in his sorrow forged this wonder, that his fleeting love may never leave this earth. With precious stones he adorned both cheek and bosom, as once of his spouse so now of her memorial.

Here is continuing life! How nobly here does wisdom speak: life ends not in death!

194   ERNST WALTER ANDRAE – RAINER MICHAEL BOEHMER

On Nos. 80–87, from SGW, 7.5.1954

Beauty in concealment. The royal palace of Babylon was nothing but a heap of earth. To the scholar's disgust, there was nothing to see but soil and broken fragments. Just occasionally was there a flash of sky-blue and white and yellow and black, molten colours, immortal, as though fresh from the kilns of great craftsmen.

A ray of hope! And the battle was on. Digging, searching, a treasure hunt: not for gold and statues, but for mere fragments bearing glittering colours. Thousands were found, but what did they mean?

The colours are so pretty! But the forms – would they be as beautiful? The struggle went on for three decades, trying to put together what two millennia had shattered, what once made up the most famous palace in the world, the goal and heart's desire of several generations. Here were the long rows of beautiful animals and plants, representations of the strength which shines from heaven to have effect on earth, to help those who seek right and strive upward.
Well, unveiled beauty – can you help mankind now?

On No. 98, from SGW 6.5.1954

Frog beauty. To a frog, is beauty song? Come to the Euphrates marsh at Afaj, which is near to the ruins of Nippur, the temple city of the god Enlil, and stay a night with the sheikh of Afaj in his guest house of woven reed. It lies not far from the reed marsh, and to reach it you must take a gondola.

CATALOGUE TO PLATES 129–152 (NOS. 199–237)

199 24. 1. 1899 – Pencil – 10.0 × 18.0
Amq Plain. (Kirk-Khan, Hamamath, etc.), Kurdish farmhouse built of reeds.

200 12. 2. 1899 – Pencil – 13.3 × 18.0
Between Abu Khrera and Hamamath. Ruins of a mosque. Minaret. Details.

201 Early 1899 – Oils – 41.6 × 30.8
Damascus. Evening.

202 19. 2. 1899 – Pencil – 33.8 × 24.6
Qal'at ar-Rakhba. Compare No. 30.

203 25. 1. 1899 – Pencil – 9.0 × 12.5
'The Armoured cruiser' on the road from Alexandretta/Iskenderun to Aleppo. Expedition member H. F. Ludwig Meyer (a Berlin carpet merchant) conducts a bird-hunt from the coach. On H. F. Ludwig Meyer, who had already accompanied Koldewey to Surghul and Al-Hiba, see RK 36, 93. In another unpublished note, Andrae reports that Meyer also tried to shoot birds at Babylon, but whenever he noticed, Koldewey would warn them off with loud calls or handclapping.

204 16. 3. 1899 – Pencil – 16.5 × 2
Ctesiphon. Taq i-Kisra from the south-west. Salman Pak in the background, on the left.

205 1899 – Pen and coloured crayon – 28 × 20.7
Babylon. First plan after pace-off the ruins. From a letter home.

206 1899 – Watercolour – 8.3 × 17.8
Babylon. Expedition house: view from Koldewey's window to the north, towards the mound of Babil, after a thunderstorm. Compare No. 60.

207 1900 – Pen – 27.7 × 17.8
Babylon. Workmen on the excavation. The fine hatching which characterizes Andrae's later reconstructions is recognizable here, though not yet fully developed.

208 1902 – Watercolour – 25.3 × 35.2
Babylon. Homera from the north. Background left lie the remains of the inner city wall.

209 1902 – Pencil – 14.1 × 15.6
Babylon. The 'Hippopotamus', Andrae's grey horse at Babylon. See also Nos. 222 and fig. 25 (and text).

210 1923 – Coloured chalk – 30.4 × 46.3
Babylon. A reconstruction.
View across the archaeologically attested Euphrates bridge to the tower and the Marduk sanctuary Esangila. A second bridge is documented in the texts, but its physical location has not yet been identified (see E. Unger, Babylon, in Reallexikon der Assyriologie (Lexicon of Assyriologie) 1 (1932), 349, §§ 75–76.
Andrae, who later came to regard the tower of Babylon as a stage-tower, here and in fig. 211 still renders it block-shaped, thus paying tribute to his teacher Koldewey. (For the various attempts of reconstruction see now H. Schmid, who has an idea of his own: H. Schmid in: Das wiedererstehende Babylon (Babylon Rediscovered), 5th edition, revised by B. Hrouda (1990), 303 ff.
Koldewey, who had come to Berlin 1917, died there. Andrae was with him right up to his last hours. On the 6th of April, 1954, he dictated some of his memories (from SGW):
'MORIBUNDUS'
Master builder with no building site, no door, no path, deprived of truth, he lay sick unto death, while in his dim eyes flickered one last spark of the will to live. It was up to me to

Babylon
2. [...] 1899.

Fig. 22 Babylon. The Euphrates by the expedition house, with sailing boats and kellek. Whitsun 1899

Fig. 23 Babylon. Expedition house. Living and bedroom, original arrangement. Whitsun 1899

guide him onto the path, to help him yet to find the right portal. So I spoke – no, no – *something* spoke from within me:

'As architects we appreciate the relationship between a circle and its centre. Now the centre of our life's circle is our essential, inalienable being. Anything which lies beyond this horizon we incorporate into that life-circle by means of an image, which we construct for this express purpose.

Now suppose that what we wish to draw into our circle is infinity – suppose it is God – then the construction is crystal clear: *His* image is *our very centre,* our essential being. We reflect it infinitely, from every facet of our being. It becomes our inner sun, the light-source of our hearts!'

This sick man smiled, and from his blue lips came softly, 'Yes, that's how it is'. His eyes opened wide, with a deep unearthly beauty, in which realisation welled darkly.

The Way, the Truth, the Life, were all found. The dying man found his way to the Father through the Son's help. And for us left on earth, there lingered that light in his eyes.'

In 1988 I (R.M.B.) had the good fortune to be able to talk about Koldewey with the last person living who had known him personally. This was Frau Wasmuth, née Püttmann (13. 10. 1901–26. 10. 1990), proprietor of the Tübingen publishing house Wasmuth, universally well known in archaeological circles.

Frau Wasmuth spent part of her childhood in late Ottoman Baghdad. Her father, Ernst Püttmann, traded there as well as being Belgian Honorary Consul. There had been a disagreement between Koldewey and the Berlin assyriologist F. Delitzsch over the double defensive wall of the Ishtar gate. After this was concluded unfavourably for Koldewey he had become morose and withdrawn (RK 170, 205–208). But when this little girl arrived at Babylon by coach from Baghdad, his face lit up. He took time off to show the child round in the friendliest manner. What Frau Wasmuth remembered most distinctly into late old age was the peculiar brightness of his eyes. And it is with reference to this particular feature that Andrae concluded the above-cited tribute to this remarkable man.

Berlin, Near Eastern Museum, SPK.

211 1923 – Coloured chalk – 30.2 × 46.3
Babylon. A reconstruction. The Processional Way by night. In the left foreground, the Marduk sanctuary Esangila, then the tower Etemenanki, the 'house of heaven and earth', reconstructed according to Koldewey. On the horizon can be seen the battlements of Nebuchadnezzar II's palace compound. Left, above Esangila, is Sirius, directly over the sanctuary is Orion.
Berlin, Near Eastern Museum, SPK.

212 1899 – Pencil – 34.2 × 18.7
Babylon. Expedition house. A window in Andrae's workroom. See also No. 56.

213 1903 – Oils – 45 × 65
Basra. Along the Shatt al-Arab. Unfinished.

214 Undated, c. 1908 – Watercolour – 34.2 × 24.7
Assur. View over Tigris after thunderstorm with rainbow rising.
See also Nos. 120. 121.

215   Undated, c. 1907/8 – Pen, pencil and coloured pencil – 13.3 × 18.0
      Assur. A royal Assyrian couple 'at home' with the excavators in the courtyard of the Expedi-
      tion house. 'Gottlieb' the young gazelle buck, butts the queen from behind, as he did all
      strange visitors.
      See LE 159 f.:
      'The gazelle buck 'Gottlieb' became a member of the household at the tender age of just a
      few days. He had to be hand-reared with a bottle, which succeeded surprisingly well,
      although to start with he was just a mere scrap with spindly legs. Mohammed, the only
      hunter in the district, must have had a hunter's sharp eyes fo find something so earth-
      coloured on the earth-coloured steppe. However, Gottlieb grew and flourished, acquired a
      stately pair of sharp horns, and became the darling of the whole household. This affection
      was not, however, shared by strangers who dared to enter the courtyard wearing one of the
      loose, earth-coloured Arab cloaks. These he used to ambush systematically, as they were
      innocently minding their own business. In a couple of classic gazelle bounds he would leap
      right across the courtyard to sink his horns in the unsuspecting victim's behind. The unfor-
      tunate would fall flat on his back, and Gottlieb would return satisfied to his sacrosanct den.
      Needless to say, this did not happen too often, as his trick was well known. So every Arab
      who came into the yard kept an eye out for Gottlieb and crept along with his back to the
      wall, which caused us nearly as much amusement as the full performance.'

216   Christmas 1907 – Pen – 7.5 × 26.0
      Assur. 'Assyrians celebrating'.

217   1912 – Pencil – 6.8 × 10.5
      Aleppo. The Baron hotel. The landlord and his brother.

218   December 1912 – Pencil – 9.5 × 11.8
      A passenger on board of the Helwan.

219   1909 – Oils – 44.8 × 64.8
      Assur. View looking south from the Assur temple to the Expedition house.
      Berlin. Near Eastern Museum, SPK.

220   1908 – Coloured chalk on tinted paper – 13.7 × 23.0
      Assur. Water-buffalo in a wooded meadow by the Tigris.

221   1905 – Oils – 32.7 × 41.3
      Assur in the snow.

222   1908 – Oils – 60.5 × 80.0
      The Euphrates south of Meskene (see also No. 24).
      Horses drinking (– for journeys by covered wagon see also figs. 24 and 25). In the fore-
      ground is a carpet of flowers: marguerites, poppies, larkspur. This brief flowering is a phe-
      nomenon of spring in the East.
      See also LE, 189:
      'We rode [from Assur] for 15 hours through green grass and all kinds of sweet-smelling

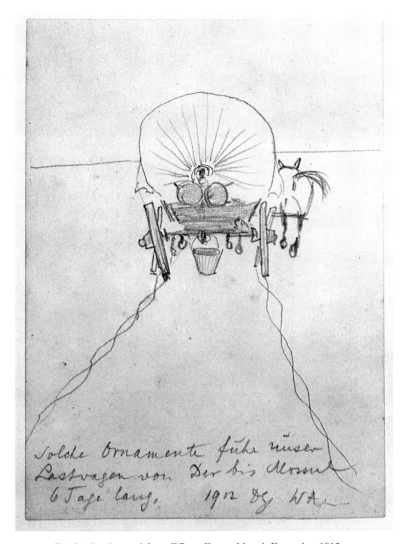

Fig. 24 On the road from Dēr ez-Zor to Mosul. December 1912

flowers. They always looked as though they had been strewn as a gift by some benificent goddess, spread over the desert ground, which showed through everywhere, not matted over like a German meadow.' – p. 191 f.: 'Through the triangular vent in the tent [at Uwenat] I look out over what seems to be a green cloth laid on a great table. The horizon is its edge ... The Flower Goddess has placed many camomile flowers on the green table ... Sometimes the scent is sweet, sometimes strong; everywhere is green, sometimes colourful, never desert. Only trees are missing: that is the only odd thing.' – p. 194 f.: 'The following

Fig. 25 On the way from 'Ain Ghazal to Tell 'Afer. – 31. 12. 1912

days afford each his particular pleasure, although the same plain and the same barren mountains form the landscape to the right. But sometimes there are huge, fiery red tulips spread out on these expanses (see Nos. 140 and 141), and sometimes huge green plants with leaves like well-manured rhubarb (see No. 141), which hardly leave room between them for anything else and nib any competition in the bud. They stretch out to the horizon, and here and there on this sea there is a particularly large leaf sticking out like an artificial wave. Next the now more undulating ground is covered with black blocks, small at first, then getting larger. The mystery ends in a small, flat valley, with nothing to indicate its presence until we were right upon it: we are riding over a basalt lava river, which flowed away over the goodly alluvium in deposits barely a meter thick, before anyone thought of building a railway over it. Here by the modest stream which winds off to the right down the mountains to the steppe, to run underground or end in a sterile salt-pan, the basalt formation can be seen in section. Cube-shaped blocks have rolled off the edge of the valley into the bed of the stream and litter it in an untidy fashion (see Nos. 141 and 142). Here and there little caves have formed under the hard, water-tight stone.'

Further to this may be mentioned Andrae's memories of spring at Assur, SGW, for 12. 4. 1954:

Two wonders of the stars:

I am lying on the flat roof of our house with my hands under my head. The Tigris gurgles gently by below. Above, the great heavenly dial rotates majestically about the pole-star, silent, but with myriad illumination, like a great, dark blue meadow full of star-flowers. Only a few have names: it is a nameless, measureless army of flowers, which beguiles me gently with sleep.

In the morning I ride up the Tigris to the meadows. Normally they are bare and hard and earth-grey. But today, overnight, they have dressed themselves wondrously in a boundless white carpet of fullblown marguerites. So thickly are the innocent white faces with golden pearls clustered together that there is hardly room between them for the green. Yes, my good grey steed (see fig. 25 and text), you wonder as I do at a starry sky below our feet, not overhead on one of our night journeys. The pony whickers contentedly. We both drink in this fortunate beauty. And, like the sun, we prance in circles through our star-meadow, into-xicated with joy.'

223 1918 – Coloured chalk – 16.9 × 10.4
Aleppo. Turkish bath.
Berlin, Staatsbibliothek, SPK, Andrae Bequest 9.

224 1917 – Coloured chalk – 15.4 × 9.9
Aleppo. Kefr Salama. Water-carrier.
Berlin, Staatsbibliothek, SPK. Andrae Bequest 9.

225 1917 – Coloured chalk – 10.2 × 16.8
Aleppo. 'Gay ladies'.

226 1916 – Coloured chalks – 13.0 × 20.7
On a voyage down the Euphrates from Aleppo to Baghdad. Ruins of a water-wheel (Na'ura) on the Euphrates.
See also p. 26, fig. 10 Nos. 165, 168.

227 Spring 1918 – Coloured chalks on tinted paper – 10.1 × 16.7
Dervish monastery (Tekke) south of Aleppo: Mashad al-Husain. E. Herzfeld: Inscriptions et monuments d'Alep (Kairo, 1955), 236–248, Pls. 94–101.
For the identification of this picture and the reference we are indebted to H. Gaube.

228 1989 – Coloured chalks on tinted paper – 10.1 × 16.5
Dervish monastery (Tekke) near Aleppo: Takiya ash-Sheikh Abu Bakr. See also Nos. 18, 154.

229 21. 12. 1918 – Coloured chalks – 11.6 × 18.0
Near Hama.

230 1918 – Coloured chalks – 10.5 × 17.9
Damascus, the old city.
Berlin, Staatsbibliothek, SPK, Andrae Bequest No. 9.

231 15. 7. 1918 – Coloured chalks – 15.7 × 11.4
Meissner Pasha. See No. 190.

From an unpublished part of LE:

'Contact with genuine pioneers definitely counts as one of the noteworthy experiences of one's life. I consider Meissner Pasha to be one such pioneer. He was billeted on us at Assur for a few days along with a small advance party prospecting the route of the Baghdad railway. In a land like Mesopotamia, entirely devoid of railways, you could call such an undertaking real pioneering work indeed. To imagine Germany without railways, I would have to go right back to my grandfathers' youth. One of them belonged among the ranks of Saxon 'pioneers', albeit in a modest way. The first railway from Dresden to Leipzig was already in existence, and grandfather was in charge of building part of the stretch from Saxony to Bohemia through the Elbe valley.

Meissner Pasha came from Saxony too: his speech betrayed it. Like many of his compatriots, he outgrew his mother-country, and his career in the East began with the building of the Mecca railway from Damascus to Medina. The Turks showered him with honour for this achievement, in the form both of his title and a large endowment. So he could feel well within his rights to smoke the best, longest, strongest cigarettes that Turkey could provide, and to fall ill once a year with nicotine poisoning so acute that he was sometimes out of action for weeks. Then smoking would be forbidden and his temper appalling. For the remaining eleven months of the year he remained the most delightful raconteur as well as a brilliantly innovative engineer.

At Assur we got to know him during his work-breaks at our table. As Europeans we rarely appreciate what a thick net of steel is spun around our earth. But here a single strand of 1,000 and more kilometres was to be laid over the uneven earth without treading on the toes of a single land-owner. The engineer embraced the earth there unequivocally, with outstretched arms, and felt his way over the goodly folds and wrinkles of her face. And then later the locomotives rolled over it. In the course of his railway-building Meissner Pasha had got to know the Turks and the other inhabitants of the country well and got on with them very well indeed. In a small way we had had the same experience. Visions of the future used to wander across our fantasies at the time. We saw the barren land developing and coming into wellbeing, for we thought this steel strand, when it first crept up to us, was an unmitigated blessing. In reality, before it reached its goal, it brought war: one of the causes of the War was the building by the Germans of the Baghdad Railway.

Today the railway culture seems to have been left behind. One can in fact travel very comfortably from Instanbul to Baghdad and Basra by Pullman-car, but the asphalt roads are the crucial carriers of traffic. The oil-wealth which came in the wake of the Second World war enabled the young Iraqi state to achieve this state of affairs.

Now these memories of the original state of the country are gradually dissolving, and pale against the very questionable Europeanisation and Americanisation which is taking place. When will that land produce pioneers of *spiritual* development? When will we Europeans produce a large enough following of the pioneers of our own *spiritual* development?

Berlin, Staatsbibliothek, SPK, Andrae Bequest No. 9.

232   – Coloured chalks – 16.1 × 9.4
Aleppo. A merchant, possibly singing. See No. 189, the same individual.

233   1988 – Coloured chalks on tinted paper – 16.4 × 10.4
Damascus. Garden by the Barada stream outside the city.

234 Spring 1918 – Pen, pencil, coloured crayon on tinted paper – 13.4 × 17.8
Flowers from the Nazareth region: asphodelus and orchid blooms, alpine pansies etc.

235 20. 2. 1917 – Pencil, coloured chalks – 12.7 × 7.5
Baghdad. Tents in a palm-grove, late evening.

236 19. 2. 1918 – Coloured chalks – 18.2 × 11.8
Nazareth. A field path in the valley: cypresses and prickly pears (see No. 173).

237 26. 9. 1927 – Coloured chalks on tinted paper – 10.2 × 16.8
Istanbul. Beikos on the Bosphorus. It was during a visit to Bogazkoy in 1927 that Andrae passed through Istanbul again and once again took up his crayons – a still very rare occurrence at this period. See also the pictures of earlier visits, Nos. 144–150, 198.

CATALOGUE OF TEXT FIGURES

22 Whitsun 1899 – Pen – 6.5 × 11.5
Babylon. The Euphrates by the Expedition house, with sailing boats and kelek.

23 Whitsun 1899 – Pen – 7.8 × 10.7
Babylon. Expedition house. Living and bedroom, original arrangement.

24 Dec. 1912 – Pencil – Original lost.
On the road from Der ez-Zor to Mosul. Covered wagon with a bucket hung on the back. The tracks show how wobbly the wheels were.
In Andrae's handwriting: 'This design followed our wagon from Der to Mosul, 6 days' journey.' For travelling by covered wagon see also No. 22 and fig. 25. LE, first edition, fig. 21.

25 31. 12. 1912 – Pencil – Original lost.
In Andrae's handwriting: 'Should we oil it, or will it be all right? On the way from 'Ain Ghazal to Tell 'Afer. My Happel [the grey horse to the right of the picture]'. For travelling by covered wagon see also No. 222 and fig. 24. On the horses at Assur Andrae writes in LE 158:
'We had riding horses which became like friends. They repaid us for this friendship when we exercised them in the roadless, fenceless region that was their natural habitat. And their spirits responded to the slightest indication from us.'
See also No. 209.
LE, first edition, fig. 22.